MENU DESIGN 2

MENU DESIGN 2

Marketing the Restaurant through Graphics

JUDI RADICE

AND THE NATIONAL RESTAURANT ASSOCIATION

Text by JACKIE COMERFORD

PBC International Inc. ● New York

Distributor to the book trade in the United States:
PBC INTERNATIONAL, INC.
One School Street
Glen Cove, NY 11542

Distributor to the art trade in the United States:
Letraset USA
40 Eisenhower Drive
Paramus, NJ 07653

Distributor in Canada:
Letraset Canada Limited
555 Alden Road
Markham, Ontario L3R 3L5, Canada

Distributed throughout the rest of the world by:
Hearst Books International
1790 Broadway
New York, NY 10019

Library of Congress Cataloging-in-Publication Data

Radice, Judi.
  Menu Design 2.

  Includes index.
  1. Menus. I. Title.
TX911.3.M45R329   1986   642'.5   86-12180
ISBN 0-86636-016-6

Cover:
Art Direction by David Bartels
Design by Buck Smith
Photography by Jim Olvera

Color separation, printing, and binding by
Toppan Printing Co. (H.K.) Ltd., Hong Kong

Typesetting by Vera-Reyes, Inc.

Printed in Hong Kong

10 9 8 7 6 5 4 3 2

Publisher: Herb Taylor
Project Director: Cora Sibal Taylor
Executive Editor: Virginia Christensen
Editor: Carolyn Edwins
Art Director: Richard Liu
Art Associates: Patty Bertram
Dan Larkin

To the Fine Art of Dining . . .

Acknowledgments

To the countless designers and restaurant owners and managers who shared their vision (especially those interviewed):

To Menu Workshop, and most particularly to Gregg Rapp, for information and insights on the design process, and for collecting all those releases.

To Russ Charpentier for helping meet another "high-noon" deadline.

To Kerby Macrae for service above and beyond what was expected and for helping pull together all the last minute details and phone calls.

To Joann Mitchell of Allan And Gray, for valuable information about paper and the paper selection process.

To the National Restaurant Association, in particular to Anne Papa, Steven Dahllos, and Jeffrey Prince for their work on the Great Menus Project.

To Diane Arpaia, for interviewing Joseph Baum and providing the article for this book.

To Michael O'Neill, for photographing the menus in this book.

And mostly, to all those who have an appreciation for the fine art of menu design.

And finally, to "The Pickle" for the late-night airport runs . . .

THANKS!

Contents

Foreword

With this book in hand, anthropologists of the future would be able to reconstruct our culture in detail. The menus in *Menu Design 2* portray our sense of style, our sense of humor, and our sense of taste. They define how we have fun and how we do business. They depict how we relax and how we romance. They keep time with our culture. Menus may be one of the most telltale artifacts we leave to future generations.

Menus today communicate more to customers than the bill of fare. They are capable of setting a mood, building interest, enticing customers, and creating excitement.

Menu Design 2 shows there is no one, correct way to design a menu. They emerge in new and unusual formats as restaurants concepts are born. The permutations are as endless as the imagination is expansive. Menus, perhaps more than any other graphic art project, put the designer to the test. Their success demands an imaginative approach yet relies on an organized, structured treatment. The hundreds of successes in *Menu Design 2* set the highest standard of excellence for the restaurateur and graphic designer.

The winners of the National Restaurant Association's 23rd Annual Great Menus Contest are included in *Menu Design 2*. They represent the most outstanding group of menus in the industry, according to a distinguished panel of industry judges. Over 600 entries in the 1986 Great Menus Contest were judged on imagination, design, and merchandising power. Only 30 entries were selected to receive "Great Menu" status from the National Restaurant Association. Take special note of these winners. Their outstanding performance in each of the judging criteria make them excellent models for your future menus.

Only tomorrow's menus decide where we go from here. That is up to you—the restaurateur and the graphic designer. If there is a motto for the restaurateur and designer to work by, it comes from Pearl Bailey, who said, "You can taste a word."

—NATIONAL RESTAURANT ASSOCIATION

Introduction

Good menus are not created by good designers alone . . .
they are the result of an intelligent and thoughtful
collaboration between the designer and the restaurateur.
Simply put, the designer channels, refines, and executes the
restaurateur's ideas. The symbiosis that occurs is a major
focus of this book.

A successful menu is a tribute to the designer's ability to
translate the restaurateur's idea into graphics and words that
will express that vision coherently to the public.
Restaurateurs are a breed apart—just as designers chose
graphic art as the best medium to express their creativity, so
restaurateurs chose restaurants. Successful communication
between two such disparate groups is not easily achieved.
But, as the menus presented in this book demonstrate, it *is*
attainable, and the results are well worth the effort.

François

SPRING
LUNCHEON MENU
March - June

1

Techniques of Menu Design

Restaurant owners often see menu design as a very minor part of planning to open a restaurant. In the view of many restaurateurs, the menu is simply a list of the dishes offered at the restaurant. The quality of the foodstuffs and the competence of the chef in preparing them seem much more important.

But a restaurant is a business and, like any other business, it must *sell* its product to the general public. Without a good, working menu—the restaurant's primary sales tool—the public will never be tempted to explore the restaurant's repertory.

This chapter discusses the entire menu design process, from the planning done by the designer and the restaurateur, to the final printing of the menu and accompanying promotional pieces. It explores each phase of the process and offers important tips and techniques.

This graphic menu for the Union Club at the University of Arizona in Tucson is the result of brainstorming sessions between graphic arts students and staff members. Not only does the mountain theme reflect the university's geographic location, but the cover artwork resembles that of many local artists.

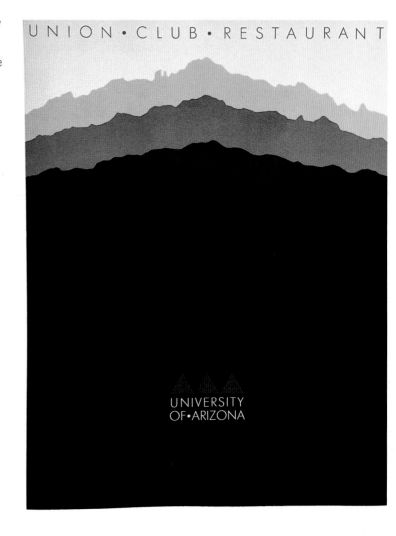

MENU PLANNING
Involving the Restaurateur

Good menu design depends upon the relationship between restaurateur and designer. Each brings a specific expertise to the design of a good menu; these skills are complementary—neither person can achieve as good a result alone as both can working together. The restaurateur should select a designer on the basis of previous work and the ability of both of them to establish a dialogue. These two individuals must be able to communicate effectively with each other. Both must also be willing to be flexible and to expend time and care in the planning and production of the menu and peripheral materials.

Whenever possible, the restaurant owner or manager should be directly involved in planning the menu. This person should be consulted and should "sign off"—that is, give approval—at each stage of the work.

Once the designer-restaurateur relationship is established, an initial meeting for the exchange of information is held. At this meeting, the restaurateur educates the designer about the restaurant and the designer educates the owner about menu program planning.

Specific areas for discussion should include: the clientele, the restaurant's interior design, the number and complexity of the menu items, what the menu should achieve, the budget, how often the menu will be changed, how soon the new menus will be needed, and personal preferences of the restaurateur regarding color and style.

The restaurateur must express to the designer what he wants the menu to achieve and how often it will change. At Chardonnay, a restaurant committed to serving fresh, seasonal foods in elegant surroundings, the menus are changed quarterly. The designer used four separate views of the same courtyard to identify the season.

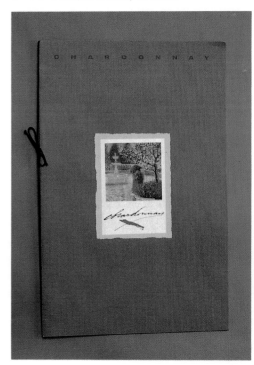

IN ROOM DINING

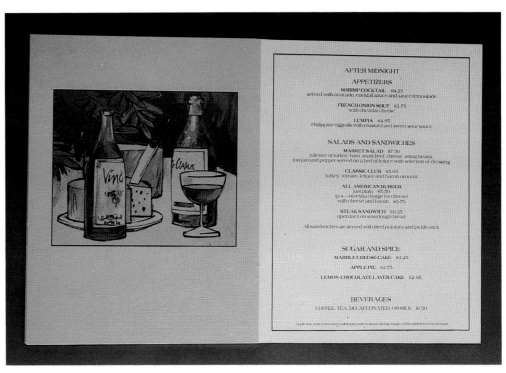

The food and beverage director at the Sheraton Premiere wanted an artistic room service menu, but needed the ability to change menu items and prices. The creative design solution was to print full-color masters and assemble them with two-color menu pages that are revised as needed.

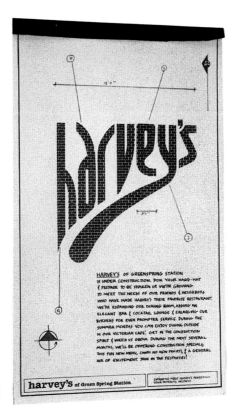

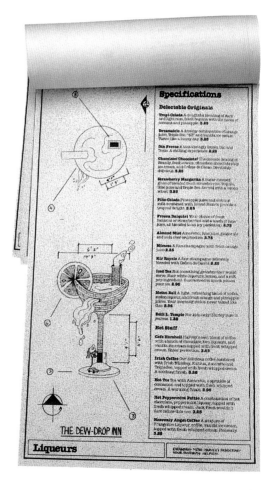

The restaurateur at Harvey's was determined to make the best of a difficult situation when construction at the restaurant threatened to disrupt dining. The menu shown here was designed to add humor to the inevitable inconvenience. Besides looking like a blueprint, the menu includes an amusing illustration of a brick building in the shape of a goblet.

Creating a Menu Program

The right menu program for a restaurant is determined by budget, the degree of flexibility needed, and the method most comfortable for the restaurateur.

Based on this information, a "lifetime" for the menu program will be established and a program method selected. A menu program, rather than a menu planned for a single printing, is almost always a good idea. Production (printing and finishing the menu) is the most expensive element in the costs associated with a new menu. It is far less expensive to print extra masters and store them for periodic updates than to reprint the entire menu each time it is changed. To facilitate the updates, elements of the menu that are expected to change should be designed for printing in one color only. One-color printing involves lower production costs than printing multiple colors.

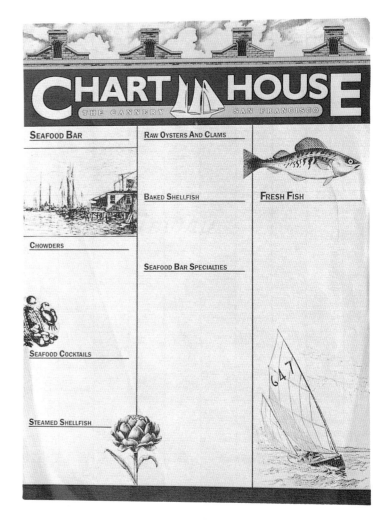

The Chart House uses menu masters pre-printed in two colors and updates them daily. The menu masters were designed to permit easy updating—the design provides large blocks of clear space that do not require careful aligning of items within them.

Creative Gourmets, Ltd., uses four menu masters pre-printed with watercolor illustrations that correspond to the seasons of the year for its catered cafeteria service. Menu items are revised as necessary on these masters.

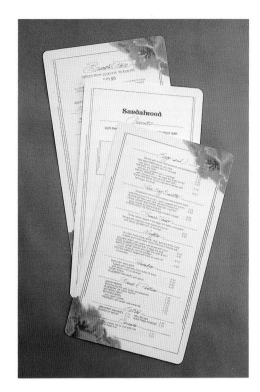

Sandalwood's basic menu, which won second place in the "Best Design" Category of the National Restaurant Association's 1986 Great Menus Contest, does not change often. But, a card listing monthly specials is inserted into a sleeve in the menu. Six seasonal cards are used—each showing the specials for one month on one side and those for another month on its other side. The dinner menu is adapted for either breakfast or lunch by inserting an appropriate card.

Pelican Pete's uses a ring binder to hold individual menu pages. One or more pages can be updated without remaking the entire menu. The menu items that vary are printed in one color on standard-sized paper.

A more formal menu program may involve inserts on which variable menu items are printed in one color. The Arbour imprints its inserts on vellum and holds them in place with pockets at the sides of the open menu.

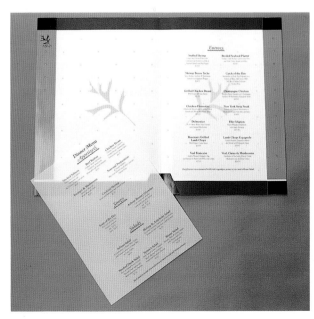

MENU DESIGN

Presenting Ideas

After the first planning meeting, the designer prepares ideas for presentation. He or she may start with many rough ideas and choose three or four for presentation. Pieces of art created for presentation are called comprehensive or linear art, more informally referred to as "comps." Rough sketches, called "thumbnails," may be presented if the designer and restaurateur are very comfortable with each other. Otherwise, more elaborate comps may be necessary.

Colored papers, magic markers, transfer type, sketches, and sometimes photographs or clip-art are used to make the comp, an actual-size model of the menu. Each comp includes the designer's recommendations for type style, paper, and colors.

The restaurateur chooses one idea, or a combination of ideas, to be developed. He or she provides the food selections to be included in the menu, along with their prices. The designer then creates a layout.

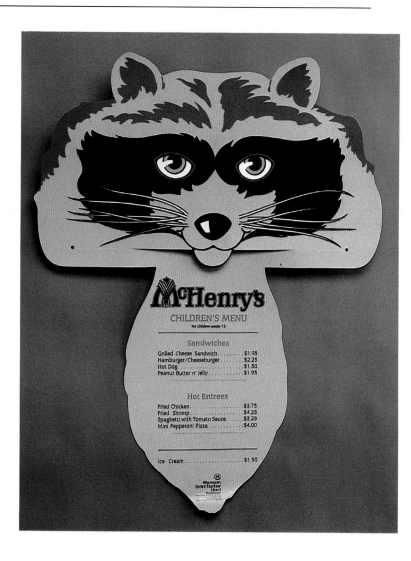

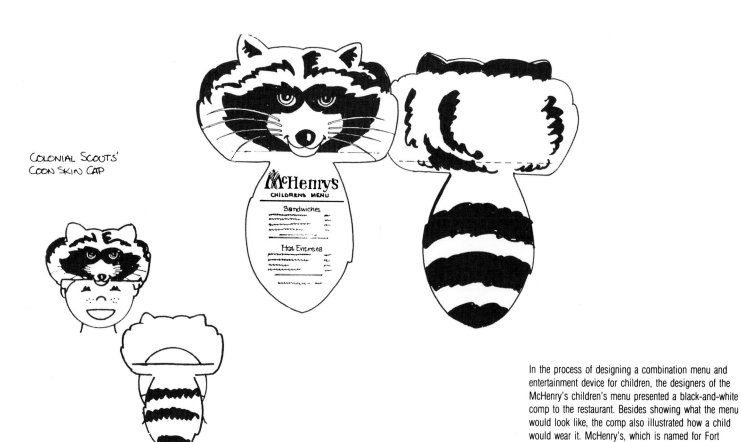

COLONIAL SCOUTS' COON SKIN CAP

In the process of designing a combination menu and entertainment device for children, the designers of the McHenry's children's menu presented a black-and-white comp to the restaurant. Besides showing what the menu would look like, the comp also illustrated how a child would wear it. McHenry's, which is named for Fort McHenry, approved the colonial coonskin cap theme and the finished menu was produced.

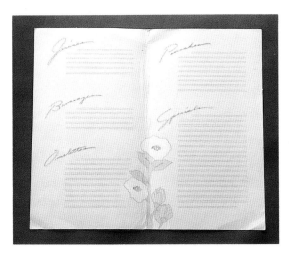

On the original comp for the interior of the Francois menu, the menu listings were positioned in two columns with an illustration of flowers in between, at the very center of the open menu. The design was ultimately modified and the final menu has listings set in three columns with illustrations of flowers positioned between columns.

Designer Dale Glasser adopted the design motif for The Pelican Club menu directly from the restaurant's decor. Recreated in her colored comp and the final menu are the latticework surrounding the dining room and the fabric design of the undercloth on the individual tables.

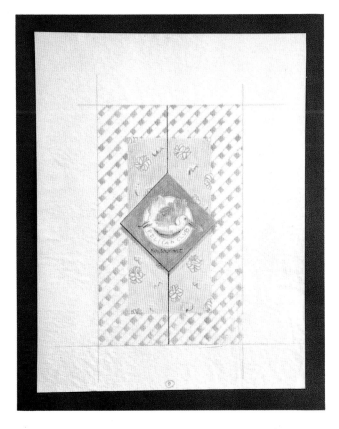

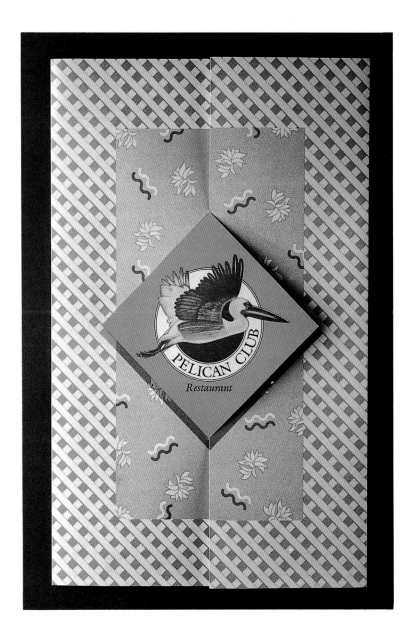

Preparing Menu Copy

Copywriting can greatly enhance the menu's effectiveness as a sales tool. A copywriter can edit the menu information for clarity, provide a humorous or historical note for the menu, or write copy that will "sell the sizzle as well as the steak."

It is important to consider how extensive the copywriting should be. A restaurant whose patrons do business over lunch or race through their meal to get back to work should use concise, straightforward language on its menu. The copy on a children's menu, on the other hand, should be entertaining.

The Company Chef, a gourmet office catering firm, uses copywriting on its menu to describe its services and to merchandise its food. Referring to the office staff as the "9 to 5 family" adds a warm personal touch.

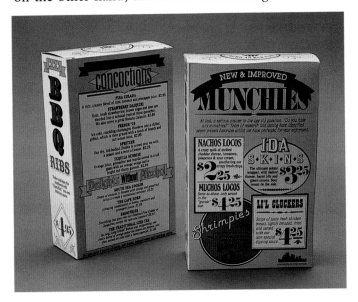

The copywriting on the Mardeck, Ltd. "New and Improved Munchies" menu is spiked with adjectives but avoids being long-winded. Every surface of this three-dimensional menu, except for the bottom, is used to sell the fare.

The colorful circular menu and accompanying table tent at Skipper's is targeted directly at its intended clientele—children. The copywriting promises a Fun Pack ® with each meal and advises, "If you're an adult, stop reading this."

From the very start of a menu project, the designer should insist that the client make all copy changes *before* typesetting. This is especially important when the type will be fit tightly into the design, as is the case with the menu at Restaurant Las Chivas, shown here. This practice will avoid additional typesetting charges, which can be substantial, and design changes.

Setting Type and Making Mechanical Art

The restaurant approves the menu copy, as well as the layout and illustrations or photography. At this point, the copy is set in type or hand-lettered. The type or lettered copy is then positioned and mechanicals are completed. Extreme care should be exercised when handling mechanical art. The least scratch or smudge will faithfully reproduce on the plates and thus on the final printed piece.

Probably the greatest frustration for any designer is the tendency of the client to revise copy after the type is set. All copy changes should be made during the *manuscript*, rather than the *mechanical*, stage of menu design. Resetting type can be very expensive and can increase the final cost of producing the menu.

Informative copywriting reinforces the colorful and detailed illustrations in "The Atlas of Wine," a specialty menu at the Hong Kong Hilton.

An important consideration in preparing copy is the positioning of prices. The Casa Lupita menu avoids lining up prices in a justified column, a practice called "price listing," and instead incorporates prices into the descriptive copy for the menu selections. Customers are thereby encouraged to base their choices on personal preference rather than cost.

Choosing Paper Stock

The menu is touched, held, and read and becomes
the diner's personal introduction to the restaurant.
And paper carries the message of the menu. Paper
characteristics can affect the menu's tactility,
durability, printability—and, ultimately, the image it
projects.

Many textured papers that enhance tactility are
available. Also, coated and uncoated papers can both
be embossed or foil-stamped with a name or a logo to
incorporate the restaurant's graphic theme
three-dimensionally.

Paper companies try to keep current with color
trends, so it is often possible to match paper color to
the other decorative components of the restaurant.
Alternatively, ink colors can be coordinated with these
elements.

Benihana's luncheon menu presents free flowing flowers
on exquisitely textured paper. It brings to mind the
delicate Japanese renderings of pastoral scenes captured
in brush and ink on rice paper.

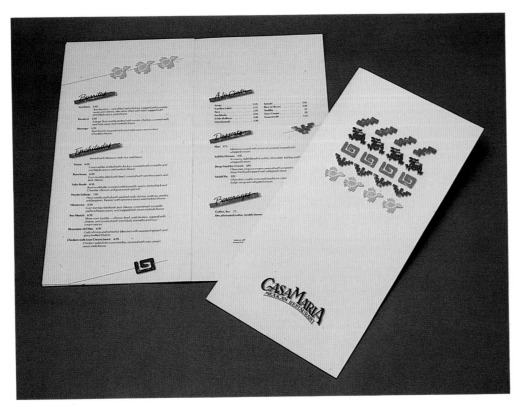

The speckled, beige paper used for the menu at Casa
Maria, a Mexican restaurant owned by the El Torito
chain, resembles flour tortillas in both texture and color.

The glossy cover of the Le Cygne menu, which bears a graceful swan represented in bas relief, is not only elegant but extremely sturdy as well. The heavy cover is constructed of two-ply stock.

There is nothing formal or delicate about the menu at Valley Deli. This sturdy menu, copies of which hang on a hook in this quaint deli, is made of the same type of paper used to line freight cars.

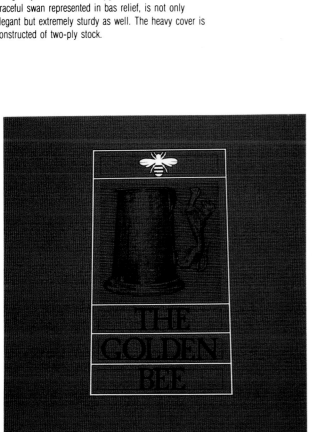

Elegance and distinction are the messages graphically communicated by the menu at The Golden Bee. Both the gold-foil-stamped bee and the exquisite ribbed paper contribute to the effect.

MENU PRODUCTION
Printing the Menu

Different types of printers are used to meet different needs. A commercial printer is most often the best choice to produce the menu masters. But a smaller print shop may be used to imprint the menu items and prices, particularly for updates when variables are printed in one color only.

It is even possible to perform these updates on word-processing equipment or a personal computer for especially fast and inexpensive changes.

Inks can be opaque or transparent, and while paper color does not show through the former, it does mix with the latter. By varying the "screens" (the density of the dot pattern formed by the ink on paper), a wide range of effects can be achieved relatively inexpensively.

Especially important in menu production are the bindery and finishing techniques that occur after printing—techniques such as embossing, lamination, foil stamping, and the use of die cuts. Judicious use of these techniques can perfect the menu design.

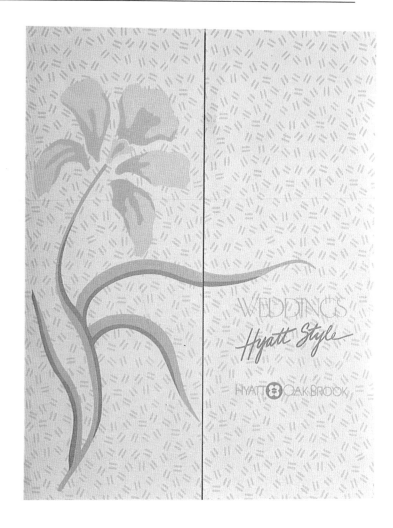

Tint screens of varying density were used in printing the Hyatt Regency wedding menu, creating a sense of depth and texture.

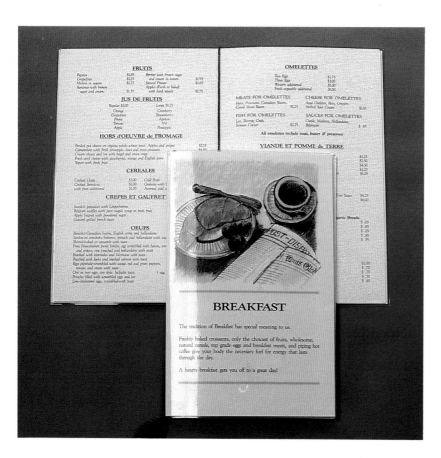

Menus usually are laminated for durability and moisture resistance, both important considerations in a restaurant setting. The cover of the Breckenridge Frontenac Hotel breakfast menu, which features an appropriate and colorful illustration, was laminated for durability.

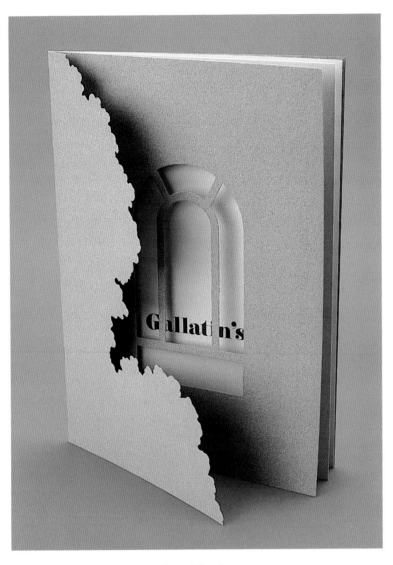

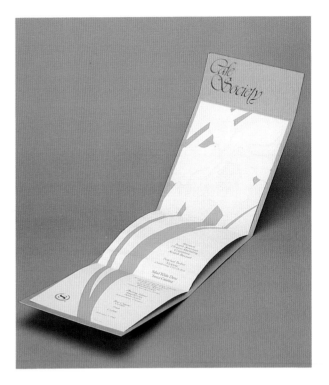

The interior of this menu, created for the Cafe Society Awards Dinner held at   Sheraton Corporate Headquarters, illustrates two printing techniques available to menu designers—the name of the event is attractively foil-stamped and the elegant white orchid is hot-stamped.

Gallatin's menu illustrates exceptional use of die cuts. The die-cut window was inspired by the dining room's many windows; the die-cut foliage, by views of the woods surrounding the restaurant. Notice the delicacy that can be created by this printing technique.

As a result of screening, the breakfast card at The Brasserie has a variety of shades, even though only two colors were used to print it.

Using Menu Art for Promotion

Menu art can be adapted for a variety of other advertising applications—postcards, newsletters, matchbooks and match boxes, guest checks, napkins, and posters. This has two advantages—it presents a consistent image, and if the restaurant has purchased rights to re-use the art and design, new art will not have to be created.

If at all possible, a restaurant's entire promotional program should be designed and produced at the same time a new menu is. Printing several pieces—for instance, the menu cover, a table tent, and a postcard—at the same time can reduce set-up charges and save on the cost of press time.

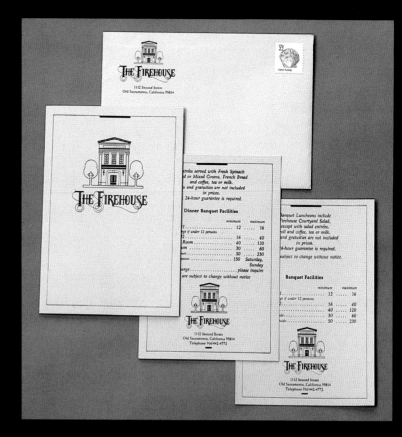

The Firehouse uses a line drawing of a firehouse as a symbol on all of its menus. The banquet menu, shown here, was designed to fit a matching envelope and is used as a promotional piece.

A mini-menu based on the full-size Sheppard's menu is used as an in-room promotional piece, a souvenir, and a direct mailer. Prices are not included in order to keep the mini-menu from becoming dated.

This miniature version of the cover of the Monique menu serves as a lightweight promotional card. Its small size and shape make it look much like a bookmark. The menu cover for Nicole, Monique's sister restaurant, has also been reproduced as a small card.

Full-color illustrations of the "Dion's Pizza Chef"—as a Valentine's Day angel, Uncle Sam, the Easter Bunny, and other seasonal characters—originally appeared on pressure-sensitive stickers that were affixed to the Dion's menu. Since then the same illustrations have been used on carry-out boxes, postcards, and posters. Two stickers and corresponding postcards are shown here.

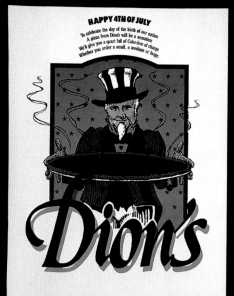

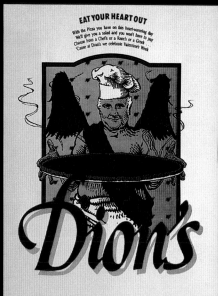

2

Interviews

Menu design is achieved through a collaboration of individuals—restaurateur, designer, consultant, printer, and the various specialists who may be involved in either design or production. The interviews in this chapter cover the same broad range of professionals.

Here, designers, restaurateurs, and the head of a turnkey design/printing concern discuss their approaches to the menu design process. Exploring how each viewpoint fits with the others provides insights into the level of interaction needed to achieve successful results. Also, the ideas expressed here can be applied by anyone involved in menu design.

Note: The menus shown in this chapter that are not referred to in the accompanying interview can be found later in the book, together with credit information and specifications.

Joseph Baum
**Restaurant Consultant, Restaurateur,
New York, New York**

"Everything must be in harmony, in balance. The menu must express that . . . it puts the ambiance to work."

Joseph Baum is a noted restaurant consultant whose creations include some of the most famous restaurants in America. Among them are New York City's Windows on the World, The Four Seasons, and, most recently, Aurora, of which he is a very active part-owner.

His personal trademark is his meticulous attention to all of the details, no matter how trifling they may seem, that contribute to the restaurant's ambiance . . . right down to china that coordinates not only with the decor but also with the colors of the foods that will be placed upon it. As consultant, he acts as a "producer/director." He works with the top talents in the field, including Milton Glaser, choosing them with their skills for the particular project in mind. He calls the group "purveyors of pleasure for profit."

The menu, "the silent salesman," as Baum calls it, is always an element in the overall scheme. He explains, "Everything must be in harmony, in balance. The menu must express that . . . it puts the ambiance to work."

Baum remarks that discussion of menus "opens a whole Pandora's Box of questions." For one, along with an appropriate design, the copy is important. Baum feels that over-defining an item is as undesirable as a lack of explanation. Also, the copy should not be trendy. For example, he feels that using words such as "market fresh" tells the customer something he or she already expects.

True to his perfectionist ways, Baum abhors menus that are "imitations" of good menus. He sticks by his high standards of appropriateness for the particular restaurant.

Baum is well known for the creation of classic restaurants. He quotes Oscar Wilde as having said, "If fashion weren't so terrible, it wouldn't have to be changed so often." Baum refers to his concepts as "an interpretation of today." This does not mean that they are trendy by any means.

For example, Aurora is the kind of restaurant that one can visit every day. Through thoughtful design, it is a comfortable place for business men and women to conduct "the power lunch," and it is also an appropriate choice for an exquisite dinner. *Everything* is custom-designed to harmonize beautifully with the total concept. Is this the culmination of years of dreaming? "Every love affair is," Baum replies with a smile.

Though his primary role at other restaurants has been as consultant, at Aurora he is a financially involved partner. What's the difference? Says Baum, "I don't work harder for myself, as people might think. But there is more risk-taking here." Why? "Because I'm responsible to myself," he says.

The menu at Aurora, designed by Milton Glaser, together with architect Phillip George, is a simple yet elegant understatement, a laminated card with four diecut semicircles to hold the neatly typed 8½″ × 11″ menu sheet in place. It includes a date, emphasizing the fact that it changes daily. Two main points in the design are clearly apparent: First, its simple construction flatters the concept of the restaurant, and second, it facilitates an easy change in menu items through the use of a word processor. Baum is certain that his well-heeled customers, about eighty percent of whom are repeat visitors, appreciate the daily changes in fare as well as the simplicity of the menu.

The staff, including Baum, meets regularly to create one-of-a-kind compositions. According to Aurora's talented chef, Gerard Pangaud, the group takes many factors into consideration, including market availability, the weather, and the staff that will be on hand. He also confides that the lunch menus are tailored to what the customers want, while the dinner menus express more of his personal creativity.

As far as the copy is concerned, Aurora's menus include the most important elements of each dish in a simple, straightforward manner that exudes style. Pangaud adds, "The secret is not in the recipe . . . it is in the experience [of the chef]."

Not all of Baum's menus have been so simple. He jokes about one he created during his early years in the industry. "The restaurant was called The Flame Room. The menu was printed with the type of ink that jumps out at you [when properly illuminated]. I learned that placing quinine water in front of the lights would produce this jumping out effect. Unfortunately," he laughs, "so did many other things, including everyone's cavities. The menu lasted one day."

Overall, Baum explains, "The menu must offer the customer an ease of choice. It shouldn't impose of the customer by requiring responses. You have to remember what the customer is in the restaurant for. It [the menu] doesn't exist to flatter the restaurateur."

Wally Ganzi

Restaurateur,
The Palm Restaurants,
New York, New York

"The menu, the caricatures on the walls, and above all, the service and quality of food must all be exactly right. Otherwise, the restaurant will never have the kind of feeling that will bring people back."

How do you take a two-outlet, intensely New York operation that restaurateur Wally Ganzi describes as "a family steak joint" and expand it to other cities without losing a flavor that's taken fifty years to create? It's not easy, but that's exactly what Ganzi has done.

Ganzi, a third generation restaurateur, and cousin Bruce Bozzi grew up in the two restaurants—The Palm and The Palm Too—that their grandfathers founded in New York City in 1926. Both restaurants are popular with the media and both are tremendously successful, but not successful enough to support six families. Ganzi and Bozzi, partly for economic reasons and partly in response to regular customer requests, wanted to expand to other cities.

Initially, they met with family opposition. So, in order to try their wings, both he and Bozzi opened their own restaurants in Manhattan. Finally, the family agreed to the expansion, and the cousins began with Washington, D.C. "We opened in Washington, D.C., without a printed menu," Ganzi recalls. "Customers didn't like it . . . they didn't like not knowing the prices."

A dinner menu was ultimately created, designed by Ganzi himself. Its cover features the cartoon-decked walls of the original Palm in New York, and it is used in all the Palms (prices are kept the same at all the restaurants). Individual restaurants are allowed flexibility with the lunch menu.

Ganzi maintains uniform quality in each Palm through personal supervision. He travels an average of thirty hours a month, monitoring operations at the various Palms and scouting new locations. He always chooses a location no farther than ten minutes from the major hotels, since the Palm's primary clientele is business travelers and persons who work in the media. Finally, he moves to the location of a new Palm for the first six months or so after it opens. "I organize the opening gala and fly in friends for the occasion," explains Ganzi. "Then I spend the next six months working out any kinks in the operation . . . training the staff, making sure things run smoothly." Personnel often transfer from city to city to work at new Palms. This contributes to the continuity of service and style.

"We want our staff to feel like part of the family," says Ganzi. "That translates into better service and a more relaxed and enjoyable meal for the customer. . . ." He feels that this is particularly important during the first few months of operation of a new restaurant. "There's a pattern that develops after a new Palm opens," he explains. "The opening gala attracts a lot of media attention and, for the first two months, we're completely booked. Customers wind up coming once a week and begin to burn out. Meanwhile, the customers that couldn't get in are turned off." At this point, the promoting must begin all over again. It's not unusual to see Ganzi himself making the rounds of the tables, checking to make sure everything is just right.

All of the Palms have the same look, which is partly attributable to Ganzi's twenty-year relationship with the same architect, and offer the same fine service. Says Ganzi, "The restaurant business is very demanding. . . . Fourteen- to sixteen-hour days are very common . . . but that's what it takes if you're going to do it right. . . . The menu, the caricatures on the walls, and above all, the service and quality of food must all be exactly right. Otherwise, the restaurant will never have the kind of feeling that will bring people back."

Dale Glasser

Designer,
Dale Glasser Graphics, Inc.,
New York, New York

"The menu should be clear and wonderful. . . . it should capture the essence of the restaurant."

Dale Glasser's first menus were designed for Bloomingdale's more than six years ago. Since then, she has worked with both small chains and independent restaurateurs on food-related projects. The most striking feature of her work is that each menu she designs reflects the place it represents. Apart from simple, clear copy, there is no stylistic clue that all the menus were conceived by the same person.

Glasser uses several strategies in developing successful menus for her clients. But the most important is laying a strong foundation of background information—about the concept, the market, the space, the food, and the client. One current client is located in Boston and has additional restaurants in Pittsburgh and Cleveland. She flies up to the headquarters at least once a month and makes frequent phone calls to keep updated.

Glasser's restaurant work involves both new projects and additions to existing programs. Ideally, she develops the menu at the same time the interior of the restaurant is designed. This allows for coordination of all the visual elements of the space, from signage to matches, and ensures a unified look. Although she works partly from renderings, she feels that two-dimensional representation can never duplicate the sense of the space itself. "I always view the location at least once," she says, "and if the interior work is far enough along, I'll take photographs, too, for future reference."

Based in New York City, Glasser finds that she has three tiers of restaurant clients: restaurant owners, restaurant consultants, and interior designers/ architects. "The owner is involved in all major presentations and always has final design approval," she explains. "The consultant most often acts as intermediary, providing me with food concept and marketing details, and screening out any extraneous material either to or from the client. And the architect and interior designers have more specific creative input, with stylistic and color suggestions."

Much of her business is referred by consultants, designers, or friends with whom she has worked before. "Most of my steady repeat business is due to good past working relationships," she says. "Only very rarely do I make cold calls—if it's a project that

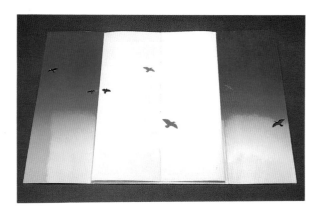

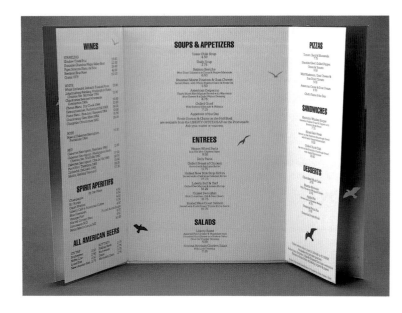

I'm lusting after, or would be perfect for me, or would be great fun to do, or would be highly visible."

Part of the reason for Glasser's success is her passion for excellence. When she recognizes that a situation demands different skills than she possesses, she hires specialists accordingly, whether they are copywriters, illustrators, retouchers, photographers, or translators. For example, she explains, "If menu items are in a foreign language, I'll work with a translator to review the descriptions, the spelling, and the grammar. If they're in English, though, I'll usually edit the copy myself."

Although capable, she doesn't often do the illustration herself. "There are millions of others," she says, "who can do it better, faster, and with much less agony than I." One notable exception is the illustration for the Safari Grill. The restaurateur wanted a menu that was a bit 1920s French in feel, but that had a sense of the contemporary. Glasser provided the Cubist still-life illustration, reminiscent of the Paris art scene of the 1920s, but ensured that the menu would have a current feeling by handling the type in a modern way.

Glasser most frequently designs for an entire menu program. "Before I set pencil to paper," she explains, "I determine how the menu will be used in the restaurant, how often it should change to reflect new items and prices." In one case where the menu changed weekly, she designed preprinted forms onto which the menu items would be photocopied with only one master sheet prepared by the chef each week. Often, her lunch and dinner menu covers can be distinguished by a change in color or scale, for ease of management and administration.

Glasser's proposals are designed to be letters of agreement and include the design fee, the scope of services, standard business conditions, and a provision that permits her to receive a credit line for her work on the menu. The proposals do not cover out-of-pocket expenses, which are estimated once the design format is established. Glasser explains, "I charge by the project, not by the hour because I can have more control over the progress of the job, since there are set limits to each phase."

In her experience, restaurants usually start with just dinner service and, if the business warrants it, usually expand to lunch, then brunch. "I frequently check back with them to see how things are going, if the menu is working, or if they need additional pieces designed," she says. "This is a good source of work and establishes a reputation for good follow-through with the client."

Regarding promotional pieces, Glasser feels that, while they have their place, not every restaurant needs them. "It's important to consider where and how to advertise, that the pieces be targeted correctly, and whether the restaurant is prepared to handle the additional volume of meals they can generate."

Like every other designer, Glasser sometimes experiences problems on design projects. She recounts one in which she encountered an all-too-frequent problem—a lack of time. The client, Il Giardino, an elegant Italian restaurant in New Jersey, needed

printed menus delivered ten days after concept approval. "There was no time to do the fine-tuning we usually do at the comp stage. In fact, there was no comp stage. The art for the rose was already drawn and color-separated, but we still had to design the background and prepare the mechanical art. The staff went into high gear. The restaurant consultant came to the office to review and sign-off on the boards, and the printer was waiting at the door to take the artwork the second it was okayed." The menu was delivered in time for the opening, but as a result, the orange dots on the cover are larger than either the restaurateur or the designer would have liked. "This problem has now been corrected," Glasser says, "and the next run will be perfect."

Glasser suspects that computers and word-processors will significantly affect menu design in the future: "Although I haven't seen anything yet that will work for a larger than legal-size format or for anything other than a strictly standardized system, I do think that the computer has great potential in simplifying the menu system once designers and programmers can work out a format that can work as both a creative and a flexible system."

This designer also sees a trend toward greater public awareness of menus. "As people are dining out more and more, increased attention is put on restaurant ambiance, of which the menu is a major focus," she explains. "It is the sole means of communicating the food items, and speaks intimately to the customers. The restaurant today is a source of social entertainment . . . not just a place for filling stomachs. And menus now seem more attuned to adding to that spirit of delight. The padded, leather-bound, gold tied, and tassled menus are seen less and less, in favor of simpler, or more inventive, pieces."

And, she insists, "the most important thing is that you clearly communicate what the place is serving. The worst thing is to bewilder, terrify, infuriate, or disgust the diner. The menu should be pleasant to experience, and easy to read. The more delight or humor, or tasteful elegance, or sense of place it brings the reader, the better."

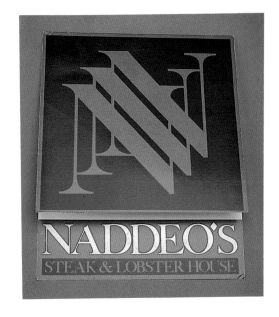

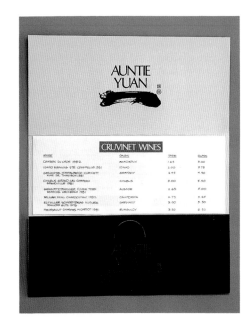

Chuck Polonsky
**Co-owner,
Associates Printing Service,
Glenview, Illinois**

"We all keep a great sense of humor. We have fun. We have a good relationship with all our clients. Communication is a lot easier when our clients feel comfortable."

Associates Printing Services has long-term clients, not one-time customers. This is because so much of its work is repeat business—whether that work involves new projects from a long-standing restaurant or hotel client or a first time design project from an organization whose new food and beverage director has previously worked with Associates Printing Service.

Chuck Polonsky and his partner, Jeffrey Harris, who together founded the company in 1973, offer "one-stop shopping" for a menu buyer. They can provide all design and production services needed to create a menu, utilizing the talents of Polonsky, as Creative Director, eight staff artists, an in-house copy copywriter, an in-house proofreader, and a staff that provides complete typography and printing services. Associates Printing Service also designs logos and signage and can produce peripheral materials such as advertisements, direct mailers, and brochures.

Polonsky believes that the secret to this organization's continued success is communication and planning. "A restaurateur," he says, "is a special breed . . . a different animal . . . after thirteen years in this business, I've learned how to speak his language . . . we can *communicate*."

Polonsky also believes very strongly in planning. As a "turnkey" operation, Associates Printing Service has the luxury of needing only four weeks to produce a menu for a restaurant. Even so, planning is a key issue.

The first step is to "communicate with the person in charge. Talk to him . . . explain how to plan ahead," Polonsky explains. Specific goals and objectives are then defined, and the "image" the restaurant must project is established. On occasion, Polonsky asks his clients to look at samples and decide what they want or what they *don't* want. "Sometimes, it's easier to identify what you don't like," he says.

In most instances, Polonsky presents several ideas. The client usually chooses one idea to develop or a

combination of the ideas presented. On the rare occasions when none of the ideas is acceptable, Polonsky presents others until the client is totally satisfied. He *guarantees* his work. In all instances, achieving the "look" sought is a group effort with both the design group and the restaurateur contributing ideas. Further communication then enables the design group to refine the selected approach into the final product.

Once an idea is selected for development, a production budget is established. The client is advised in advance of the development cost for that idea; if satisfied, he is given an estimate of the cost to produce the menu in the quantity needed.

The quantity is determined by considering several factors, which include the number of seats in the restaurant and the rate of turnover, the type of usage (fine dining or coffee shops, for example), expected spoilage and waste (wear and tear) and expected length of usage.

Polonsky prefers to view many of the "problems" associated with the menu design business as "challenges." He has, for example, had a client call him Tuesday, needing a printed menu by Friday. Of course, in such cases, he says, "There is only so much you can do in a certain amount of time!" Yet he prides himself on his staff's ability to produce near-miracles. "If we can't produce it in time, you know it can't be done!"

Polonsky has reason for his pride. He establishes a trusting and trustworthy relationship with clients whenever possible. He guarantees his clients' satisfaction. Most importantly of all, he tries to educate his clients on how to plan a successful menu program.

Because of the broad range of his clients, Polonsky can see several trends in the restaurant industry and consequently in menu design. He feels that heavy, leather-bound menus contradict the simplicity of the current trends in American cuisine, which include the increasing popularity of Southwestern and other regional American cooking styles.

He also sees that specials are currently selling very well—a factor that directly affects menu design. He feels that word processing is well suited for restaurants needing the flexibility to change items—whether these items are specials or dishes containing extremely perishable foods that are no longer available.

Finally, Polonsky encourages the use of the "mini-menu." "It's an excellent form of advertising," he explains. "It maximizes the use of your menu as a promotional aspect of your restaurant."

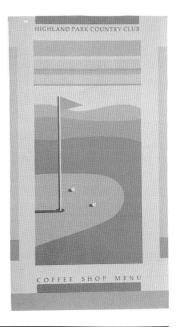

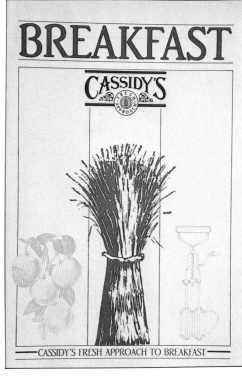

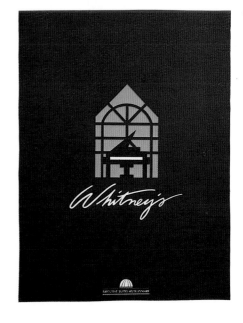

Diane Richards
Art Director, Marketing Department, El Torito Restaurants, Irvine, California

"El Torito has a recognizable company style."

Mexican food is as much a part of the California lifestyle as surfing or the movies. Because Mexico borders the southern edge of the state, many Californians have visited Mexico and, like Texans and residents of other bordering states, have become fairly sophisticated about Mexican culture and food.

By extension, this means that when a California-based chain of Mexican restaurants goes national, it faces new marketing challenges. Rather than simply presenting the food, it must also educate the consumer about the nature of the food—how to eat it, how to combine different dishes for an enjoyable meal, even how to pronounce the names of the dishes. At the same time, the company's marketing on the home front must become increasingly sophisticated to meet the needs of more knowledgeable patrons.

That's quite an assignment for any company. And, when the company's art department consists of one Art Director and three designers who develop all the point-of-purchase material, ads, and menus, it's a very tall order indeed. Yet that's what El Torito's Diane Richards does and, as the selection of menus here demonstrates, she does it very well.

El Torito uses a variety of specialty menus for drinks, desserts, and the different seasons. Richards' role is to develop a creative direction, find the right people to execute it, and ensure that the end product meets company design standards and is ready on time. She finds the variety an exciting part of her job.

El Torito tracks sales in the various menu categories on a national basis. When one area seems to be lagging, a point-of-purchase item is sought. "A problem faced by all restaurants is a decline in liquor sales," Richards says. "The Polar Relief Kit was our answer to this problem . . . We addressed it to a particular audience we thought would be found in our cantinas." The Polar Relief Kit was the second place Grand Prize winner in the National Restaurant Association's 1986 Great Menus Contest. Aimed at a young, fun-loving crowd, it is a humorous rendition of a standard first-aid kit. Inside, the customer finds "bandages," "potions," and other medical paraphernalia to "cure the winter cold." All of the items are warm and comforting, and employ

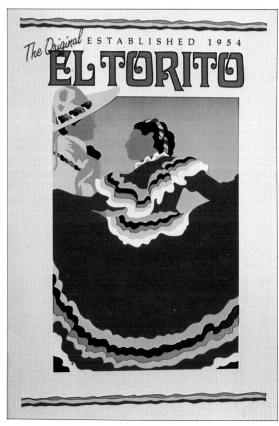

name-brand liquors and liqueurs in their manufacture. The copy is humorous but brief, and no prices are listed. "It was kept light and fun," Richards explains, "and we went easy on the Mexican theme because of my observation that all the menus in the [restaurant] environment are so permeated with the theme that any intermediate menu . . . will stand out."

Not all El Torito's marketing efforts have been as successful. For Rosa Corona, a restaurant in Indianapolis, the menu was carefully geared to educate the consumer on Mexican cuisine. Local sentiment for American foods proved too strong and the restaurant closed and reopened as the Keystone Grill, a contemporary American restaurant. The interior of the Rosa Corona menu, with its two bright red roses atop the menu selections, is shown here.

A specialist in food-related projects and previously an art director with Carnation Company, Richards enjoys working with in-house clients. She says, "The advantage of in-house advertising is that one has the opportunity to really *know* the client and the concept they want to communicate. It also provides for a working relationship with the operations side which shows the results of the promotion. There is also the opportunity to build on past successes and continue to improve."

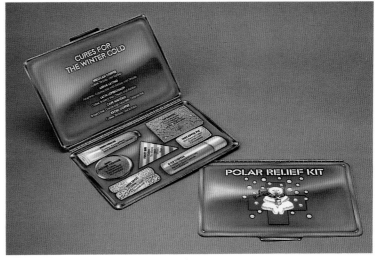

Gordon A. Sinclair

Restaurateur
Gordon, Chicago, Illinois
Sinclair's, Lake Forest, Illinois
Sinclair's American Grill, Jupiter, Florida

"Businessmen are used to risk. . . . It is up to the graphic designer to make it more comfortable for the businessman [restaurateur] to deal with the danger of a graphic designer."

In 1976, Gordon A. Sinclair changed careers, moving from public relations and advertising into the restaurant business. He opened Gordon, his first restaurant, in a then-unusual location. "The area was most charitably described as 'colorful'," he explains. Gordon was Chicago's first sophisticated storefront restaurant. The lack of a printed menu and printed prices was not popular with the clientele.

By the time Sinclair opened his second restaurant, Sinclair's, in Lake Forest, he had met David Bartels, who still does the graphic design, including menu covers, for all his restaurants.

Juxtaposition of the incongruous is an important feature of Sinclair's restaurants. Gordon, for example, is quite posh, but the restroom walls are covered with graffiti. The menu covers are designed to startle, elicit conversation, and generally enhance the experience.

Sinclair's background in the advertising and public relations fields has, he feels, enabled him to successfully interact with graphic designers. For those without such a background, his advice is, "Surrender!"

In Sinclair's view, the menu can make a statement about a restaurant and can say, "This place is fun, this place is attractive." He feels that the lighting, the ambiance, the temperature, even the flowers on the table, all mount up to "yes, I'd like to come back" or "no, I wouldn't." "What we're trying to do as businesspeople," he says, "is design things that will contribute to the experience so that they [the patrons] will *want* to come back."

Design by committee doesn't work for Sinclair. He has a definite idea of the direction he wants a menu to take and prefers to work directly with the designer. He feels that a menu should spark conversation and be fun, but it should also be legible. "If a menu cannot be read by the available light, even if it is candlelight," he says, "the meal is immediately off to a bad start." He prefers menus that incorporate the price into the body of the item description. He feels that, because his establishment provides "dining as theater, extravagance," price should not be a primary consideration and therefore, there is no reason to position the prices out in a column by themselves. He also feels that use of a printed menu, instead of a daily

written menu, gives the kitchen time to perfect its repertoire and affects food cost favorably.

Sinclair also makes extensive use of promotional materials based on art he has had created for a menu cover or another purpose. For example, the postcard of "Rosemary and Mr. Chicken" was first a free poster distributed to customers as a souvenir immediately following the expansion of his restaurant, Gordon. "It was just getting more mileage out of art we'd already bought," he explains. The art for that postcard was created by artist-illustrator Roy Carruthers.

Sinclair has a budget for menu design separate from his advertising budget. He also uses direct mail and is planning a newsletter to regular restaurant customers. He feels that advertising media should be carefully selected to reflect the type of restaurant one has; for fine dining, radio coverage and billboards are not appropriate. Film or television mentions, however, can be very effective. His restaurant, Gordon, has appeared in a cameo role in several films.

Sinclair feels that word processing and computers can be, but need *not* be, a threat to designers. In his view, the designer must provide the refinement and taste to *enhance* the use of word processing in menu composition, but not permit word processing to dictate the design.

Restaurants today are big business—equipment can cost up to a million dollars. Sinclair feels that anyone who is at all "savvy" to the needs of a restaurant as a business must understand the need for a designer. "A menu is another sales tool," he explains.

After more than ten years in the restaurant business, Sinclair has assembled the right chef, the right ambiance, and the right design elements. He understands and consistently addresses his audience. He was the recipient of the Ivy Award from *Restaurants and Institutions* magazine in 1986. This is the most prestigious award available to a restaurateur; that says it all.

3

Theme Menus

The theme restaurant uses decorative motifs, appropriate
entertainment, and sometimes clever descriptive menu copy
to create its ambiance. Because this type of
restaurant is the embodiment of a total vision, it is important
that the menu be a logical extension of the overall concept.

Although theme restaurants are often light-hearted and
entertaining, the theme can also be tied to location,
specialized collections, or activities offered at the restaurant.
The menus in this chapter feature cuisines ranging from
simple burgers to nouvelle cuisine to the best of fine dining.
Yet each incorporates a special and unique vision that extends
far beyond the choice of food served.

RESTAURANT: Scotch n' Sirloin
LOCATION: Boston, Massachusetts
DESIGNER: In-house designer
SPECIFICATIONS:
SIZE: 10"(l) x 4½"(w) x 7¼"(h) (lunch box)
MEDIUM: Clear acetate

This restaurant is located in a former print shop opposite the Boston Garden. The decor emphasizes the print shop theme, though the presses have been replaced with broilers. The industrial theme is further enhanced by the use of a worker's lunch box as a three-dimensional medium for the menu. The menu is produced by silkscreening onto clear acetate, which is then sealed onto the lunch boxes. Good food in an informal atmosphere draws both an older crowd and some spillover traffic from the sporting events at the Garden.

RESTAURANT:	Pittsburg Millie's Grand Opera House
LOCATION:	Pittsburg, Pennsylvania
DESIGNER:	Kathy Grubb
FIRM:	Gray, Baingarten Layport, Inc.
ILLUSTRATORS:	Vann Jennings, Sharon Thompson

SPECIFICATIONS:

SIZE:	7½″ x 14″
PAPER:	70# Carnival Groove/Khaki
PRINTER:	New Image Press

Pittsburgh Millie's is located in the newly renovated Warner Centre in the heart of downtown Pittsburgh. The Warner Centre originally was a grand old theater, and the theatrical architectural elements are still visible throughout the new shops and restaurants in the building.

Though primarily serving a young office crowd, Millie's hearkens back to Pittsburgh's proud past as a mill town. This is particularly evident in the slightly brash menu copy. Many dishes are named for prominent Pittsburgh residents of the past.

The cover establishes the restaurant as a light-hearted drinking place by showing a Toulouse-Lautrec poster detail. The entertainment theme is further enhanced by performances reminiscent of old dance-hall times .

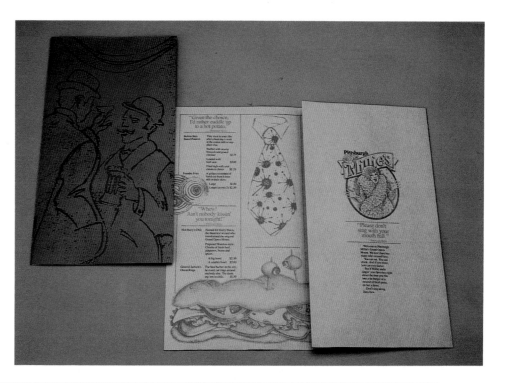

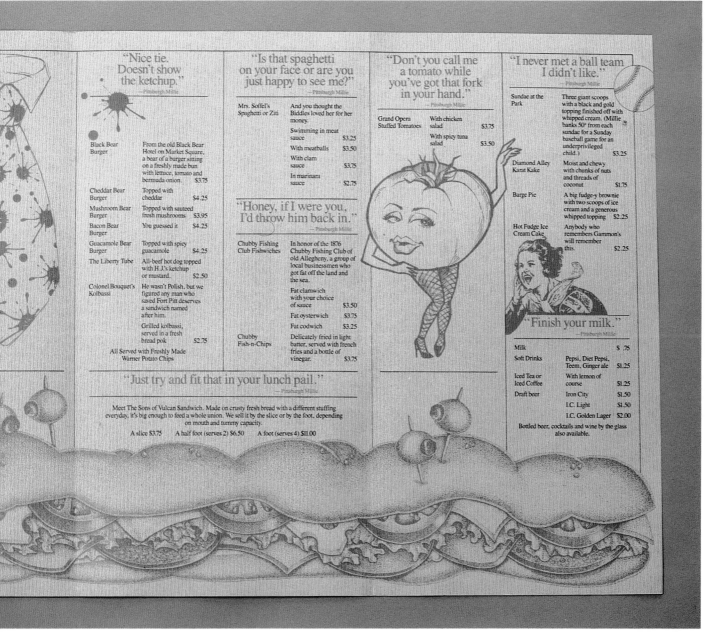

MENU

DAISY FLOUR MILL

1880 Blossom Road   Rochester, New York

APPETIZERS

CLAMS CASINO Six beauties broiled with butter, chopped green pepper and bacon served on hot rock salt
4.50

SHRIMP ON THE ROCKS Four large chilled shrimp on ice with a zippy cocktail sauce
5.75

of ground meats and
d sauce

DESSERTS
Made here by our own "blue ribbon" baker using DAISY PASTRY FLOUR

DAISY FLOUR MILL

1880 Blossom Road   Rochester, New York

AFTER DINNER COFFEES

$3.00

DAISY COFFEE
a blend of freshly
brandy, Kahlua and a do
me

ANISH COFFEE
with Tia Maria

ICAN COFFEE
with Kahlua

RUBY'S
an exciting com
nd rums - it alwa

WINE LIST

DAISY FLOUR MILL

1880 Blossom Road   Rochester, New York

RESTAURANT: McGuffey's
LOCATION: Asheville, North Carolina
DESIGNER: Michael Gaffney
FIRM: Young Creative Associates, Inc.
ILLUSTRATOR: Michael Gaffney
SPECIFICATIONS:
SIZE: 6½" x 8"
PAPER: Case bound book (cover); 80#
Valley Forge Olde Natural Cover
(interior)
PRINTER: The R.L. Bryan Company

This menu won second place in the "Most Imaginative" category of the National Restaurant Association's 1986 Great Menus Contest. The name of the restaurant is drawn from the McGuffey Reader, which was used to teach generations of American children the basics of reading. The restaurant's theme is traditional American cooking. The educational motif is carried out via chalkboard specials, which also appear at each table on individual slates similar to those pioneer children used in learning to write.

The menus are relatively expensive to produce—each costs sixteen dollars. But, the use of case bound books as a medium for the menus makes them as sturdy as the original readers. Clever copywriting leads the diner through a "lesson plan," beginning with "academic appetizers" and continuing through such areas as "elective courses" and "supplemental studies."

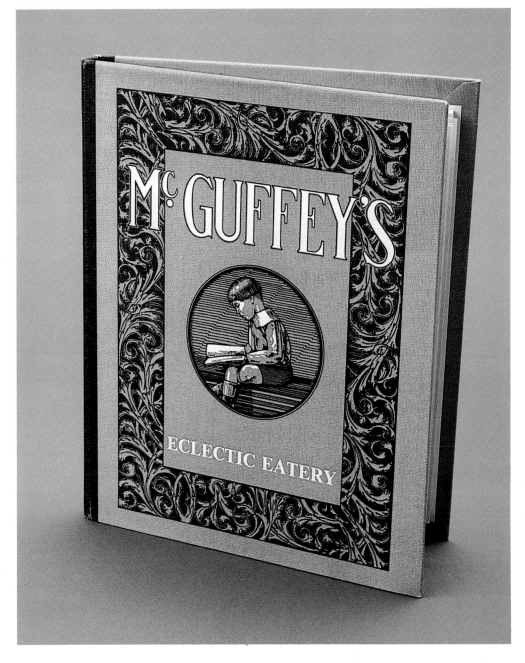

◄ RESTAURANT: Daisy Flour Mill Restaurant
LOCATION: Rochester, New York
SPECIFICATIONS:
SIZE: 8½" x 13"
PRINTER: Eric Venas

The Daisy Flour Mill was a working flour mill into the twentieth century. Though it has become a restaurant specializing in elegant traditional cuisine, it remains listed on the National Register of Historic Places. The menu pays homage to the mill's five-pound flour sack by using a replica to hold the three menu list inserts. On the back of the sack is a brief history of Daisy Flour Mill and its various owners. The mill theme is continued at the restaurant with the downstairs Mill Race Bar and the miller's houses, which still stand around the mill itself.

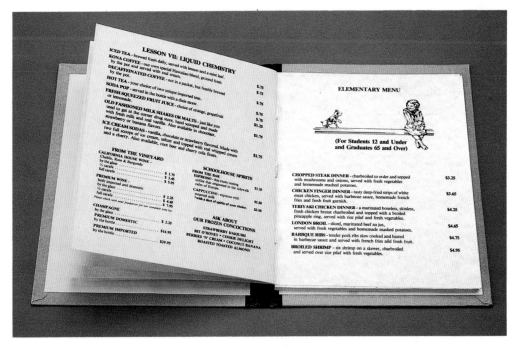

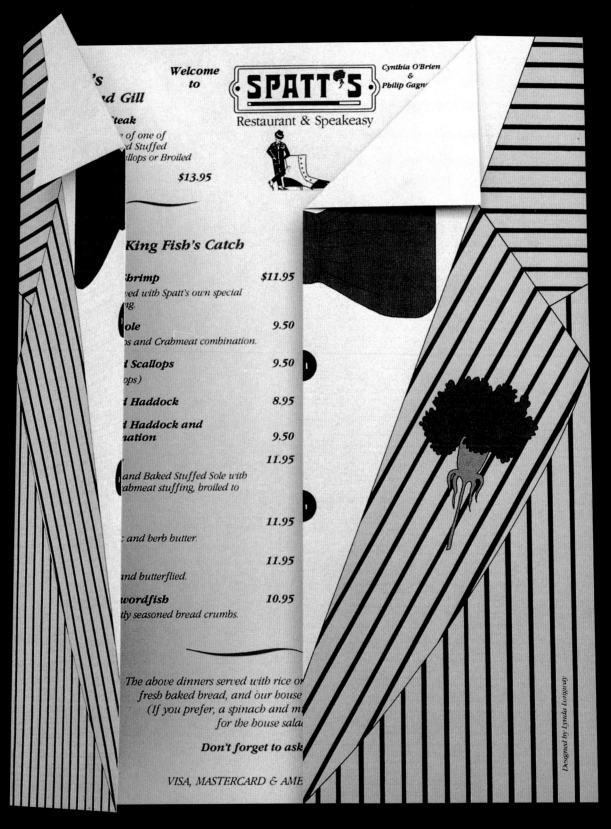

Welcome to

·SPATT'S·
Restaurant & Speakeasy

Cynthia O'Brien
&
Philip Gagn

's
d Gill

teak

of one of
d Stuffed
llops or Broiled

$13.95

King Fish's Catch

brimp	$11.95
ed with Spatt's own special ng.	
ole	9.50
s and Crabmeat combination.	
Scallops	9.50
ps)	
Haddock	8.95
Haddock and ation	9.50
	11.95
and Baked Stuffed Sole with abmeat stuffing, broiled to	
	11.95
and herb butter.	
	11.95
and butterflied.	
wordfish	10.95
tly seasoned bread crumbs.	

The above dinners served with rice or
fresh baked bread, and our house
(If you prefer, a spinach and m
for the house sala

Don't forget to ask

VISA, MASTERCARD & AME

Designed by Lynda Langway

RESTAURANT: Spatt's Restaurant & Speakeasy
LOCATION: Manchester, New Hampshire
DESIGNER: Linda Langway
FIRM: Keyston Press
SPECIFICATIONS:
SIZE: 8½" x 11"
PRINTER: Keyston Press

The front cover of this delightful menu, which deservedly credits the designer, features a wing collar and boutonniere that effectively convey the restaurant's theme of the 1930s and early 1940s. The design invites the diner to open the natty striped jacket and discover what's inside. The menu cover splits, logically, right through the shirt buttons. The restaurant walls are decorated with movie stills of "gangster" actors such as Humphrey Bogart and glamourous co-stars like Lauren Bacall.

RESTAURANT: Liberty Cafe

LOCATION: New York, New York

DESIGNER: Dale Glasser

FIRM: Dale Glasser Graphics, Inc.

ILLUSTRATOR: Dale Glasser

SPECIFICATIONS:

SIZE: 10″ x 14″

PAPER: Chromolux, coated one side, film-laminated, die-cut and blind embossed (cover); 100# Mohawk Superfine, bright white (interior)

Seagulls float in graduated shades of blue, some printed on the cover, others die-cut to reveal the inside front cover. The three-color interior forms were designed to permit one-color updates. The restaurateur requested and got a menu that accurately reflects the sense of air and light that characterizes the restaurant. Although the menu interior incorporates everything from the wine list to main courses to desserts, there is plenty of space around each section. The seagull motif is repeated for interest. A pleasant blend of serif and sans serif type styles and the incorporation of prices into the copy describing the main course selections further distinguish the overall menu design.

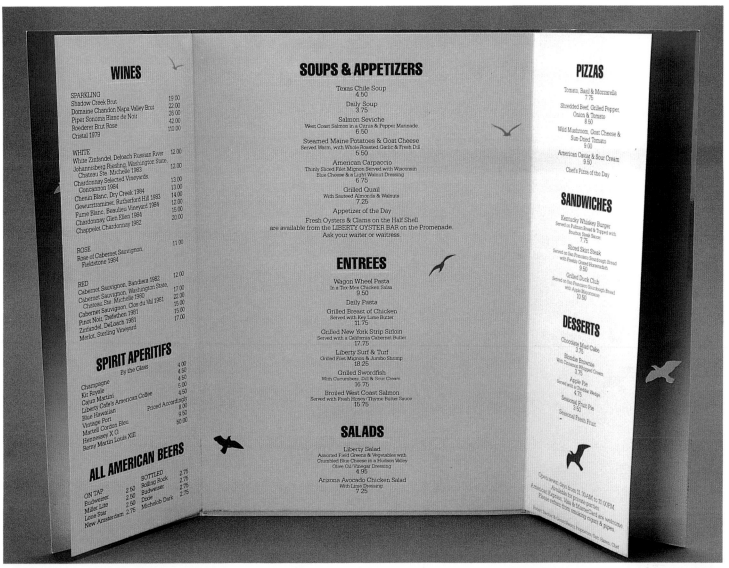

WINES

SPARKLING
Shadow Creek Brut   19.00
Domaine Chandon Napa Valley Brut   22.00
Piper Sonoma Blanc de Noir   26.00
Roederer Brut Rose   42.00
Cristal 1979   110.00

WHITE
White Zinfandel, Deloach Russian River   12.00
Johannisberg Riesling, Washington State,
   Chateau Ste. Michelle 1983   12.00
Chardonnay Selected Vineyards,
   Concannon 1984   13.00
Chenin Blanc, Dry Creek 1984   13.00
Gewurztraminer, Rutherford Hill 1983   14.00
Fume Blanc, Beaulieu Vineyard 1984   12.00
Chardonnay, Glen Ellen 1984   15.00
Chappelet Chardonnay 1982   20.00

ROSE   11.00
Rose of Cabernet Sauvignon,
   Fieldstone 1984

RED
Cabernet Sauvignon, Bandiera 1982   12.00
Cabernet Sauvignon, Washington State,
   Chateau Ste. Michelle 1980   17.00
Cabernet Sauvignon, Clos du Val 1981   22.00
Pinot Noir, Trefethen 1981   15.00
Zinfandel, DeLoach 1981   15.00
Merlot, Sterling Vineyard   17.00

SPIRIT APERITIFS
By the Glass   4.00
                                                                     4.50
Champagne   4.50
Kir Royale   5.00
Cajun Martini   4.50
Liberty Cafe's American Coffee
Blue Hawaiian   Priced Accordingly
Vintage Port   8.00
Martell Cordon Bleu   9.50
Hennessey X.O.   50.00
Remy Martin Louis XIII

ALL AMERICAN BEERS

ON TAP		BOTTLED	
Budweiser	2.50	Rolling Rock	2.75
Miller Lite	2.50	Budweiser	2.75
Lone Star	2.50	Dixie	2.75
New Amsterdam	2.75	Michelob Dark	2.75

SOUPS & APPETIZERS

Texas Chile Soup
4.50

Daily Soup
3.75

Salmon Seviche
West Coast Salmon in a Citrus & Pepper Marinade
6.50

Steamed Maine Potatoes & Goat Cheese
Served Warm, with Whole Roasted Garlic & Fresh Dill
5.50

American Carpaccio
Thinly Sliced Filet Mignon Served with Wisconsin
Blue Cheese & a Light Walnut Dressing
6.75

Grilled Quail
With Sauteed Almonds & Walnuts
7.25

Appetizer of the Day

Fresh Oysters & Clams on the Half Shell
are available from the LIBERTY OYSTER BAR on the Promenade.
Ask your waiter or waitress.

ENTREES

Wagon Wheel Pasta
In a Tex-Mex Chicken Salsa
9.50

Daily Pasta

Grilled Breast of Chicken
Served with Key Lime Butter
11.75

Grilled New York Strip Sirloin
Served with a California Cabernet Butter
17.75

Liberty Surf & Turf
Grilled Filet Mignon & Jumbo Shrimp
18.25

Grilled Swordfish
With Cucumbers, Dill & Sour Cream
16.75

Broiled West Coast Salmon
Served with Fresh Honey/Thyme Butter Sauce
15.75

SALADS

Liberty Salad
Assorted Field Greens & Vegetables with
Crumbled Blue Cheese in a Hudson Valley
Olive Oil/Vinegar Dressing
4.95

Arizona Avocado Chicken Salad
With Lime Dressing
7.25

PIZZAS

Tomato, Basil & Mozzarella
7.75

Shredded Beef, Grilled Pepper,
Onion & Tomato
8.50

Wild Mushroom, Goat Cheese &
Sun-Dried Tomato
9.00

American Caviar & Sour Cream
9.50

Chef's Pizza of the Day

SANDWICHES

Kentucky Whiskey Burger
Served on Pullman Bread & Topped with
Bourbon Steak Sauce
7.75

Sliced Skirt Steak
Served on San Francisco Sourdough Bread
with Freshly Grated Horseradish
9.50

Grilled Duck Club
Served on San Francisco Sourdough Bread
with Apple Mayonnaise
10.50

DESSERTS

Chocolate Mud Cake
3.75

Blondie Brownie
With Cinnamon Whipped Cream
3.75

Apple Pie
Served with a Cheddar Wedge
4.75

Seasonal Fruit Pie
3.50

Seasonal Fresh Fruit

Open seven days from 11:30AM to 11:00PM
Available for private parties
American Express, Visa & MasterCard are welcome
Please refrain from smoking cigars & pipes

Robert Reebin & Gerald Bertox Proprietors; Sam Hazen, Chef

RESTAURANT: Champions
LOCATION: San Luis Obispo, California
DESIGNER: Julie Patricio Block
SPECIFICATIONS:
　　SIZE: 17″ x 9″ (closed)
　　PAPER: Palomino
　　PRINTER: Winken's Printing

Foil-stamping brightens the cover of this menu, which is die-cut to resemble a pennant. The excitement of sports is the focus of this restaurant and bar, which is equipped with a satellite dish and two ten-foot television screens. The sports theme is evident in both the menu's copywriting and food offerings. A number of hearty appetizers are offered for those unable to tear themselves away from the on-screen action in the bar. The menu was recently changed in response to customers' reluctance to purchase extra-large portions of steak. These are still available but are mentioned in a footnote, rather than formally listed in the menu.

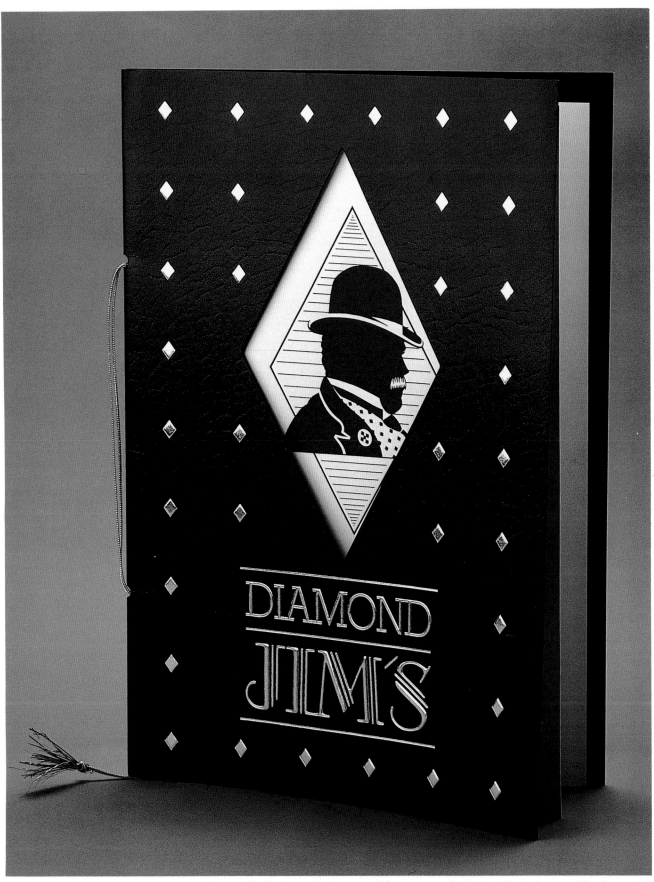

RESTAURANT:	Diamond Jim's
LOCATION:	Las Vegas, Nevada
DESIGNERS:	Dyane Grady, Michael A. Severino, Jr.
FIRM:	Nevada Business Forms, Inc.
SPECIFICATIONS:	
SIZE:	10½" x 15"
PRINTER:	Nevada Business Forms, Inc.

Diamond Jim Brady was famed as a prodigious eater in an era—the gay '90s—that produced many hearty trenchermen. He is a good choice as an emblem for a fine dining room in a Las Vegas Hotel. Brady was famous for the many and elaborate banquets he hosted; generosity and a zest for life were his trademarks. The restaurant's cuisine is traditional and sumptuous—no cuisine minceur here. The designer used the diamond as a motif in both the foil embossing on the cover and a die-cut window revealing a cameo of Diamond Jim himself on the menu's front page. The menu covers are sturdy. The interiors are printed in one color and are held in place by silver cord. This arrangement permits easy replacement of the more fragile interior forms.

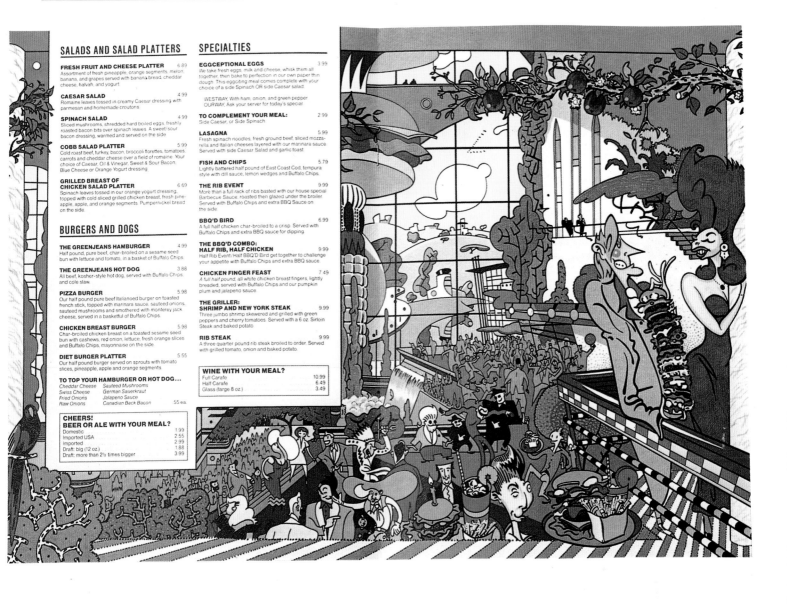

SALADS AND SALAD PLATTERS

FRESH FRUIT AND CHEESE PLATTER 6.89
Assortment of fresh pineapple, orange segments, melon, banana, and grapes served with banana bread, cheddar cheese, halvah, and yogurt.

CAESAR SALAD 4.99
Romaine leaves tossed in creamy Caesar dressing with parmesan and homemade croutons.

SPINACH SALAD 4.99
Sliced mushrooms, shredded hard boiled eggs, freshly roasted bacon bits over spinach leaves. A sweet/sour bacon dressing, warmed and served on the side.

COBB SALAD PLATTER 5.99
Cold roast beef, turkey, bacon, broccoli florettes, tomatoes, carrots and cheddar cheese over a field of romaine. Your choice of Caesar, Oil & Vinegar, Sweet & Sour Bacon, Blue Cheese or Orange Yogurt dressing.

GRILLED BREAST OF CHICKEN SALAD PLATTER 6.69
Spinach leaves tossed in our orange yogurt dressing, topped with cold sliced grilled chicken breast, fresh pineapple, apple, and orange segments. Pumpernickel bread on the side.

BURGERS AND DOGS

THE GREENJEANS HAMBURGER 4.99
Half pound, pure beef, char-broiled on a sesame seed bun with lettuce and tomato, in a basket of Buffalo Chips.

THE GREENJEANS HOT DOG 3.88
All beef, kosher-style hot dog, served with Buffalo Chips, and cole slaw.

PIZZA BURGER 5.98
Our half pound pure beef Italianoed burger on toasted french stick, topped with marinara sauce, sauteed onions, sauteed mushrooms and smothered with monterey jack cheese, served in a basketful of Buffalo Chips.

CHICKEN BREAST BURGER 5.98
Char-broiled chicken breast on a toasted sesame seed bun with cashews, red onion, lettuce, fresh orange slices and Buffalo Chips, mayonnaise on the side.

DIET BURGER PLATTER 5.55
Our half pound burger served on sprouts with tomato slices, pineapple, apple and orange segments.

TO TOP YOUR HAMBURGER OR HOT DOG...
Cheddar Cheese ... Sauteed Mushrooms
Swiss Cheese ... German Sauerkraut
Fried Onions ... Jalapeno Sauce
Raw Onions ... Canadian Back Bacon ... .55 ea.

**CHEERS!
BEER OR ALE WITH YOUR MEAL?**
Domestic 1.99
Imported USA 2.55
Imported 2.99
Draft: big (12 oz.) 1.88
Draft: more than 2½ times bigger 3.99

SPECIALTIES

EGGCEPTIONAL EGGS 3.99
We take fresh eggs, milk and cheese, whisk them all together, then bake to perfection in our own paper thin dough. This eggciting meal comes complete with your choice of a side Spinach OR side Caesar salad.

WESTWAY, With ham, onion, and green pepper OURWAY, Ask your server for today's special

TO COMPLEMENT YOUR MEAL: 2.99
Side Caesar, or Side Spinach

LASAGNA 5.99
Fresh spinach noodles, fresh ground beef, sliced mozzarella and Italian cheeses layered with our marinara sauce. Served with side Caesar Salad and garlic toast.

FISH AND CHIPS 5.79
Lightly battered half pound of East Coast Cod, tempura style with dill sauce, lemon wedges and Buffalo Chips.

THE RIB EVENT 9.99
More than a full rack of ribs basted with our house special Barbecue Sauce, roasted then glazed under the broiler. Served with Buffalo Chips and extra BBQ Sauce on the side.

BBQ'D BIRD 6.99
A full half chicken char-broiled to a crisp. Served with Buffalo Chips and extra BBQ sauce for dipping.

**THE BBQ'D COMBO:
HALF RIB, HALF CHICKEN** 9.99
Half Rib Event/Half BBQ'D Bird get together to challenge your appetite with Buffalo Chips and extra BBQ sauce.

CHICKEN FINGER FEAST 7.49
A full half pound, all white chicken breast fingers, lightly breaded, served with Buffalo Chips and our pumpkin plum and jalapeno sauce.

**THE GRILLER:
SHRIMP AND NEW YORK STEAK** 9.99
Three jumbo shrimp skewered and grilled with green peppers and cherry tomatoes. Served with a 6 oz. Sirloin Steak and baked potato.

RIB STEAK 9.99
A three quarter pound rib steak broiled to order. Served with grilled tomato, onion and baked potato.

WINE WITH YOUR MEAL?
Full Carafe 10.99
Half Carafe 6.49
Glass (large 8 oz.) 3.49

RESTAURANT: Mr. Greenjeans/The Kalen Group
LOCATION: Toronto, Ontario, Canada
Benito,
FIRM: Reactor
SPECIFICATIONS:
SIZE: 9″ x 12½″
PAPER: 100# Plainfield Homespun
PRINTER: Baker, Gurney & McLaren Press

This menu won third place in the "Restaurants: Average Check Between $5.00–10.00 Per Person" category of the 1986 Great Menus Contest sponsored by the National Restaurant Association. Greenjean's Digest uses a wildly futuristic cartoon universe as a backdrop for its menu items. The restaurant's high-energy, quick turnover atmosphere is reflected in the menu design. The paper chosen for this menu is highly textured, which contributes to the overall impression of urgency. Sleek aircars rush through bright yellow skies. Many menu items are finger foods or quickly prepared light snacks. Since the restaurant's clientele is generally young, the speed of food preparation and consumption is a plus.

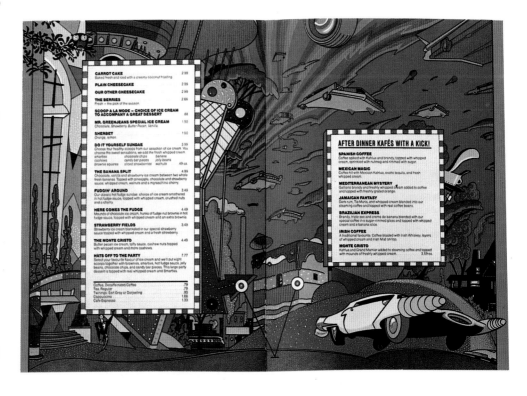

RESTAURANT: Maggie Mae's (Roadhouse & Creekhouse)

LOCATION: Pittsburgh, Pennsylvania

DESIGNER: Kathy Grubb

FIRM: Gray, Baumgarten & Lamport

PHOTOGRAPHER: Ron Layport

ILLUSTRATOR: Kathy Grubb

SPECIFICATIONS:

SIZE: 12¼" square (exterior), 13" x 11¾" (interior)

PAPER: 12 pt. Carolina, coated one side, 4-color process, with ultraviolet coating (exterior); Carnival Cover (interior)

PRINTER: Kelley & Company

A combination of clip art and illustration set the tone of this "record album" menu. The Roadhouse attracts a young, fun-loving crowd later in the evening. The menu selection, with its emphasis on munchies, sandwiches, and burgers, caters to this clientele. The choice of a record album cover may have been inspired by a local radio campaign to establish the character of Maggie Mae. The Creekhouse menu complements the Roadhouse's "Greatest Hits II." The menu insert slips out of the "album cover." Updates to the insert are tracked by the simple addition of a roman numeral so that there are Maggie Mae's Greatest Hits II and III, and so on.

RESTAURANT: Harvey's

LOCATION: Baltimore, Maryland

DESIGNER: W. Scott Mahr

FIRM: Great Scott Graphics

SPECIFICATIONS:

SIZE: 8½" x 14⁵⁄₁₆"

PAPER: White offset

This temporary menu was designed for use during construction of a patio for outdoor dining. The restaurateur wanted to make a virtue out of necessity and play up the humorous aspects of the inevitable inconvenience caused by construction. Because the menu was designed for short-term use only, inexpensive paper stock and printing methods were used. There was no typography cost because type was picked up from existing menus.

Top and side views of fanciful "buildings" such as the Dew Drop Inn, a brick goblet complete with chimney, add an amusing element to the menu. During the construction of the new patio, which ran four months, rather than the one month initially anticipated, the servers all wore hardhats and construction overalls. The blueprint look was achieved with a solid 10% screen and an airbrush-stipple effect.

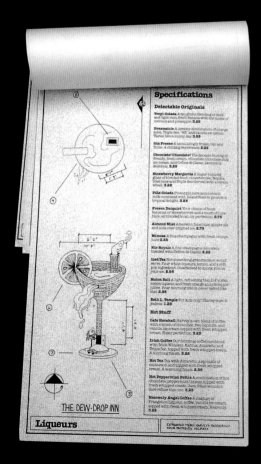

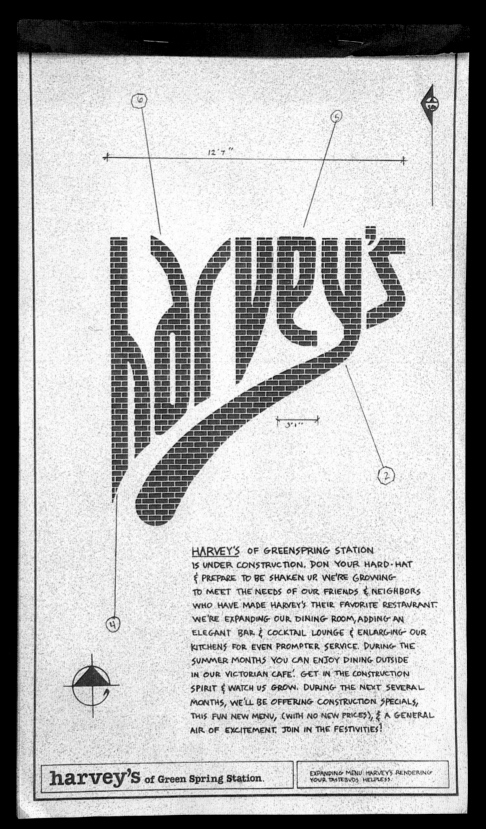

HARVEY'S OF GREENSPRING STATION IS UNDER CONSTRUCTION. DON YOUR HARD-HAT & PREPARE TO BE SHAKEN UP. WE'RE GROWING TO MEET THE NEEDS OF OUR FRIENDS & NEIGHBORS WHO HAVE MADE HARVEY'S THEIR FAVORITE RESTAURANT. WE'RE EXPANDING OUR DINING ROOM, ADDING AN ELEGANT BAR & COCKTAIL LOUNGE & ENLARGING OUR KITCHENS FOR EVEN PROMPTER SERVICE. DURING THE SUMMER MONTHS YOU CAN ENJOY DINING OUTSIDE IN OUR VICTORIAN CAFÉ. GET IN THE CONSTRUCTION SPIRIT & WATCH US GROW. DURING THE NEXT SEVERAL MONTHS, WE'LL BE OFFERING CONSTRUCTION SPECIALS, THIS FUN NEW MENU, (WITH NO NEW PRICES), & A GENERAL AIR OF EXCITEMENT. JOIN IN THE FESTIVITIES!

harvey's of Green Spring Station.

EXPANDING MENU: HARVEY'S RENDERING YOUR TASTEBUDS HELPLESS.

RESTAURANT: Max & Erma's
LOCATION: Columbus, Ohio
DESIGNER: David Browning
FIRM: Browning Design
ILLUSTRATORS: Michel Sennett (cartoonist),
David Browning

SPECIFICATIONS:
SIZE: 8½" x 14"
PAPER: 80# Vintage Cover Gloss
PRINTER: West-Camp Press

This menu took second place in the 1986 National
Restaurant Association's Great Menus Contest in
the category of "Restaurants: Average Check
Between $5.00–10.00 Per Person." An unabashedly
"funky" place, Max & Erma's is located in an old
warehouse adorned with Tiffany-style lamps and a
wacky assortment of incongruous objects. This
entertaining approach is reflected in the menu's
cartoons and the broad range of food offered.
Because the menu is composed of three separate
sheets slipped into cafe covers any sheet can be
updated independently of the others.

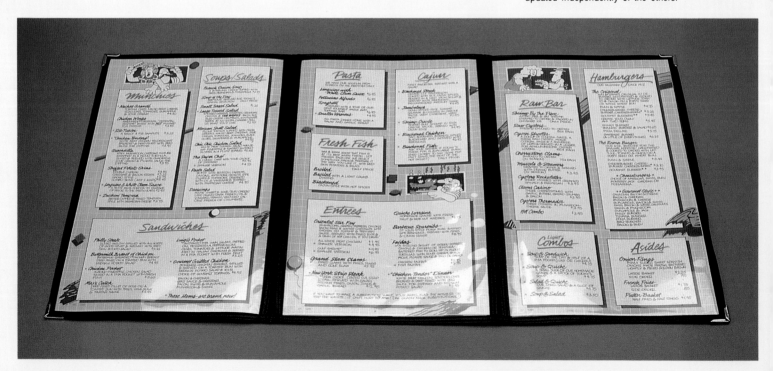

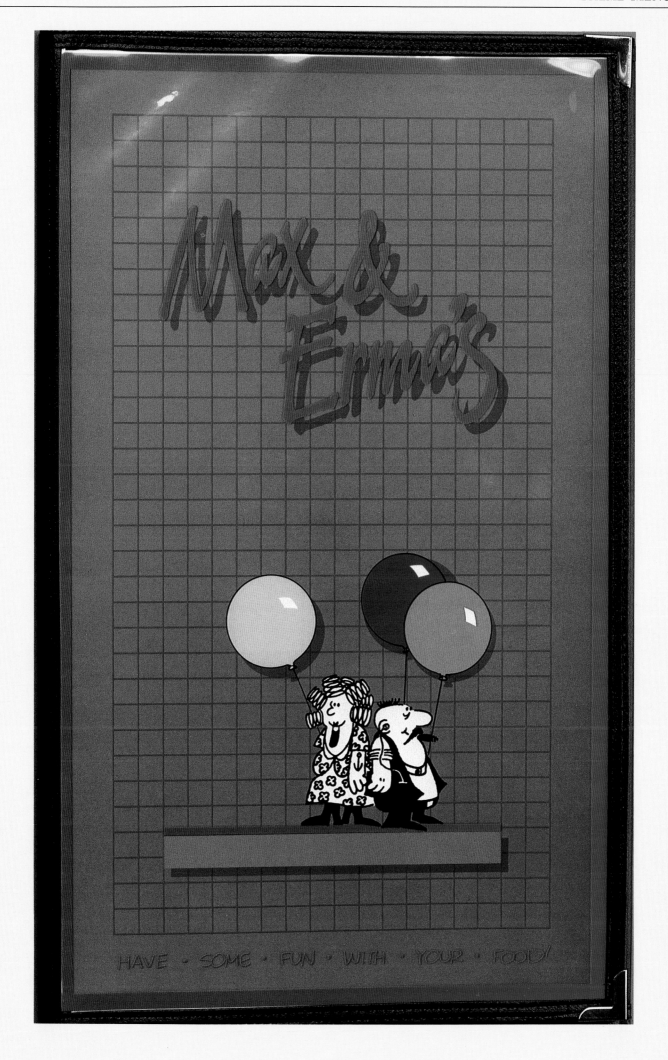

P.G. BARNUM'S RESTAURANT · 6505 BELCREST ROAD · HYATTSVILLE MARYLAND 20782

Barnum's

ADMIT ONE

GOOD EATING ANYTIME

779·5448

SWEET ENDINGS

I SCREAM: All natural flavors **1.25**

CIRCUS PARFAITS: Chocolate fudge, strawberry, butterscotch **1.25**

HOMEMADE CARROT CAKE: Cream cheese icing **.95**

APPLE CRISP: Served hot **.75** A la mode **1.25**

CHOCOLATE MOUSSE PIE 1.25

HOMEMADE SOUR CREAM COFFEE CAKE .95

THE GRAND FINALE

COFFEE, TEA OR MILK .50

ICED COFFEE OR TEA .50

PEACHES & CREAM: Non-alcoholic drink **.95**

IRISH COFFEE: Kahlua, Irish whiskey & whipped cream **1.50**

DUTCH COFFEE: Vandermint & whipped cream **1.50**

AMARETTO TEA: Orange Pekoe & Amaretto topped with whipped cream **1.50**

GOLDEN CADILLAC: Galliano, white creme de menthe & ice cream **1.50**

ALEXANDER COCKTAIL: Brandy, creme de cocoa & ice cream **1.50**

GRASSHOPPER: Green creme de menthe, white creme de cocoa & ice cream **1.50**

POUR ON THE PRAISE

DRAFT BEER BY THE PITCHER 2.95

SANGRIA BY THE PITCHER 2.95

OR BY THE GLASS: Beer **.75** Wine **1.00**

P.G. BARNUM'S RESTAURANT

Private party rooms are available for groups of 25 to 175 people. For information, contact our dining room manager or telephone 779-5448.

6505 BELCREST ROAD · HYATTSVILLE MARYLAND

GOOD·BYE

THE GREATEST GLOW ON EARTH

DRINK OF THE MONTH: Please ask your server

UN-WINE-DER: Burgundy wine & 7-Up **1.25**

STRAWBERRY KIR: Chablis & strawberry cordial **1.50**

PERRIER SIPPER: Non-alcoholic sparkling water **1.25**

MUNCHIES

THE MARKET BASKET: Fresh seasonal vegetables served with your favorite dip—Guacamole (spicy avocado), curried yogurt or herbed garlic **2.50**

THE CALIFORNIA: Tangy bowl of chili with corn chips **1.95**

NACHOS: Crisp tortilla chips baked with Monterey Jack cheese, green chilies & Jalapeno peppers **1.50**

FRESH VEGETABLE TEMPURA: Crisp fried vegetables in the Oriental manner **2.25**

SOUPS

FRENCH ONION SOUP GRATINEE 1.25

SOUP-OF-THE-DAY: Two expertly prepared soups each day served in your own individual kettle **1.25**

SOUP SPECIALS:
Soup & ½ special overstuffed sandwich of the day **2.95**

Soup & small salad **1.95**

Soup & quiche **2.95**

GARGANTUA'S SALADS

DELI SALAD BOWL: Salami, Swiss cheese, avocado, mushrooms & alfalfa sprouts **3.25**

ALMOND TURKEY SALAD: Almonds, turkey, apples, raisins & celery **2.75**

SALAD NICOISE: White meat tuna, string beans, sliced potatoes, tomatoes, olives & anchovies **2.95**

BLOODY MARY SALAD: Garden vegetables, sea shells & diced ham served with a pitcher of Bloody Mary **4.50**

SPINACH SALAD ORIENTAL: Spinach, water chestnuts, mushrooms, beansprouts, sesame seeds, hard boiled egg & fried noodles **2.95**

QUICHE ME QUICK

All served with a mixed garden salad.

QUICHE OF THE DAY: Please ask your server for our daily special **2.10**

LORRAINE: The classic quiche with bacon, onions & Swiss cheese **2.10**

THE PERFORMING DOGS

Jumbo kosher-style hot dogs served with chopped onions upon request at no additional charge. All dogs perform with three-ring circus fries.

ROVER: Your basic hot dog **1.95**

PEDRO: The chili dog **2.25**

GIGI: The cheese dog **2.25**

SCHULTZIE: The Kraut dog **2.25**

THE EGG & OMELETTE SIDE SHOW

All served with three-ring circus fries.

THE STRONGMAN: Green chili salsa, tostada shell & Monterey Jack cheese **1.95**

THE FAT LADY: Green peppers, onions, celery, tomatoes, diced ham & bananas **2.25**

THE HURDY GURDY: Italian sausage, tomato sauce & mozzarella cheese **2.65**

THE GREAT ALMONDINI: Onions, bell peppers, tomato & almonds **1.95**

THE SWORD SWALLOWER: Mushrooms, Cheddar cheese & bacon **2.50**

THE BARKER'S CHOICE: A blend of Monterey Jack, Cheddar, & Swiss cheeses **2.10**

THE THIN MAN: Broccoli, cauliflower, zucchini, onions, tomato sauce, mozzarella & Parmesan cheeses **2.45**

IN THE CENTER RING

Our star entrees are served with a choice of two—three-ring circus fries, vegetable or salad.

MEXI-COMBO: Taco, burrito & refried beans platter **3.95**

FRIED SHRIMP: Crisp, batter-fried **5.25**

MONTEREY JACK BAKE: Medley of fresh vegetables & Monterey Jack cheese **4.25**

CHARBROILED CHOICE RIB STEAK: Broiled to perfection **5.95**

SEA CATCH OF THE DAY: Please ask your server **4.95**

CHOPPED STEAK: Delicately charbroiled with sauteed mushrooms or onions **3.95**

UNDER THE BIG TOP

Special overstuffed sandwiches served on either freshly baked Kaiser roll, onion roll, seeded rye or whole wheat bread and served with our three-ring circus fries.

THE P. G. BARNUM: Tuna salad, alfalfa sprouts, mushrooms, tomatoes & melted Cheddar cheese on toasted English muffin **2.50**

PRIDE OF THE MIDWAY: Hot kosher-style corned beef on your choice of bread **2.50**

THE GREATEST SHOW ON EARTH: The classic Reuben sandwich baked in phyllo pastry **2.95**

THE FLYING CALZONE: Italian sausage, onions & green peppers, baked in pizza dough **2.75**

LION TAMER: Roast beef, Bermuda onion & horseradish dressing **2.65**

CIRCUS BURGERS

All served with lettuce, tomato & three-ring circus fries on freshly home-baked Kaiser, onion or French roll. For the diet conscious, a lettuce raft and cottage cheese may be substituted for your roll at no extra charge.

THE TIGHTROPE WALKER: Guacamole & Monterey Jack cheese **2.65**

THE FLYING WALLENDA'S: Boursin cheese **2.75**

THE DRUMBEATER: Teriyaki sauce & sauteed onions **2.45**

THE ANNIE OAKLEY: Sauteed onions & Cheddar cheese **2.45**

THE BARE BACK RIDER: Broiled to your order with no toppings **2.10**

RINGLING'S RELIABLE: Bacon & American cheese **2.50**

THE WEARY WILLIE: Sauteed mushrooms **2.25**

THE IMPRESARIO: Pizza sauce & mozzarella cheese **2.25**

MORE ATTRACTIONS →

RESTAURANT: P.G. Barnum's

LOCATION: Hyattsville, Maryland

DESIGNER: Dale Glasser

FIRM: Dale Glasser Graphics, Inc.

ILLUSTRATOR: Dale Glasser

SPECIFICATIONS:

SIZE: 8½″ x 17″, die-cut ticket shape

Peanut shells on the floor and circus artifacts mounted on the walls and suspended from the ceiling establish a circus mood in this reasonably-priced restaurant. One look at the menu demonstrates that the diner has been "admitted" to a good time. The format of the menu interior was designed to permit inexpensive updates as menu items are imprinted in only one color, red.

Set Sail

POTATO BOATS 3.25
Unsinkably Chip Potato Skins Set Afloat with Chili Con Queso, Guacamole and Picante Sauce.

BURIED TREASURE 2.50
A Treasure of Batter-Dipped Fried Mushrooms Served with Spicy Orange Marmalade Sauce.

TEXAS TIDAL WAVE 2.75
Tostada Chips Covered with a Wave of Cheddar Cheese, Black Olives and South Texas Spices.

SPANISH GALLEON 3.95
Crisp Tostada Chips Launched with Refried Beans, Cheddar Cheese, Guacamole and Sour Cream.

QUESADILLAS 2.75
Toasted Flour Tortillas Filled with Monterey Jack Cheese and Served with Ranchero Sauce.

ISLAND COMBO 4.95
Spicy Jalapeño Peppers Topped with a Combo of Crabmeat and Cheddar Cheese.

GULF COAST PLEASURE 3.95
One of the Island's Delicious Pleasures, Iced and Spiced Gulf Shrimp, Served by the Quarter Pound.

Warming Trends

SHE CRAB SOUP 2.25
A Hilton Specialty. Tender Crabmeat Served in a Rich, Sherried Cream Sauce with a Touch of Nutmeg.

BLACK BEAN SOUP 1.95
An Authentic Island Favorite. Served with Rice and Sour Cream.

The Mainsails

SPINNAKER 4.95
French Onion Soup and Today's Quiche. Served with a Glass of Our House Wine.

SAIL MAKER 5.50
Baked Brie in Puff Pastry. Served with French Bread and Fresh Fruit.

HIGH TIDE FRIED SHRIMP 7.95
Rollin' in with the Tide. Jumbo Butterfly Shrimp, Delicately Fried Golden Brown. Served with French Fries.

CHIMICHANGA 4.95
Refried Beans and Onions Rolled Inside a Large Flour Tortilla and Deep Fried. Served with Lettuce, Cheddar Cheese, Tomatoes, Sour Cream and Picante Sauce.

AUTHENTIC TEXAS CHILI 2.95
A Windjammer's Specialty. Hot and Spicy!

NAVIGATOR'S CHICKEN STICKS 4.75
Find Your Way to Our Breaded Sticks of Boneless Filet of Chicken, Deep Fried and Charted with Honey-Mustard Dressing and Cole Slaw.

Starboard Side

STEAK AHOY! 5.75
Thinly Sliced Sirloin Steak Covered with Swiss Cheese, Grilled Onions, Bell Peppers and Mushrooms, Aboard a Large French Roll.

THE BEACH CLUB 5.25
Join Our Exclusive Club with a Triple Decker of Thinly Sliced Turkey Breast, Jellied Cranberry Sauce, Bacon Strips, Lettuce and Toasted Pecans on Buttered Toast.

THE LANDLUBBER 5.25
For Those Without Their Sea Legs. Sliced Breast of Turkey, Tomatoes, Mild Cheddar and Avocado Covered with Mornay Sauce and Served Open Face on Puff Pastry.

WINDJAMMER'S BURGER 4.25
A Choice Ground Sirloin Patty, Broiled and Served on a Sesame Seed Bun with Homemade French Fries and Melted Cheese.

POLYNESIAN CHICKEN 4.75
A Tropical Delight. Marinated Chicken Breast, Broiled and Served on a Grilled Sesame Seed Bun with Pineapple Wedges.

WALK THE PLANK 5.75
Off You Go, Mate, with Baby Bay Shrimp, Sliced Avocado, Fresh Sprouts, Tomatoes and Cucumber Slices on a Large Croissant.

BARNACLE BURGER 4.50
A Burger Smothered in Mushrooms and Onions Sautéed in Wine, and Melted Provolone Cheese.

BILGE BURGER Priced Accordingly
You Build the Burger, Whatever's Your Personal Favorite.

The Port Side

BEER BATTER ONION RINGS 1.50
FRENCH FRIES 1.25

The Sand Bar

COFFEE, TEA, SANKA .95
MILK .95   **SOFT DRINKS** .95

The Sweet Fleet

Ask About Windjammer's Daily Dessert Specials.

RESTAURANT: Windjammers Beachfront Cafe

LOCATION: South Padre Hilton Resort, South Padre Island, Texas

DESIGNER: Ann Werner

FIRM: Associates Printing Service

ILLUSTRATOR: Ann Werner

SPECIFICATIONS:

SIZE: 11" x 8"

PAPER: Curtis Linen Cover, double thick

PRINTER: Associates Printing Service

Die-cut macaws and palm trees provide a tropical flavor for this beach-theme menu. The paper is a pale sand. Category headings continue the tropical beach theme in both their content and their color and texture, which suggest tropical blooms. Many of the individual menu items have been named so as to further emphasize the theme. The accompanying wine list repeats the macaws-and-palms illustration and has a pattern of tiny palm trees as well. A clear, easy-to-read sans serif typeface is used on both.

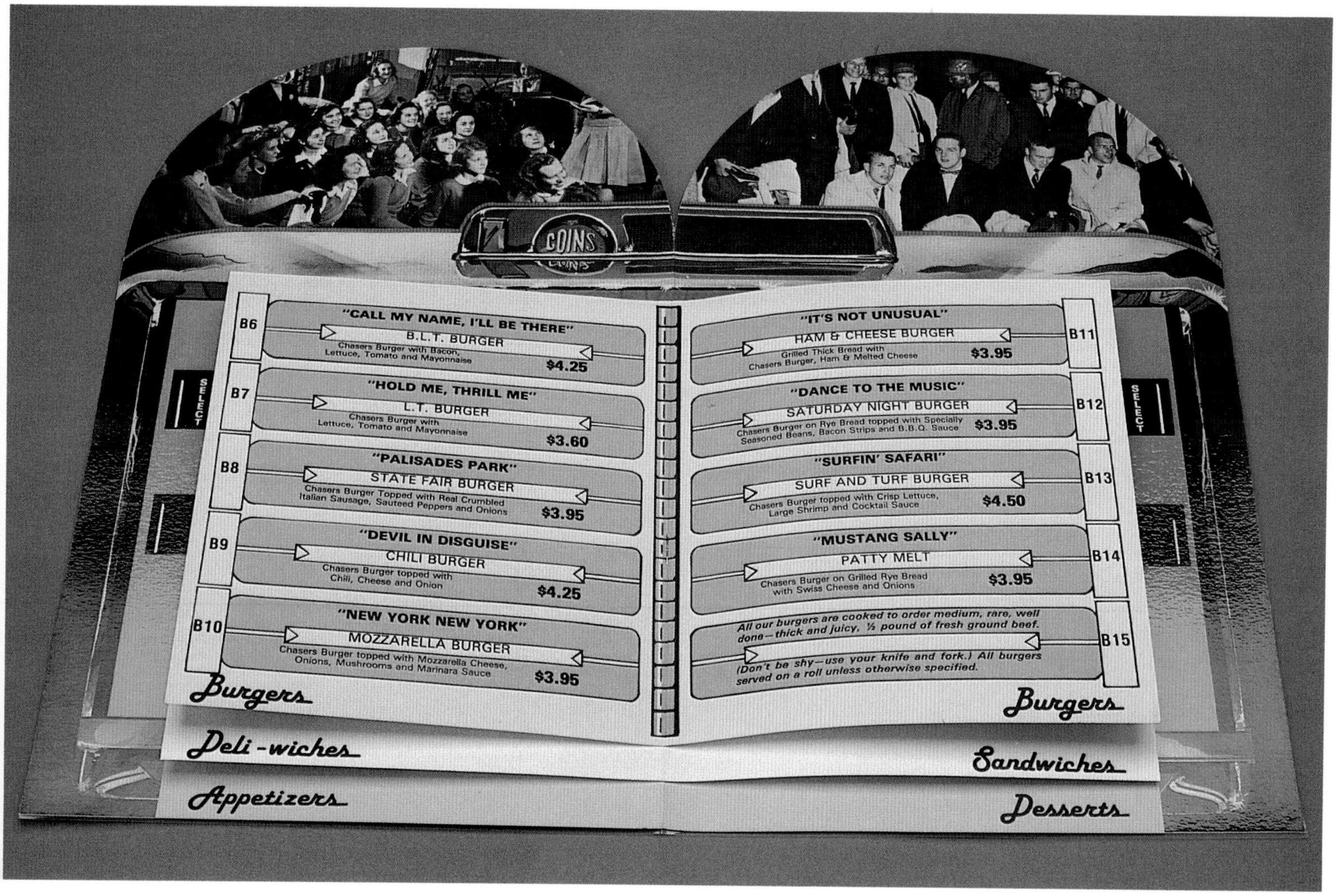

RESTAURANT: Chasers
LOCATION: Syracuse, New York
DESIGNER: James F. Brown
COPYWRITER: James F. Brown
SPECIFICATIONS:
SIZE: 8" x 13½" (cover die-cut);
6¼" x 8½" (inserts)

This menu won first prize in the "Most Imaginative" category of the National Restaurant Association's 1986 Great Menus Contest. The cover photo proudly displays the restaurant's jukebox. The interior sheets are color-coordinated to match the restaurant's decor and are stapled into the covers to permit quick and inexpensive updating of any or all sheets. The servers, costumed as cheerleaders, take orders based on the jukebox listing—for example, B-5 is a B.L.T. Cheeseburger. At the bar are a pair of actual jukeboxes that display menu inserts.

James F. Brown has been in the restaurant business all his life and also collects menus from all over the world. He wanted a menu that was completely different. The black-and-white photos inside the menu are of female students at Syracuse University in 1959 and of the national champion football team, Syracuse University, 1959.

RESTAURANT: St. Louis Union Station
Biergarten
LOCATION: St. Louis, Missouri
DESIGNERS: David Bartels, Buck Smith
FIRM: Bartels & Carstens, Inc.
ILLUSTRATOR: Paul Wolf
COPYWRITER: Cathy Williams
SPECIFICATIONS:
SIZE: 5½" x 12" (folded)
PAPER: 100# Enamel
PRINTER: Colorart Printing

St. Louis has a strong German heritage; it's noted for its beer and, of course, for its biergartens. For the uninitiated, a biergarten is an outdoor restaurant and night spot with dancing, German "oom-pah" music, authentic German cooking, and of course, beer. This one is located in St. Louis' famous Union Station. For reasons not yet fully understood by social historians, at the Union Station Biergarten, people do a dance called "The Duck," which is the inspiration for the duck in Tyrolean cap and lederhosen illustrated on the menu cover. The menu is written with just enough German to maintain an authentic touch, without overwhelming. Note, too, that a "duck-bill" is provided for authentic "Duck Dancing."

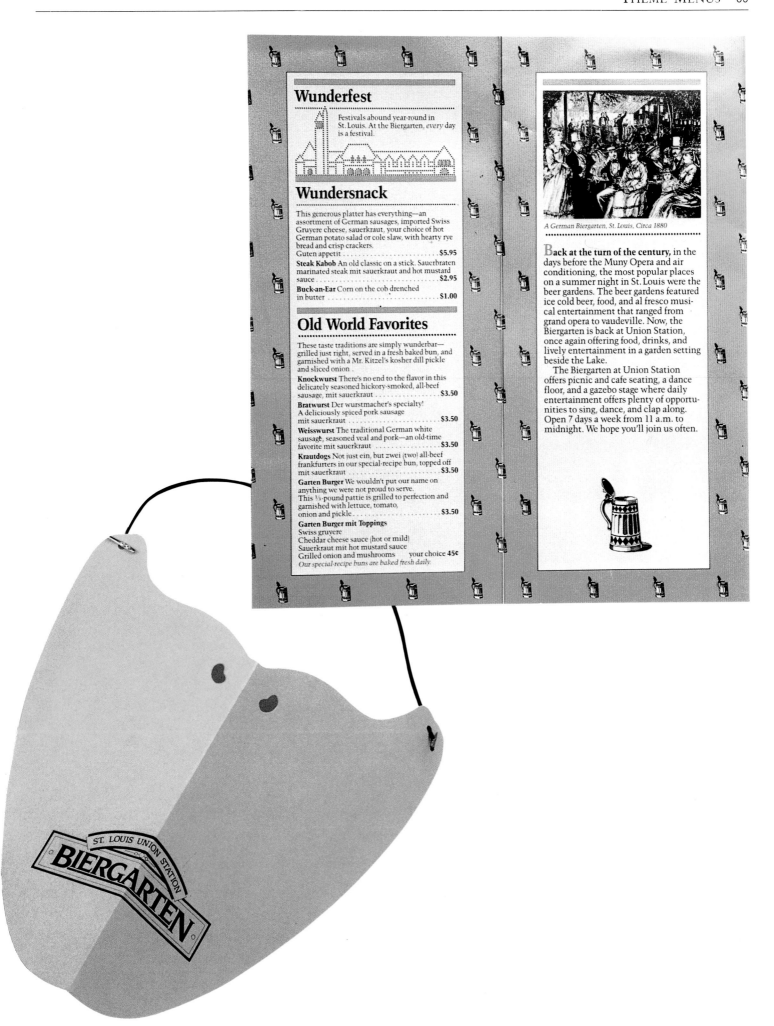

Wunderfest

Festivals abound year-round in St. Louis. At the Biergarten, *every* day is a festival.

Wundersnack

This generous platter has everything—an assortment of German sausages, imported Swiss Gruyere cheese, sauerkraut, your choice of hot German potato salad or cole slaw, with hearty rye bread and crisp crackers.
Guten appetit $5.95

Steak Kabob An old classic on a stick. Sauerbraten marinated steak mit sauerkraut and hot mustard sauce $2.95

Buck-an-Ear Corn on the cob drenched in butter $1.00

Old World Favorites

These taste traditions are simply wunderbar—grilled just right, served in a fresh baked bun, and garnished with a Mr. Kitzel's kosher dill pickle and sliced onion .

Knockwurst There's no end to the flavor in this delicately seasoned hickory-smoked, all-beef sausage, mit sauerkraut $3.50

Bratwurst Der wurstmacher's specialty! A deliciously spiced pork sausage mit sauerkraut $3.50

Weisswurst The traditional German white sausage, seasoned veal and pork—an old-time favorite mit sauerkraut $3.50

Krautdogs Not just ein, but zwei (two) all-beef frankfurters in our special-recipe bun, topped off mit sauerkraut $3.50

Garten Burger We wouldn't put our name on anything we were not proud to serve. This ⅓-pound pattie is grilled to perfection and garnished with lettuce, tomato, onion and pickle $3.50

Garten Burger mit Toppings
Swiss gruyere
Cheddar cheese sauce (hot or mild)
Sauerkraut mit hot mustard sauce
Grilled onion and mushrooms   your choice 45¢
Our special-recipe buns are baked fresh daily.

A German Biergarten, St. Louis, Circa 1880

Back at the turn of the century, in the days before the Muny Opera and air conditioning, the most popular places on a summer night in St. Louis were the beer gardens. The beer gardens featured ice cold beer, food, and al fresco musical entertainment that ranged from grand opera to vaudeville. Now, the Biergarten is back at Union Station, once again offering food, drinks, and lively entertainment in a garden setting beside the Lake.

The Biergarten at Union Station offers picnic and cafe seating, a dance floor, and a gazebo stage where daily entertainment offers plenty of opportunities to sing, dance, and clap along. Open 7 days a week from 11 a.m. to midnight. We hope you'll join us often.

ST. LOUIS UNION STATION
BIERGARTEN

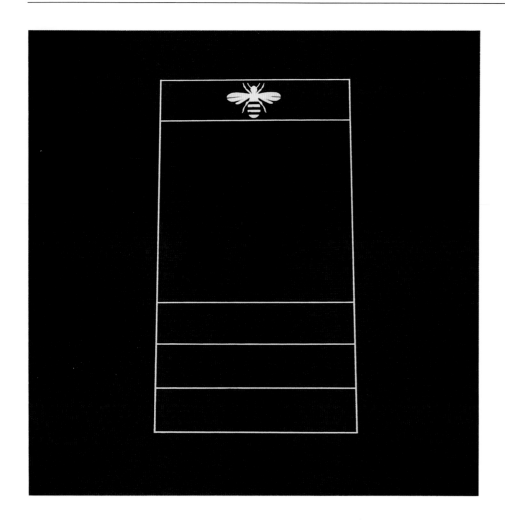

RESTAURANT: The Golden Bee

LOCATION: The Broadmoor,
Colorado Springs, Colorado

DESIGNER: Juli Jamison

FIRM: The Broadmoor Advertising Agency

ILLUSTRATOR: Juli Jamison

SPECIFICATIONS:

SIZE: 8½″ x 8½″

PAPER: Beckett Ridge Duplex

PRINTER: Scott Printing

The cover illustration of a tankard in the style of a steel engraving establishes the theme of The Golden Bee, an English-style pub that serves light sandwiches, pub specialties, and beer and wine. This theme is enhanced by the description of the "Yard of Ale," which used to be handed up to coachmen on the box of the English cross-country stages. The beautiful paper used for the menu lends a touch of distinction. The bee itself appears gold-foil-stamped on the cover and as an unobstructive design motif inside.

SOUPS

Soup Du Jour in Cup 1.75
  Broadmoor French Bread
Soup Du Jour in Tureen 2.25
  Broadmoor French Bread
Soup Du Jour in Cup 3.75
  With Mixed Green Salad and
  Broadmoor French Bread
Soup Du Jour in Cup 4.50
  With One-Half Sandwich of
  Ham, Liverwurst, Smoked Sausage,
  Cheese or Turkey or Roast Beef
  Corned Beef, Pastrami,
  or Combo . . . . Add .50

SANDWICHES

Served on Rye, White, or French Bread with Lettuce, Tomato, Kosher Pickle and a Choice of Potato Chips or Potato Salad. Half Orders Upon Request.

Ham 5.25
Corned Beef 6.00
Pastrami 6.00
Sliced Turkey Breast 5.25
Liverwurst 5.25
Roast Beef 5.25
Smoked Sausage 5.25
Sandwich with Cheese . . . . Add .50
Cheese Sandwich 4.25
  (Swiss, American, Cheddar)
Ham Corned Beef/Cheese Combo . 6.00
Sandwiches To Go . . . . . . Add .50

PUB SPECIALTIES

Beef & Kidney Pie with Salad 7.00
Chili (Cheese & Chopped Onion) . 5.50
  With Salad
Open Face California Sandwich . 6.00

Try our Imported English
Pickled Onions .75

SALADS

Small Luncheon Salad 2.50
Luncheon Salad 3.50
Chef's Salad (For 2) 8.00
Chef's Salad 4.75

Dressing Selection:
Broadmoor (Creamy Garlic with Herbs and Spices) Ranch, Bleu Cheese, Oil & Vinegar; Thousand Island, Italian (Lite)

DESSERTS

Hot Apple Pie 1.25
  with Cheese 1.50
Hot Apple Pie A La Mode 2.00
Ice Cream 1.25
Ice Cream With Strawberries 1.65
  with Chocolate 1.50

BEVERAGES

Coffee, Tea, Decaffeinated Coffee and
  Tea, Milk, Sanka 75
Perrier 1.75
Soft Drinks 1.25

BEER & ALE

ON DRAUGHT
Bass Ale (Imported)
Guiness Stout (Imported) Served at 45°F
  Coors   Coors Light
BOTTLED
Moussy Non-alcoholic
Henninger Dark (Imported)
Heineken Light (Imported)
Budweiser   Budweiser Light
  Michelob   Miller Lite

YARD OF ALE

Half yard and full yard of ale glass is a reproduction of the yard ale glasses used in England in the 17th and 18th centuries. They were used to celebrate events of national importance and it is recorded that, in 1685, the High Sheriff of Kent and his officers, following the proclamation of the accession to the throne of James III, drank to the health of His Majesty from glasses a yard in length.

Although these glasses were used extensively for local celebrations and competitions, there is little doubt that their main function was that of a long glass that could be easily handled, by the potman or barmaid, to the stage coach driver so he could remain on the box and in control of his horses.

WINE
BY THE GLASS

SPARKLING WINE

Almaden Blanc de Blanc 3.00
  A California Sparkling White Wine from the Santa Clara Valley. Crisp, Clean Flavor. Perfect for any Occasion.
Black Velvet 3.25
  Champagne and Guiness Stout.
Henkell (Piccolo Only) 4.50
  A German Sparkling Wine with a Zestful Character.

WHITE WINE

Almaden Chardonnay 3.00
  A Light, Dry White Wine from the Santa Clara Valley. This Wine Is Well-balanced with a Slight Toasty Flavor.

Sutter Home White Zinfandel 2.75
  A "Blush Wine" Made with Red Grapes. A Clean Aromatic Flavor.

RED WINE

Beaujolais Villages, Louis Latour . . . 3.75
  One of the Most Widely Enjoyed Red Wines in the World. This Light-Bodied Red Wine is from the Southern Burgundy Region of France.

RESTAURANT: Oscars

LOCATION: Sheraton Premiere Hotel, Universal City, California

DESIGNERS: Paul Harnagy, Barry Berlin

FIRM: Art Group Inc.

ILLUSTRATORS: Al Himes, Lynn Candy

FIRM: Art Group Inc.

SPECIFICATIONS:

SIZE: 9¼″ x 5¾″ (folded); 9¼″ x 23″ (open)

PAPER: 70# Mohawk Irish Linen Cover

PRINTER: Ripple Printing/TH Enterprises

Hooray for Hollywood! A restaurant named Oscars at a hotel called the Premiere, near the major studios . . . of course the menu is presented in an envelope sealed with wax. You, too, can feel like an Academy Award presenter. A nice die-cut on the first fold opens to display the hotel's logo at the bottom of the fully unfolded menu, presumably to bring the diner back to reality before he or she stands up to make an acceptance speech.

4

Ethnic Dining

Every culture has its own symbols and color schemes. The most effective ethnic menus take advantage of these generally recognized visual cues to reinforce the cuisine.

Each menu discussed in this chapter makes a powerful visual statement about the culture whose cuisine it represents. The images range from delicate brush strokes of ink on rice paper, which typify Asia, to the vivid colors and geometric shapes associated with Aztec art in Mexico.

RESTAURANT: Monique
LOCATION: Omni Hotel, Washington, D.C.
DESIGNER: Cindia Sanford-Garte
FIRM: Grigg Printing Service
ILLUSTRATOR: Cindia Sanford-Garte
SPECIFICATIONS:
SIZE: 8¼″ x 16″ (folded)
PAPER: 80# Caress Cover
PRINTER: Grigg Printing Service

Like its sister restaurant, Nicole, in New York, Monique is an Omni Hotel restaurant. The menus differ only slightly. In both instances, a real effort has been made to present authentic French regional food. Among the house specialties are Cassoulet, a hearty country-style stew of beans and at least three kinds of meat. Cassoulet is a favorite dish in the southern provinces of France, and sauerkraut is traditional in both Alsace and Lorraine. It is encouraging to many that we are beginning to see more French regional cuisine, not just the haute cuisine associated with Paris.

SOUPS & SALADS

Soups

Salads

Salads from the Sea

HOUSE SPECIALTIES

Fajitas Lupita

Arroz con Pollo

Chili Verde

Enchiladas Suizas

Pollo de Rey

Flautas

Soufflé de Mexico

CASA LUPITA

Refreshers · Appetizers · Soups & Salads
House Specialties · Traditional Mexican
Specialties · Seafood · Traditional American
Specialties · Desserts · Special Attractions

RESTAURANT:	Casa Lupita
LOCATION:	Restaurant chain headquartered in Dayton, Ohio
DESIGNERS:	Lynne Ginsberg, Jim Basirico
FIRM:	Geer, DuBois, Inc.
ILLUSTRATOR:	Nick Gaetano
COPYWRITER:	Sara Slater
SPECIFICATIONS:	Main menu
SIZE:	10¼" x 15¼" (folded)
PAPER:	Kimdura Boxcalf
PRINTER:	Progressive Printers

Colors vary from one type of menu to another but all fall within the range associated with the tropics—lots of sunshine yellow with bright reds and oranges, all played against a sandy paper with a pleasantly grainy texture, transport the diner (in spirit, at least) to Mexico. The theme is held together with images drawn from Mexico's Aztec and Mayan folk art.

Each menu features the same border of birds, cactus, flowers, sun symbols, and stylized representations of both gods and men. The designer has chosen to lay out the copy in square blocks, with prices completing the lower right-hand border of each block, a highly effective sales technique. The object of the menu is to sell the food, not the price. In the program, there are menus for appetizers, lunch, dessert, and summer.

RESTAURANT: Casa Gallardo
LOCATION: Columbus, Ohio
DESIGN FIRM: Seattle Menu Specialists
SPECIFICATIONS: Lunch menu
SIZE: 7¼″ x 16½″ (folded)
PAPER: Lustro Gloss (cover); Kimdura (insert)
PRINTER: Seattle Menu Specialists

A third-place winner in the 1986 National Restaurant Association's Great Menus Contest in the category of "Restaurants: Average Check Under $5.00 Per Person," this luncheon menu makes use of simple, but vividly colored illustrations. The desert landscapes at the bottom of each page lead the diner from sunrise at the appetizer section through sunset at the desserts and drinks page. Restaurant specials are printed on a card positioned on the inside of the front cover.
This is an inexpensive updating system that still harmonizes with the rest of the menu.

Create a Combo

Create your favorite Mexican combination plate including one of the following side dishes: rice, refried beans, mixed vegetables, green beans or a fresh vegetable relish.

ONE TACO, ENCHILADA, BURRITO, FLAUTA, TAQUITO OR MINI-TACO SALAD
2.95

ONE MINI-CHIMICHANGA, CHILE RELLENO, OR BURRITO MACHACA
3.95

ANY TWO ENTRÉES 4.75   ANY THREE ENTRÉES 5.75

Lunch Specialties

Served with a fresh vegetable relish and your choice of rice, refried beans, mixed vegetables or green beans.

TACO y ENCHILADA   3.95
A beef or chicken taco and a beef or chicken enchilada topped with our Pipian sauce and shredded cheese.

BURRITO MACHACA   3.95
Special shredded beef rolled in an extra-large flour tortilla with cheese, lettuce and tomatoes and topped with chile con queso.

TAQUITOS   3.25
Crisp flour tortillas rolled and filled with special shredded beef and topped with chile con queso. Served with sour cream and guacamole.

CHIMICHANGA   5.95
A large tortilla filled with beef and pork or chicken, lightly fried and covered with guacamole, sour cream, cheese, tomatoes and green onions.

FLAUTAS   3.25
Two corn tortillas filled with beef or chicken, rolled and fried to a golden brown. Topped with guacamole and sour cream.

MUCHO TACO   3.95
A large flour tortilla filled with beef, lettuce, tomatoes, sour cream, guacamole and cheese.

Salads

TACO SALAD   3.95
A flour tortilla basket filled with refried beans, special shredded beef or chicken, lettuce, tomatoes and hard-boiled egg slices. Served with a light avocado dressing.

CHICKEN AND AVOCADO SALAD   3.95
Fresh chicken salad on a bed of shredded lettuce laced with fresh mushrooms, avocado slices, hard-boiled egg slices and tomatoes. Served in a flour tortilla basket with a light avocado dressing.

TOSTADA   3.50
A flour tortilla shell layered with refried beans, beef and pork, special shredded beef or chicken, plus lettuce, tomatoes, cheese, spicy sauce and green onions.

HOUSE SALAD   1.95
Crisp lettuce topped with mushrooms and avocado slices. Served with oil and vinegar dressing.

Sandwiches

CASA BURGER   2.95
One-half pound (pre-cooked weight) ground chuck burger, served on a toasted Mexican roll with lettuce and tomato.

FUNDIDO BURGER   3.95
The Casa Burger topped with chile con queso and served with steak fries.

BORDER BURGER   4.25
A Casa Burger topped with melted cheese and bacon and served with steak fries.

Sides

FRESH VEGETABLE RELISH	.85	MIXED VEGETABLES	.85
CASA SALAD	.95	GREEN BEANS	.85
MEXICAN RICE	.85	GUACAMOLE small .45 large 1.25	
REFRIED BEANS	.85	SOUR CREAM small .45 large 1.25	
STEAK FRIES	.85		

RESTAURANT: Caramba!

LOCATION: New York, New York

DESIGNER: Paul Seaman
(part owner of the restaurant)

SPECIFICATIONS:

SIZE: 8½″ x 14″ (folded in half)

PAPER: Melon Offset

The Mexican food served at Caramba! is good but the festive atmosphere makes the restaurant memorable. Caramba's specialties include three sizes of margaritas. In such an environment, spilled drinks and water damage to the menus are inevitable. Caramba! solves this problem by printing its menus on standard offset sheets and replacing the menus at frequent intervals. The restaurant's logo has a wonderful pattern of spots that recalls bullet-pocked walls after the Mexican revolution.

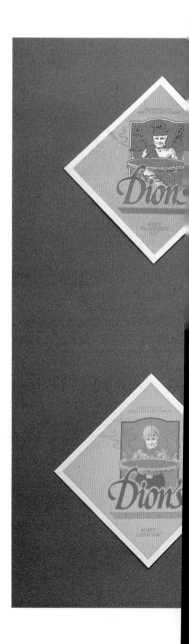

RESTAURANT:	Dion's Pizza
LOCATION:	Alb, New Mexico
DESIGNER:	Steven Wedeen
FIRM:	Vaughn/Wedeen Creative, Inc.
ILLUSTRATORS:	Russ Ball, Steven Wedeen
SPECIFICATIONS:	
SIZE:	Various
PAPER:	80# Karma Cover Creme, plus crack 'n peel labels
PRINTER:	Academy Printers

Dion's wanted an inexpensive way to have full-color menus. Pressure-sensitive stickers, featuring the theme character, were designed for various holidays—Halloween, St. Patrick's Day, Valentine's Day, etc.—and were affixed to the covers of printed menus ten days before the particular holiday. The preprinted inside of the menu was a simple two-color affair. The "Dion's Pizza Chef" starred as the Easter Bunny, Uncle Sam, and so on, providing continuity and humor.

Eventually, Dion's became such a success that the number of menus needed leaped from 5,000 to 40,000. Hand-affixing became unrealistic; on the other hand, four-color process printing was easily justified. The labels are now used on carry-out boxes. There are also postcards and posters using the same "Dion's Chef" character.

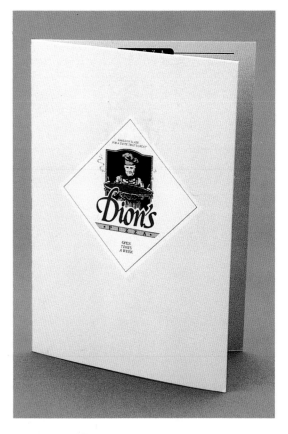

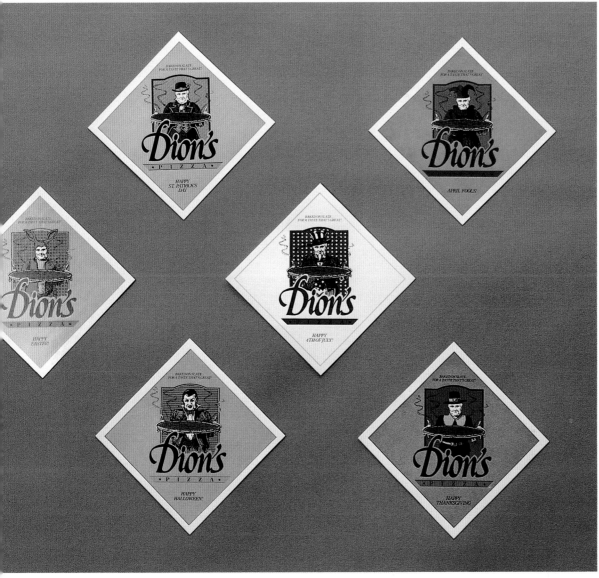

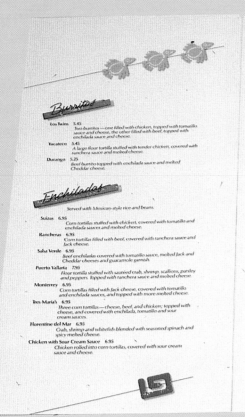

RESTAURANT: Casa Maria

LOCATION: Owned by El Torito, a
nationwide chain headquartered
in Irvine, California

DESIGNER: Claude Prettyman

ART DIRECTION: Diane Richards (El Torito
in-house creative dept.)

ILLUSTRATOR: Claude Prettyman

SPECIFICATIONS:

SIZE: 7½" x 15¼"

PAPER: Gainsborough Wheat

PRINTER: The Dot Printer

Bright colors and symbols drawn from Aztec
bas-reliefs provide the motif for this menu. The
speckled paper recalls the texture and appearance
of flour tortillas. Category headings and design
symbols are set at an uphill slant. Prices are
printed immediately following the item, but *before*
the description to avoid "price listing."

THE JAPANESE STEAKHOUSE

RESTAURANT: Benihana Steak House
LOCATION: Nationwide restaurant chain
DESIGNER: Ted Tanaka (in-house designer)
SPECIFICATIONS: Lunch and dinner menus
SIZE: 6″ x 14″
PAPER: Curtis Eggshell Cover, double thick (lunch menu); 15 pt. Appleton Super Tuff (dinner menu)
PRINTER: Continental Graphic

In a departure from the usual philosophy of restaurant chains, each Benihana location has a different menu, each produced locally. Pictured here are the luncheon and dinner menus from the Miami location. The two menus are stylistically quite different but both are quintessentially Japanese. The luncheon menu, with its free-form flowers on a beautifully textured paper, emulates the pastoral scenes done with brush and ink on rice paper which typify, to the Westerner, Japanese art. The dinner menu, done in bold red and black geometrics, shows the modern, high-tech face of Japan. Both menus feature a "Florida Cooler" under the specialty drinks. This provides a nice local flavor.

RESTAURANT: El Rio Grande
LOCATION: New York, New York
DESIGNER: John Nordland
SPECIFICATIONS:
SIZE: 10″ x 18″
PAPER: 12 pt. Carolina Cover
PRINTER: a/DEL

For this bright and cheerful menu, the designer has extended the "I" in the restaurant's name to suggest the Rio Grande itself. It comes looping across the cover in a sassy swirl of red. The restaurant is located on the first level of a high-rise apartment building above Third Avenue in New York City. The kitchen itself, inside this truly "authentic Mexican" restaurant, forms a symbolic "Rio Grande" dividing the two seating areas. A mural of El Rio Grande adorns the dining room walls.

RESTAURANT: Inn of Happiness
LOCATION: Hilton International, Singapore
DESIGNER: McCann Erickson
SPECIFICATIONS:
SIZE: 8″ x 13½″
PAPER: Artcard
PRINTER: Ho Printing

This menu won first place for "Best Design" in the National Restaurant Association's 1986 Great Menus Contest. Beautiful watercolors and delicately brushed calligraphy adorn each page of this exquisite menu. The style of cooking is generally Chinese, but the extensive menu reflects the broad range of ingredients available in Singapore. The watercolors convey a sense of happiness as the artist has captured playful carp, a strutting rooster, and delightful yellow chrysanthemums on the various pages.

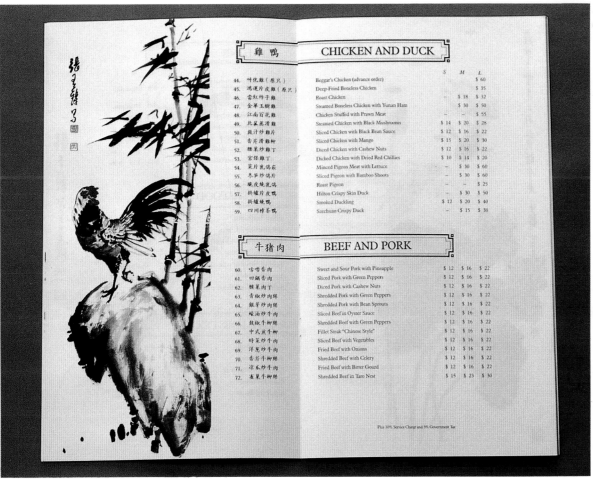

雞 鴨　　CHICKEN AND DUCK

			S	M	L
44.	叫化雞（原只）	Beggar's Chicken (advance order)	–	–	$ 60
45.	鴻運片皮雞（原只）	Deep-Fried Boneless Chicken	–	–	$ 35
46.	雲紅炸子雞	Roast Chicken	–	$ 18	$ 32
47.	金華玉樹雞	Steamed Boneless Chicken with Yunan Ham	–	$ 30	$ 50
48.	江南百花雞	Chicken Stuffed with Prawn Meat	–	–	$ 55
49.	北菰蒸滑雞	Steamed Chicken with Black Mushrooms	$ 14	$ 20	$ 28
50.	鼓汁炒雞片	Sliced Chicken with Black Bean Sauce	$ 12	$ 16	$ 22
51.	杏片滑雞柳	Sliced Chicken with Mango	$ 15	$ 20	$ 30
52.	腰果炒雞丁	Diced Chicken with Cashew Nuts	$ 12	$ 16	$ 22
53.	宮保雞丁	Diced Chicken with Dried Red Chillies	$ 10	$ 14	$ 20
54.	菜片乳鴿崧	Minced Pigeon Meat with Lettuce	–	$ 30	$ 60
55.	冬筍炒鴿片	Sliced Pigeon with Bamboo Shoots	–	$ 30	$ 60
56.	脆皮燒乳鴿	Roast Pigeon	–	–	$ 25
57.	掛爐片皮鴨	Hilton Crispy Skin Duck	–	$ 30	$ 50
58.	掛爐燒鴨	Smoked Duckling	$ 12	$ 20	$ 40
59.	四川樟茶鴨	Szechuan Crispy Duck	–	$ 15	$ 30

牛猪肉　　BEEF AND PORK

60.	咕嚕香肉	Sweet and Sour Pork with Pineapple	$ 12	$ 16	$ 22
61.	回鍋香肉	Sliced Pork with Green Peppers	$ 12	$ 16	$ 22
62.	腰果肉丁	Diced Pork with Cashew Nuts	$ 12	$ 16	$ 22
63.	青椒炒肉絲	Shredded Pork with Green Peppers	$ 12	$ 16	$ 22
64.	銀芽炒肉絲	Shredded Pork with Bean Sprouts	$ 12	$ 16	$ 22
65.	蠔油炒牛肉	Sliced Beef in Oyster Sauce	$ 12	$ 16	$ 22
66.	鼓椒牛柳絲	Shredded Beef with Green Peppers	$ 12	$ 16	$ 22
67.	中式煎牛柳	Fillet Steak "Chinese Style"	$ 12	$ 16	$ 22
68.	時菜炒牛肉	Sliced Beef with Vegetables	$ 12	$ 16	$ 22
69.	洋蔥炒牛肉	Fried Beef with Onions	$ 12	$ 16	$ 22
70.	芹片牛柳絲	Shredded Beef with Celery	$ 12	$ 16	$ 22
71.	涼瓜炒牛肉	Fried Beef with Bitter Gourd	$ 12	$ 16	$ 22
72.	雀巢牛柳絲	Shredded Beef in Taro Nest	$ 15	$ 23	$ 30

Plus 10% Service Charge and 3% Government Tax

RESTAURANT: Nicole
LOCATION: Omni Hotel,
New York, New York
DESIGNER: Cindia Sanford-Garte
FIRM: Grigg Printing Service
ILLUSTRATOR: Cindia Sanford-Carte
SPECIFICATIONS:
SIZE: 8¼″ x 16″ (folded)
PAPER: 80# Caress Cover
PRINTER: Grigg Printing Service

The daily specials, wines, desserts, and aperitifs and digestifs appear in two columns flanking the main menu. They are set off by having been handwritten while the rest of the items have been typeset. An elegantly Parisian "fin de siècle" lady adorns the cover.

RESTAURANT: Top O' Texas

LOCATION: Dallas, Texas
(one of three locations)

DESIGNER: Turner Duncan

FIRM: Duncan Design Associates

SPECIFICATIONS:

SIZE: 9¼" x 11½" (folded)

PAPER: 65# Hammermill Text (in cafe covers)

This menu placed second in the "Restaurants: Average Check Under $5.00 Per Person" category of the 1986 National Restaurant Association's Great Menus Contest. The star logo on the cover, outlined in yellow against black, typifies Texas, the Lone Star State. The inside of the menu, using cartoons of a "Texas cowboy," provides entertaining information for the diner. Humorous copywriting carries out the Tex-Mex theme.

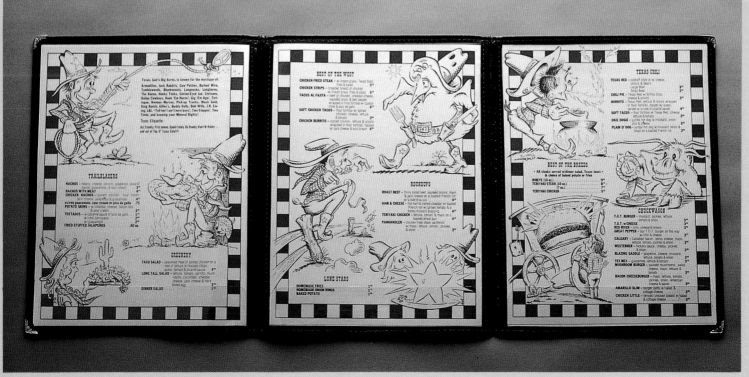

RESTAURANT: Auntie Yuan

LOCATION: New York, New York

DESIGNER: Dale Glasser

FIRM: Dale Glasser Graphics, Inc.

CALLIGRAPHER: Jean Keh (cover), Dale Glasser (insert)

SPECIFICATIONS:

SIZE: 11½″ x 8¾″ (folded)

PAPER: 12 pt. Coated Cornwall, laminated (cover); 70# Mohawk Superfine Eggshell (interior)

PRINTER: Lorshelle Graphics

The elegant decor of this chic and contemporary Chinese restaurant is directly reflected in its menu. The restaurant's walls are black, and its plates exactly match the tan of the inside cover. The "chops" (personal stamps) imprinted in red on both the cover and the insert translate to Auntie Yuan. The calligraphic brush stroke is by the owner's wife, Jean Keh, a student of this technique. The menu inserts were designed for easy updating in one color; the red category heads were printed on the menu masters and do not change.

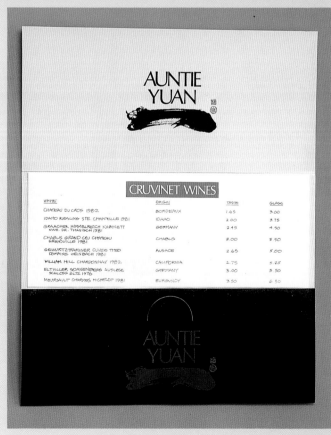

TGI FRIDAY'S

PREPARED WITH CAJUN SPICES AND BLACKENED IN A CAST IRON SKILLET

BLACKENED ENTREES

SCALLOPS	$10.25
SHRIMP	$12.50
ORANGE ROUGHY	$7.95
CHICKEN	$7.95
NEW YORK STRIP	$11.95

BLACKENED SANDWICHES

CHICKEN	$5.95
FISH	$5.95
STEAK	$6.45

FRIDAY'S BARBECUE ITEMS

St. Louis cut pork ribs, marinated in our homemade barbecue sauce or a roast beef brisket smothered in the same delicious sauce.

BARBECUE RIB APPETIZER	$4.75
FRIDAY'S RIB PLATES	
Large	$8.50
Small	$5.95
BARBECUE BRISKET	$7.50
COMBINATION PLATE	$8.50

CAJUN RECIPES

RESTAURANT: T. G. I. Friday's

LOCATION: Nationwide chain headquartered in Dallas, Texas

SPECIFICATIONS: Cajun Recipes Menu

SIZE: 7½" x 9¾"

This special menu devoted to Cajun-style cooking uses a die-cut cast iron skillet, the essential tool for blackening food in this popular Louisiana style cuisine, as the menu shape. When produced in quantity for national distribution, something as specialized as this becomes cost effective. Because so many people instantly recognize the visual image of the skillet as an essential of the cuisine, it is an extremely effective merchandizing tool.

5

Fine Dining

The ambiance of the restaurant is second only to the excellence of the food in creating the experience we call "fine dining." From the lighting and appointments to the service, to the menu, the elements that create the illusion of being, for just one night, "master (or mistress) of all one surveys" must be complete. One jarring note can burst the bubble and bring the diner back to reality.

The fine dining menu must be a perfect extension of the restaurateur's vision for the illusion to be perfect. This does *not*, however, imply that the menu designer has only to follow orders in the execution of the menu design. On the contrary, an imaginative designer can, through the use of beautiful paper stocks, textiles, or leathers and the judicious selection of type fonts and special bindery techniques, enhance the restaurateur's vision.

The designer can look at the restaurant with new eyes, noting such details as lighting level, type of lighting (candlelit tables need small menus to minimize the risk of fire), and table size. This fresh viewpoint can assist the restaurateur in the creation of a unique and effective menu.

RESTAURANT: The Penrose Room
LOCATION: The Broadmoor,
Colorado Springs, Colorado
DESIGNER: Kim Brill
FIRM: The Broadmoor Advertising
Agency
PHOTOGRAPHER: David Beightol
SPECIFICATIONS:
SIZE: 10⅛″ x 16⅛″
PAPER: Supertuff
PRINTER: Williams Printing

This restaurant presents classic continental cuisine in elegant surroundings. That is what they are selling and that is the feeling engendered by the menu. The cover is illustrated with a beautiful photograph of the place setting, complete with gold-plated flatware. The simplicity of presentation continues inside the menu where gold-colored borders frame but do not overpower the black-on-white menu listings.

RESTAURANT: The Arbour

LOCATION: Guest Quarters Hotel, Charlotte, North Carolina

DESIGNER: John P. Stasick, Director of Food and Beverage

SPECIFICATIONS: Breakfast, lunch, and dinner menus

SIZE: 9½" x 13½" (lunch and dinner menus, folded); 7" x 13½" (breakfast menu, folded)

PAPER: Coated one side (covers); Vellum (inserts)

This elegant menu program uses the same pattern—graphic leaves inspired by the trees surrounding the restaurant—with three different pastels: a soft rose for breakfast, mint green for lunch, and a soft cadet blue for dinner.

The covers are designed as folders so that the inserts can be slipped into place by hand. The vellum insert forms have similarly colored category headings to coordinate with the covers. The menu items that vary are printed in one color for easy updates.

Both the breakfast and the luncheon menus use a single sheet for insertions. The dinner menu is on two separate vellum pages so that the entrees may be varied while the accompaniments to the meal remain unchanged. The typeface is clear and legible, with the menu items set in boldface. Prices are centered under the description of each dish so that the diner can focus on the entrees, not the price.

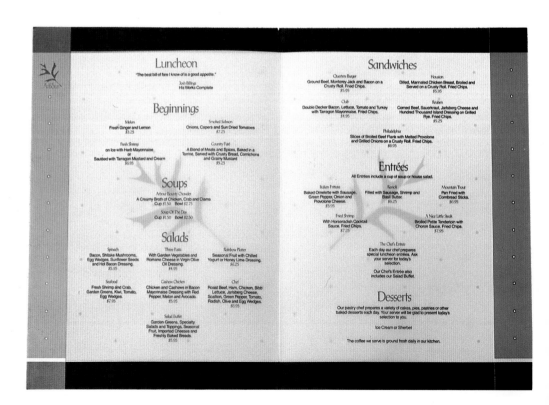

RESTAURANT: Ambrosia
LOCATION: Sheraton Kensington Hotel, Tulsa, Oklahoma
DESIGNERS: Paul Harnagy, Ray Milligan
FIRM: Art Group Inc.
SPECIFICATIONS:
SIZE: 9" x 13½"
PAPER: Appleton Super Tuff
PRINTER: Ripple Printing/TH Enterprises

The cover art on this menu is a detail of one of the paintings commissioned for the dining room. The silver foil-stamping is repeated on the vellum cover sheet inside. The beautifully textured insert sheets have been tinted pink to match the restaurant's walls. The room is rather dimly lit, so, the copy was imprinted in deep brown for legibility.

RESTAURANT: Naddeo's Steak and Lobster House

LOCATION: Crystal Pavilion, New York, New York

DESIGNER: Dale Glasser

FIRM: Dale Glasser Graphics, Inc.

SPECIFICATIONS:

SIZE: 9¾" x 12" (folded)

PAPER: 12 pt. Cornwall, coated two sides

PRINTER: Lorshelle Printers

The monogram-like logo reflects the multi-level design used in the restaurant's interior. The decor in marble, brass, and green plush was picked up in the colors used on the menu. Food preparation and presentation are traditional and formal, and the menu layout accurately reflects the restaurant's approach to food. The menu opens with a short fold so that the restaurant's name remains visible at the bottom of the menu. The brass-colored ink plays nicely against the green and cream colors.

RESTAURANT: Square One
LOCATION: San Francisco, California
DESIGNER: Gerald Reis
FIRM: Gerald Reis & Company
SPECIFICATIONS:
SIZE: 8½" x 11"
PAPER: White offset inserted into cafe covers
PRINTER: Lithography by Design

A stylized two-color graphic element appears both on the cover and at the head of each of the insert pages. This element could also be used for other applications. The menu is specifically designed to be updated frequently. The wine list cover uses background reversal to distinguish it from the main menu while carrying out the elegantly simple theme.

RESTAURANT: The Firehouse

LOCATION: Old Sacramento, California

DESIGNER: Sheree Lum Orsi

FIRM: The Dunlavey Studio

PHOTOGRAPHER: Unknown—photos all date from the 19th century

SPECIFICATIONS: Lunch and dinner menus

SIZE: 9″ x 12″ (lunch and dinner menus, folded)

PAPER: Chromolux Bronze Metallic (covers); 70# Curtis Brightwater Riblaid Text (inserts)

PRINTER: Fong & Fong

Located on "Two" Street in historic Old Sacramento, The Firehouse was once a working firehouse. Its bar area is decorated with old photos similar to those used as a frontispiece in each menu. The historic feeling of the place is echoed in the elegant corners and spines that adorn the outside of each menu and the marbled paper on the inside of each cover. A graceful, yet legible italic typeface, which works well with the vertically watermarked paper, was selected.

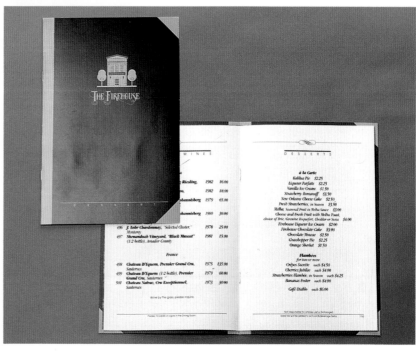

RESTAURANT: Alexis

LOCATION: Alexis Hotel,
Seattle, Washington

DESIGNER: Mike Wagner

FIRM: The Menu Workshop

SPECIFICATIONS: Main and peripheral menus

SIZE: 8½″ x 14″ (main menu);
6″ x 9″ (peripheral menus)

PAPER: Quintessence Gloss Cover
(covers); Matte (interiors)

PRINTER: Sterling Engraving Co.

A simple graphic on each front cover provides instant identification of the hotel's peripheral menus. The rising sun for breakfast and "high noon" for lunch are particularly clever. The dinner menu and the accompanying wine list feature formal black covers to continue this theme. This was designed as a full menu program, planned for easy and relatively inexpensive updates. The menus are pleasant to read because the layout provides plenty of open space to soothe the eye and the typeface is extremely legible.

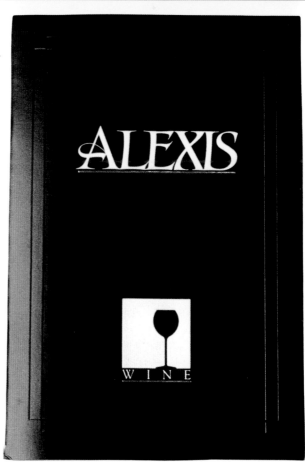

RESTAURANT: Raphael's
LOCATION: Ramada Renaissance Hotel, Washington, D.C.
DESIGNER: Ann Werner
FIRM: Associates Printing Service
ILLUSTRATOR: Roberta Warehan
LETTERING: Ann Werner
SPECIFICATIONS:
SIZE: 8½" x 13" (folded)
PAPER: Strathmore Rhododendron Cover, double thick
PRINTER: Associates Printing Service

The pattern of the restaurant's carpet, taken from an actual swatch, is repeated on the outside of the dinner menu and is used as a border around the name on the cover of the lunch menu. The pattern reappears on the dinner menu inserts, screened down considerably. Over 1,000 cover shells were printed. Updates are imprinted in two colors, in batches of 200 to 300, as needed.

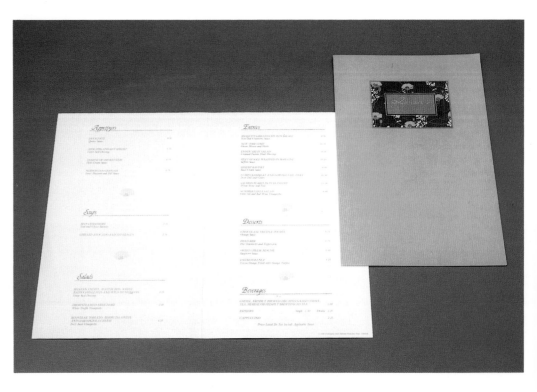

LaVilla

Fresh Oysters or Clams on the Half-Shell ½ Dozen 4.95
Scallops with Pimiento Butter 5.00
Arizona Rarebit 4.75
Shrimp with Cilantro and Tequila 6.75

Fisherman's Chowder 2.25
La Villa Soup Tureen 2.25

Pasta Salad with Seafood 6.95
Cobb Salad 6.25
Boston Bibb Salad 2.95

Fresh Fish
Mesquite Broiled
Swordfish 11.50
Sea Bass 10.50

Sautéed
Salmon 9.95
Snapper 11.00

Grilled
Lemon Sole 9.25
Blue Fish 8.75
Catfish 8.75
Halibut 10.25

La Villa Specialties
Baby Chicken in Clay 11.25
New York Steak, La Villa Style 13.95
Filet Mignon 13.95
Lamb Loin Chops 14.95

RESTAURANT: La Villa
LOCATION: Westin La Paloma, Tucson, Arizona
DESIGNER: Cynthia Lehman
FIRM: Associates Printing Service
SPECIFICATIONS:
SIZE: 9½" x 15"
PAPER: Strathmore Rhododendron Cover, double thick
PRINTER: Associates Printing Service

The menu items were handwritten, rather than typeset, before this menu was printed. The dishes offered are merely listed, not described. This simple menu is obviously designed to be supplemented by information provided personally by the server. Since personal service is the point, the choice of handwritten copy is a nice touch. Above all, this menu is beautifully coordinated with the restaurant it represents. Menu masters are in stock for future imprinting to allow frequent updates.

RESTAURANT: Chardonnay
LOCATION: Park Terrace Hotel,
Washington, D.C.
DESIGNER: Scott Mahr
FIRM: Great Scott Graphics
PAINTER: Barbara Marcos
SPECIFICATIONS: Breakfast, dinner, and dessert
menus
SIZE: 10″ x 10″ (breakfast menu);
10″ x 15″ (dinner menu);
4″ x 8½″ (dessert menu)

The menus for this elegantly appointed restaurant
are changed quarterly, as the cuisine is based on
fresh, seasonal ingredients. Four separate views of
the same courtyard were painted to identify each
season. The mauve and green used on the menus
coordinate with the restaurant's color scheme. The
wine list is updated often on a computer and
printed directly on the paper inserted in the wine
list binder. The wine list cover is the actual fabric
used on the restaurant chairs, and the binders are
protected with plastic covers. This restaurant is
committed to serving fresh, seasonal food in
exquisite surroundings. That same care is
evidenced in their menu program.

RESTAURANT: Gallatin's
LOCATION: Radisson Hotel,
Minneapolis, Minnesota
DESIGN FIRM: Graphic World
SPECIFICATIONS: Dinner menu
SIZE: 12¼″ x 13″
PAPER: Gainsborough and Beckett
Cambric
PRINTER: Graphic World

The lunch menu, with its smaller size and die-cut
foliage and window, became *too* popular. Diners
liked it so much that the restaurant constantly had
to replace copies of it. Though the die-cuts,
inspired by the dining room's many windows and
views of a heavily wooded area outside, were
beautiful, they were delicate and the menus became
frayed and were easily bent.

The dinner menu retains the restaurant's logo of a
tree, blind embossed on the cover and repeated on
a vellum overlay inside the front cover. The cover
of this menu is of sturdier material in a peach
color that harmonizes with the restaurant's interior.
The menu inserts are updated quarterly. Daily
specials are on a card attached to the left inside
cover of the menu.

◀ **RESTAURANT:** Remick's
LOCATION: Owned by El Torito, a
nationwide chain headquartered
in Irvine, California
SPECIFICATIONS: Main and small menus
SIZE: 9" x 15" (main menu);
5½" x 10" (small menu)
PRINTER: Printers Ink

RESTAURANT: Ray's Boathouse
LOCATION: Seattle, Washington
DESIGNER: Mardi Murvin
SPECIFICATIONS: Main, wine, and dessert menus
SIZE: 11½" x 11½" (main menu);
8½" x 7" (wine and dessert
menus)
PAPER: Laid finish, laminated in plastic

The restaurant's specialty is fish. This is
announced with the cover illustration of a single
fish that extends the full width of the open menu
cover. A smaller fish appears on the dessert menu.
For both menus real fish were used in making the
original prints.

This two-story restaurant serves American and
Cajun specialties in a setting reminiscent of New
Orleans. The glass-enclosed structure depicted on
the smaller menu cover houses a grand staircase
that leads up to the bar. Two terraces open off the
bar, while a third, opposite the downstairs dining
room, opens for outdoor dining in warm weather.
The fuchsia flowers depicted on the front cover of
the main menu and inside flaps are based on
those that surround the restaurant.

RESTAURANT: The Greenhouse Restaurant and Wine Bar

LOCATION: Vista International Hotel, New York, New York

DESIGN FIRM: F. G. I. Graphics Company

SPECIFICATIONS:

SIZE: 7¾" x 14"

PAPER: 100# White Vellum Bristol Cover

PRINTER: B. R. Doefler Company

The Greenhouse has glass walls and various plants for a conservatory effect. This theme is continued in the menu design. A tropical flower not only adorns the cover but is repeated inside. The prix-fixe meals are highlighted on both the lunch and the dinner menus, and for the year 1986, the restaurant's "A Taste of Liberty" promotion highlighted a different national culture each month. With the rededication of the Statue of Liberty in July, the Greenhouse featured American culture for that month.

Château Ste Michelle

SAVE A LADY
IN DISTRESS

Vista International • New York
and
Château Ste Michelle
will each contribute $1.50
for every bottle of
Château Ste Michelle Wine
sold during the month
in the Greenhouse
Restaurant and Wine Bar

APPETIZERS

Oysters and Clams on Half Shell
Cocktail Sauce 6.50

Herring Salad on Garden Greens with
Apples, Onions and Sour Cream Dressing 4.50

American Prosciutto, Fresh Pineapple 5.50

A Selection of Chilled Melons 4.25

Poached Shrimp with
Cocktail or Brandy Sauce 7.95

SOUPS

Chicken Broth with Vegetables and Chives 3.25

Seafood Gumbo 3.60

SALAD AND SANDWICHES

A Seasonal Sampler of Fresh Fruits with
Frozen Yogurt or Lemon Sherbet, Nut Bread Finger Sandwiches 9.25

COLD

Smoked Salmon on Bagel, Dilled Cream Cheese 9.50
Club Sandwich with Turkey, Bacon, Lettuce, Tomato and Egg 9.50
Combo of Egg and Tuna Salad on Toasted English Muffin 7.75
Shrimp and Avocado on a Croissant 9.75
Rare Roast Beef on Rye, Horseradish Mayonnaise 9.25

HOT

A Hamburger of Freshly Ground Beef,
Sliced Tomatoes and Onions 8.75

with Cheddar Cheese 9.00   or   Crisp Fried Onions 9.00

A TASTE OF LIBERTY

Coquille Saint Jacques à la Parisienne 12.95

From our French Heritage comes this Baked Scallop Classic
as served at our Liberty Dinner Celebrations
every Friday and Saturday Night during February

MAIN COURSES

Our Featured Roast of the Day
A Platter 10.75   A Sandwich 9.50
Charcoal Broiled 10-Ounce Sirloin Steak,
Garlic Herb Butter, French Fried Potatoes 18.25
A Three Egg Omelette with Smoked Salmon,
Mushrooms, Mixed Herbs or "your own" style 9.25
Broiled Salmon Steak, Dilled Butter Sauce 13.75
Lamb and Mushroom Kabobs served on Ratatouille 13.95
Calf's Liver Steak with Fried Onions and Crisp Bacon 14.25
Sautéed Pork Tenderloin, Green Peppercorn Sauce
and Buttered Linguine 13.25
Cornflaked Fried Shrimp with Soya Mayonnaise and Fried Rice 14.50
Catch of the Day 12.95

Entrées Served with a Mixed Green Salad with Tomatoes, Oil and Vinegar, French Dressing,
Blue Cheese Vinaigrette or Garlic Mayonnaise

FEATURED FOR THE SEASON

Citrus Cocktail, Honey Ginger Dressing 3.95
Soup of the Day 3.25

Broiled Swordfish on a Skewer, Cabbage Salad 12.75
Chili con Carne with Tortilla Chips and Garnish 8.50
Cheese and Walnut Tortellini with Bolonaise Sauce 8.75
Virginia Ham and Mushroom Quiche 8.50
Reuben Sandwich 8.95
Chicken and Snow Peas Fricassee served with Rice 11.50

Cranberry Orange Tart 3.40
Sweet Potato Pie 3.25

THE GREENHOUSE DINNER

Roast Prime Ribs of Beef, Natural Juices

Baked Potato with Sour Cream, Chives & Bacon Bits

Your Selection from The Salad Buffet

A delightful Dessert of your choice from the Buffet

Freshly Brewed Regular or Decaffeinated Coffee

A glass of Heineken Beer or a glass of Red or White Wine

24.25

DESSERTS

The Freshly Baked Pie or Layer Cake of The Season 3.25
Chocolate Fudge Layer Cake 3.50   Vista's Own Cheesecake 3.50
Greenhouse Chocolate Mousse Pie 3.40
Traditional Apple Pie 3.25   Chocolate Fudge Brownie 2.95
Fresh Ripe Fruit, Berries and Melon from "The Bowl" 2.95
Desserts Served à la mode 1.50

SUNDAES AND ICE CREAMS

Frozen Yogurt with Fresh Strawberries, Toasted Pistachios 3.40
Our Own Hot Fudge Sundae with Chocolate Chip Ice Cream 3.95
Old Fashioned Banana Split with Three Flavors of Ice Cream,
Fresh Strawberries and Pineapple 4.25
Ice Creams - Chocolate, Vanilla,
Chocolate Chip, Coffee or Strawberry 3.25
Lemon or Raspberry Sherbet 3.25
Traditional Ice Cream Sodas
Chocolate, Black and White, Coffee or Strawberry 3.25
Rich Ice Cream Milk Shakes
Chocolate, Coffee, Strawberry or Fresh Fruit 3.25

BEVERAGES

Freshly Brewed Regular or Decaffeinated Coffee 1.60   Cappuccino 2.25
Espresso: Single 1.60   Double 2.00   Pasteurized Milk 2.00
A Pot of Darjeeling Tea 1.60   Iced Tea or Coffee 1.60
Soft Drinks — A Selection 2.00   Mineral Water 2.50

Gratuity and 8.25 Tax Not Included.

This Month's Featured Non-Alcoholic Beverages

Peach Polynesian — This refreshing blend of
Cling Peaches, Pineapple and Coconut is truly a
slice of paradise 3.50

The Dorothy Rose — A tall, sparkling refresher
fashioned from Fresh Orange Juice and Ginger Ale
with the pomegranate blush of Grenadine 3.25

A Toast To Liberty

Parisienne Spritzer — A tall drink of Sparkling
Water topped with Blonde or Red Dubonnet 3.50

French "86" — Gin and Champagne
could not have been better 4.50

Greenhouse Wine Bar

BIN NO.	WHITE	Glass	Half	Bottle
700	River Oaks, Table Wine Estate Bottled, 1984 Alexander Valley	2.25	—	9.00
701	Robert Mondavi, Fume Blanc 1983/1984 Napa Valley	3.50	8.50	13.50
720	Stag's Leap, White Riesling 1983/1984 Napa Valley	2.50	—	10.50
702	Sebastiani, Chardonnay Reserve 1982/83 Sonoma Valley	3.75	—	18.25
734	Alexander Valley, Chardonnay 1982/1983 Sonoma County	4.00	—	19.50
737	Clos du Bois, Chardonnay 1984 Sonoma County	3.50	8.75	16.75
756	Dry Creek, Fume Blanc 1983/84 Sonoma Valley	3.75	9.50	18.00
733	Ste. Michelle, Fumé Blanc 1982/1983 Washington State	3.50	8.50	16.50
802	Bolla Soave Veneto, Italy	2.50	6.00	10.00
800	Bouchard Père & Fils, Chablis 1983 Burgundy, France	3.00	8.00	14.00
	RED			
500	Robert Mondavi, Table Wine 1982/1983 California	2.25	—	9.00
522	Corbett Canyon, Zinfandel 1983 Amador County	2.50	—	10.50
524	Beringer, Cabernet Sauvignon 1981 Knights Valley	3.50	—	16.00
530	Ste. Michelle, Cabernet Sauvignon 1980/1981 Washington State	3.75	—	18.50
504	Rutherford Hill, Merlot 1981/1982 Napa Valley	4.00	—	19.00
515	Trefethen, Pinot Noir 1981/1982 Napa Valley	3.75	—	16.50
602	Antinori, Chianti Classico Riserva Ducale Tuscany, Italy	3.00	8.00	14.00
600	Bouchard Père & Fils Beaujolais Villages 1983 Burgundy, France	2.50	6.00	11.00
	ROSE			
521	Robert Mondavi 1983/1984 California	2.25	—	9.00
531	Sanford Vin Gris (Pinot Noir) 1983 Santa Barbara	2.75	—	12.00
613	E & J, Château D'Ay 1983/1984 Rhône, France	3.00	8.00	14.00
	SPARKLING			
882	Brut Dargent, Côte de Jura, n.v. France	3.50	—	18.00
880	Domaine Chandon, Napa Valley Brut n.v.	3.00	—	26.00
888	Martini & Rossi, Asti Spumante	—	12.00	22.00
883	Louis Roederer Cour-Royal Brut n.v. Champagne, France	9.75 (split)	21.00	38.00
884	Moet et Chandon, Brut Imperial n.v. Champagne, France	9.75 (split)	22.00	40.00

2/86

RESTAURANT: The Safari Grill
LOCATION: New York, New York
DESIGNER: Dale Glasser
FIRM: Dale Glasser Graphics, Inc.
ILLUSTRATOR: Dale Glasser
SPECIFICATIONS:
SIZE: 10½" x 14"
PAPER: Laminated

This trendy uptown Manhattan restaurant used leopard skin as the inspiration for its carpet, added some animal skin touches, and finished the decor with deco-style lighting and green marble columns. Diners sit in oversized white wicker chairs. These eclectic design elements are incorporated into the menu design. A cubist illustration features a zebra skin napkin and place with a leopard print border. The buff on the menu exactly matches the walls; the green, the marble columns. The back of the menu is printed in one color and designed for periodic updates as part of the menu program. ▶

RESTAURANT: Crystal Swan
LOCATION: Novi Hilton Hotel,
Novi, Michigan
DESIGNER: Ann Werner
FIRM: Associates Printing Service
SPECIFICATIONS: Lunch and dinner menus
SIZE: 8½" x 15" (lunch menu);
7¼" x 14¼" (dinner menu, folded)
PAPER: Rhododendron Cover, mounted on 50 pt. board (lunch menu); Kromekote (dinner menu)
PRINTER: Associates Printing Service

A stylized, blind embossed graphic swan distinguishes both the lunch card and the more formal dinner menu. The dinner menu owes its simple elegance to the swan, the easy-to-read typeface, the glossy paper, and the airiness of the layout and design. There is nothing busy about this menu. Hairline rules beneath the category headings, and screen tints at the top and bottom of each page subtly define the menu area. The special insert page is printed in one color and stapled in for easy updating. The lunch card is even simpler, but uses a two-color linen weave stock that is embossed and mounted and feels appropriately businesslike for daytime use.

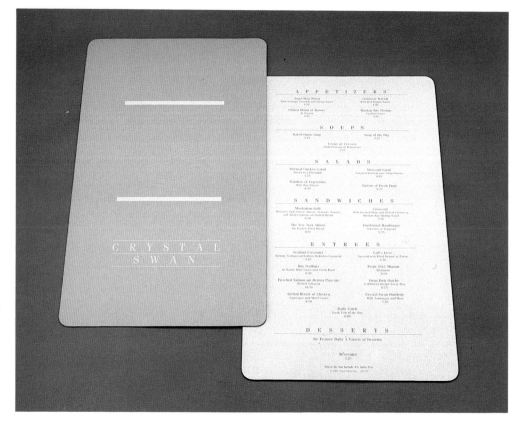

RESTAURANT: The Dome Grill
LOCATION: The Westin Paso del Norte,
El Paso, Texas
DESIGNER: Don Clark
FIRM: Visual Communications Systems,
Inc.
ILLUSTRATOR: Doug West
SPECIFICATIONS: Dinner menu
SIZE: 9" x 13¼" (closed)
PRINTER: Visual Communications
Systems, Inc.

The colors used in the menu are drawn from and
intended to enhance the hotel's Tiffany-style glass
dome. Violet foil stamping on the cover frames a
die-cut revealing a serigraph of the Southwestern
landscape by artist Doug West. The restaurant
encourages the current trend toward
"grazing"—choosing several appetizers instead of
a full meal. Appetizers make up over half the menu
listings. Menu items also are selected to take full
advantage of locally available ingredients. Menu
items that will vary are printed in one color for
easy updates.

RESTAURANT: Sheppard's
LOCATION: Sheraton Harbor Island Hotel,
San Diego, California
DESIGNER: Paul Harnagy
FIRM: Art Group, Inc.
ILLUSTRATOR: Paul Harnagy
SPECIFICATIONS:
SIZE: 9" x 12"
PAPER: 80# Mohawk Superfine Soft
White Cover
PRINTER: Ripple Printing/T H Enterprises

The light-hearted illustration on the menu cover is
designed to counterbalance the formal and elegant
atmosphere of the restaurant. Two-color menu
inserts are printed as needed. The item names are
printed in a much brighter color than the prices, a
nice merchandising touch. A mini-menu with a
one-color interior and without prices was also
produced. This is used as an in-room promotion
and can also be a souvenir or direct mailer. The
absence of prices will keep it current as long as
the menu selections do not change. This type of
promotional piece becomes very cost-effective
when printed at the same time as the menu
masters.

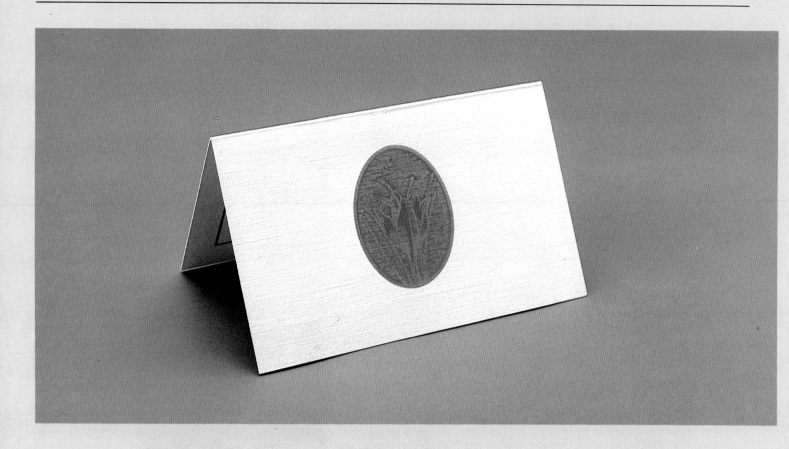

RESTAURANT: Saffron

LOCATION: Sheraton New Orleans Hotel,
New Orleans, Louisiana

DESIGNER: Paul Harnagy

FIRM: Art Group Inc.

ILLUSTRATOR: Paul Harnagy

SPECIFICATIONS:

SIZE: 8″ x 14″ (folded)

PAPER: Strathmore Rhododendron

PRINTER: Ripple Printing/TH Enterprises

One illustration of the saffron flower was reproduced in varying sizes and techniques for this elegant menu. It appears embossed on the cover, gold-foil-stamped and reproduced in lavender ink on vellum on the first page, as a pattern in lavender ink on the outside of the two-color menu insert, and as a graphic motif separating the menu categories. It is also used in the restaurant's signage, which is made of polished brass, and on the customed-designed matchbooks. The effect of all the repetition is elegant and understated because the image is not too complex. The menu cover matches the gray fabric walls of this elegant continental restaurant.

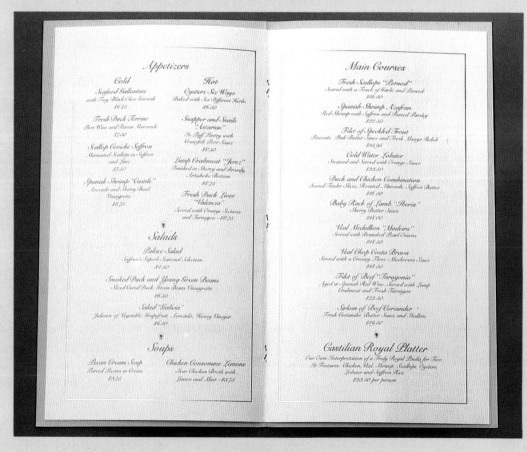

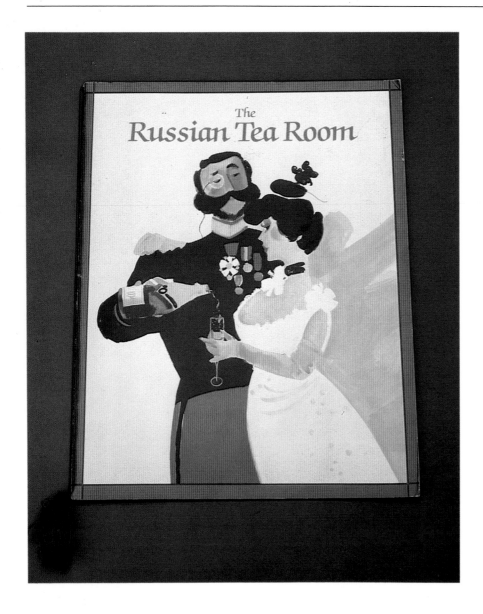

RESTAURANT: Russian Tea Room
LOCATION: New York, New York
SPECIFICATIONS:
    SIZE: 9⅝″ x 12½″
    PAPER: White Tours and Royale Cover
           Gloss (cover); 80# Peterboro
           White Vellum (insert)
    PRINTER: Ramsbee Print

Founded by members of the Russian Imperial Ballet in 1926, the Russian Tea Room features an exuberantly Russian menu. A silhouette of the traditional samovar (tea urn) adorns the short gatefolded section devoted strictly to vodkas. The Russian theme is further enhanced by use of a menu box in the shape of an onion dome, traditional on Russian Orthodox churches. The playful cover art—a monocled officer pouring champagne for an elegantly clad lady—helps conjure up images of past Russian aristocrats enjoying a wonderful night out. The vivid red continues the Russian theme. Wisely, the menu designer resisted the temptation to use a Russian-looking typeface, which would have been difficult to read.

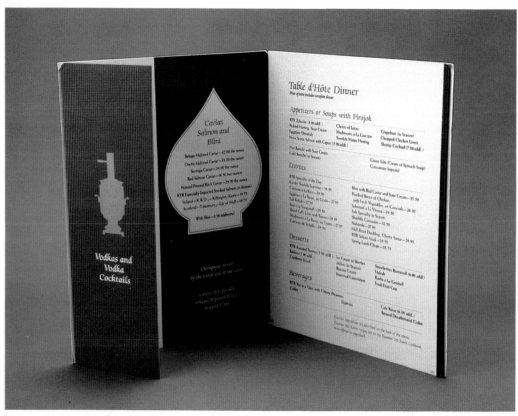

RESTAURANT: Lion & Compass
LOCATION: Sunnyvale, California
DESIGNER: Gerald Reis
FIRM: Gerald Reis & Company
SPECIFICATIONS:
PRINTER: Venture Graphics

This restaurant's audience is the Silicon Valley business community. For this reason, the breakfast menu is as extensive and unusual as the lunch and dinner menus. Breakfast meetings are very popular in the software design community. An open, legible typface has been used very effectively on the menu cards. Daily specials for all three meals are listed on a blackboard. Menus can be easily updated because only the restaurant logo is in a second color. The overall menu design is straightforward. Business people have little time to plough through stories and descriptive copy. Such elements would be inappropriate here, and so, they are not used.

Lunch

RESTAURANT: The Old Poodle Dog Restaurant
LOCATION: San Francisco, California
DESIGNER: Gerald Reis
FIRM: Gerald Reis & Company
SPECIFICATIONS:
PRINTER: Lithography by Design

The Old Poodle Dog Restaurant began life as the "Poulet d'Or" (the Golden Chicken), but San Franciscans of the 1890s soon mangled the name into "The Old Poodle Dog" and the name stuck.

The unofficial "club" of the French community for years, it has closed three times: once after the earthquake and fire of 1906 destroyed it; once for prohibition ("great cuisine cannot be served without wine," declared the chef); and once after the second generation owner's wife died in 1980. Reopened in luxurious new surroundings by the third generation, it needed a beautiful new menu.

The elegantly simple menu inserts slide into actual leather covers, and the pattern of the endpapers is picked up in bars on the inserts. The inserts are unusual, as they are printed on only one side and folded to fit into the menu covers. The menus were designed to coordinate with the tabletops and the general decor of the restaurant.

Menu

Smoked Salmon Omelet with Sautéed Apples	8.00
Leek Tart with Ham and Sundried Tomatoes	9.00
Filet of Petrale Sole with Chives Troisgros	13.00
Grilled Lamb Chops with Rice Pilaf	14.00
Poached Breast of Chicken "A La Ritz"	11.00
Fresh Seafood Chowder with Garlic and Basil	12.00
Rex Sole "Poodle Dog"	7.50
Grilled Ribeye Steak with Roasted Potatoes	12.00
Fresh Pasta	.....
Fresh Fish	.....
Caesar Salad	8.50
Smoked Fish and Avocado Salad	10.50
Shrimp Louis Coutard	10.50

Francois

SPRING
LUNCHEON MENU
March - June

RESTAURANT: Francois

LOCATION: Arco Plaza,
Los Angeles, California

DESIGNER: Tim Claffey

FIRM: Associates Printing Service

ILLUSTRATOR: Tim Claffey

SPECIFICATIONS:

SIZE: 7½" x 13¾" (closed cover)

PAPER: Kromekote

PRINTER: Associates Printing Service

Sunny flowers provide an appropriate design subject for this Southern California restaurant that specializes in locally produced foods. The production of this menu was a somewhat difficult task, but was carried out successfully—matching the two halves of the flower illustrations that appear when the three-fold menu is first unfolded was tricky but well-executed. The menu is reprinted several times a year. Featured are the spring menus for luncheon and dinner.

RESTAURANT: American Festival

LOCATION: Omni International Hotel, Orlando, Florida

DESIGNER: Cindia Sanford Garte

FIRM: Grigg Printing Service

ILLUSTRATOR: Cindia Sanford-Garte

SPECIFICATIONS:

SIZE: 9⅞" x 13" (cover, folded); 9¾" x 12⅞" (inserts)

PAPER: 80# Bianco White Cover (cover); Aquabee (insert)

PRINTER: Grigg Printing Service

This restaurant celebrates the abundance of American food and the variety of American cooking. While the nouvelle cuisine it offers has little to do with "Mom's apple pie," the cover playfully starts at the left with an image of a blue and white gingham table cloth and floats squares across the menu, borrowing pieces from the still-life of raw foodstuffs at bottom right. The effect is that of a jigsaw puzzle, assembling and recombining itself for new effects. Since American cooking is a recombining of other cuisines for new effects, the menu cover design is a nice touch. The interior forms are on parchment, secured on the center panel only; the menu items that will vary are printed in one color.

AMERICAN
Festival

ntrees

quet of Fresh Fruit
l Fresh Fruit with Champagne Sorbet

ked Chicken 2.95
reens and Rotini Pasta with Hazelnut Vinaigrette

Coast Salad 2.95
ted Seafood on Field Greens with Garden Vegetables

Coho Salmon
cold with Herb Mayonnaise and Avocado

kened Swordfish Salad
Vinaigrette and Garden Vegetables

ed Shrimp, Scallops and Mussels
per Linguini with Garden Vegetables and White Wine Garlic Sauce

d Red Snapper
l Seed Butter

kled Gulf Trout
and served with Lemon Chive Sauce

d Lamb Chops
y Jack stuffed Banana Pepper with Sauce Picante

ed Chicken and Linguini 1.25
uini, Wild Mushrooms and Madeira Cream Sauce

llions of Beef Tenderloin 1.75
Shallots and Red Wine Sauce

Breast of Chicken 1.25
ento Sauce

Sausage and Pasta 1.85
le Sausage and Fettucine with Tomato and Garlic Sauce

n Ragout
Chicken, Wild Mushrooms and Polenta in a Bourbon Sauce

ur entree will be complemented by the Chef's selection of accompaniments.

Please refrain from Pipe and Cigar Smoking.

Catering and Special Feasts

A catering menu is the caterer's promotional brochure. Unlike the menu for a restaurant, the catering menu will be given away, often as part of a mailed promotional package. These considerations govern the size, paper stocks selected, and quantity of menus produced. A catering menu can be a self-mailer, or mailed in an envelope as part of a kit.

In the case of hotels and private clubs, the catering menu may be part of a package that includes rental rates, rules for use, provisions for entertainment, and the like. In such cases, a folder with inserts for the various information booklets may be used.

At the other end of the scale are special occasion menus, designed for one-time-only use. Selection of medium and type for these is limited only by the budget and the designer's imagination. Examples pictured in this chapter range from the exquisite to the most simple.

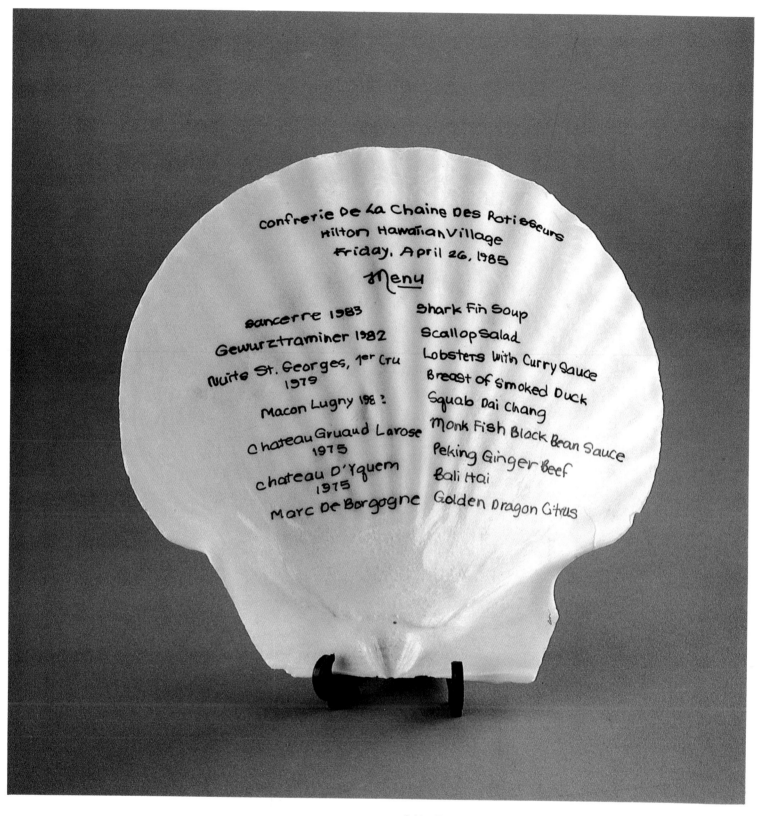

Confrerie De La Chaine Des Rotisseurs
Hilton Hawaiian Village
Friday, April 26, 1985
Menu

Sancerre 1983	Shark Fin Soup
Gewurztraminer 1982	Scallop Salad
Nuits St. Georges, 1er Cru 1979	Lobsters With Curry Sauce
	Breast of Smoked Duck
Macon Lugny 198?	Squab Dai Chang
Chateau Gruaud Larose 1975	Monk Fish Black Bean Sauce
	Peking Ginger Beef
Chateau D'Yquem 1975	Bali Hai
Marc De Borgogne	Golden Dragon Citrus

RESTAURANT: Golden Dragon

LOCATION: Hilton Hawaiian Village, Honolulu, Hawaii

SPECIFICATIONS:

MEDIUM: Hand-painted on an actual seashell

This menu was hand-lettered on an actual seashell. The Hilton Hawaiian Village has several calligraphers on staff and prides itself on the imaginative use of materials in designing special dinner menus. For this dinner party, for a group of professional chefs, wines were selected in advance to accompany each course. The wines are listed on the left, dishes on the right. A wooden plate stand supports the shell for easy reading.

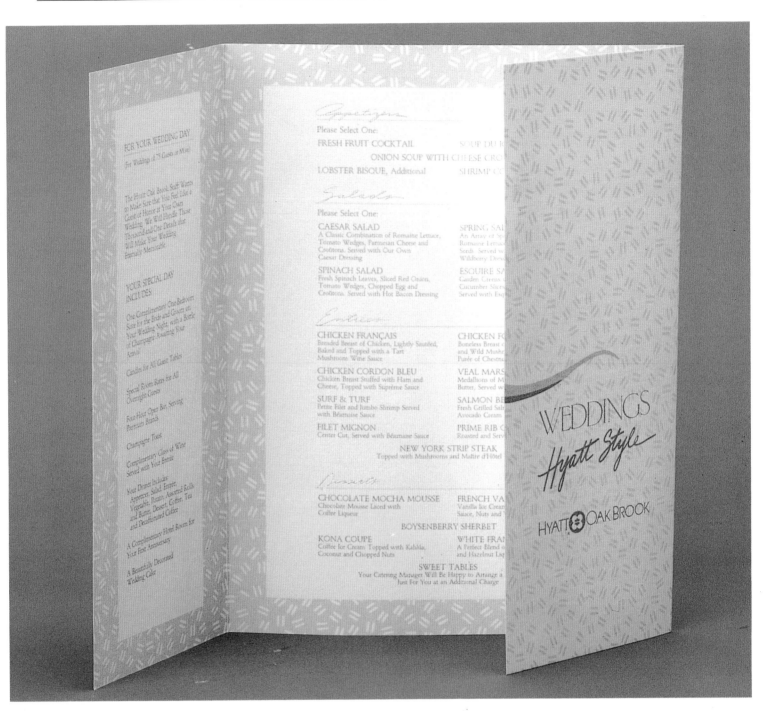

RESTAURANT: Hyatt Oakbrook
LOCATION: Oakbrook, Illinois
DESIGNER: Roberta Warehan
FIRM: Associates Printing Service
ILLUSTRATOR: Roberta Warehan
SPECIFICATIONS: "Weddings Hyatt Style" Menu
SIZE: 8½" x 11" (folded)
PAPER: Rhodondendron
PRINTER: Associates Printing Service

The use of only two colors and a beautifully textured paper stock makes this special catering menu look as special as everything associated with a wedding should be. The center section lists the menu, the left-hand fold lists the other considerable benefits included in the "Hyatt style" package, and the right-hand side provides information on payment and guarantees. The information has been organized very logically. This is just the sort of merchandising likely to appeal to a busy bride-to-be, since the menu is a multiple-choice affair—pick one from each category. The menu works not only to sell the hotel's catering facilities but also to sell bar services and rooms, too.

The Company Chef Concept

The news is spreading fast—The Company Chef is revolutionizing carry-out dining.

Telephone calls, meetings, deadlines and a hundred other tasks leave little time for long leisurely meals. Nevertheless, your demand for fresh, healthy food does not stop when you get to the office. Now you can have the advantage of tantalizing breakfast, lunch and dinner fare close to your office. You need never spend precious time traveling to find quality cuisine. With The Company Chef, you have gourmet to go.

In addition to carry-out convenience, special touches enhance The Company Chef experience: a small, informal dining area; newspapers and magazines to enjoy while you eat; and an efficient, friendly staff to serve you. Yet the best part of eating at The Company Chef is found in the menu: fresh breads and fruit for breakfast; hot entrees, salads, and desserts for lunch and a convenient carry-out service for take-home dinner. An extensive beverage list features freshly brewed coffee, beer and wine. Open from 7:00 a.m. to 6:00 p.m., we're there whenever you need us.

In addition to regular services, there are some unique surprises you might not expect to find. Catering is available for

home and office parties, and each location has a gourmet mini-market offering fresh produce, pastas, jams and jellies. These same gourmet items are found in creatively designed gift baskets.

At The Company Chef, we feel our job is to make your job more enjoyable. We do that by providing some of the freshest, most innovative cuisine, at your doorstep. Just think of us as your company chef.

Today's Market Report

You'll be making a healthy investment when you shop the Gourmet Market at The Company Chef. Playing this market is no gamble—only the freshest produce, bread, jams and jellies are sold. You'll be tempted with gourmet mustards and chocolates and an amazing array of food items you wouldn't expect to find at your office carry-out! Best of all, your dividends at our market are guaranteed—mouth-watering delicacies available right where you work.

When It Comes to Lunch We Mean Business

Your company means business and so do we. We understand the pressures of the working world, and know that as a discriminating diner you're looking for more than something "off the grill." You are health conscious and demanding, but up until now its been difficult to satisfy your gourmet needs on busy days. The Company Chef has changed that. The same great tasting foods that you expect to find at a quality restaurant are now available right where you work. You can carry out or eat in and enjoy the casual atmosphere complete with daily newspapers and magazines. Either way, the selection of soups, salads, entrees, sandwiches and enticing desserts will make your lunch at The Company Chef an out-of-the-ordinary event!

Home Team Wins

You'll never strike out if you cross home plate with a take home dinner from The Company Chef. More and more working people are discovering that today's busy lifestyle makes a quality take-out service a must. Whether you take home fresh produce and pasta to cook yourself, or choose from a variety of prepared entrees, salads and sandwiches; your dinner from The Company Chef is bound to be a hit. The next time you need a quick dinner for the home team, or something to get you through a late night at the office, The Company Chef has the winning game plan every time.

We Cater to Your Every Need

Special occasions for your "9-5 family" such as promotions, business lunches, birthdays, holidays and recognition awards deserve the very best in gourmet catering. At The Company Chef, we offer a wide range of catering services designed to make any office celebration truly special because business catering is our specialty.

Our sumptuous party platters and luncheon trays include hors d'ouevres, deli sandwiches, fruit and cheese trays, and a full complement of tempting desserts. To reflect our commitment to meeting all of your catering needs, we even offer picnic baskets and fruit baskets for gift giving.

If you're looking for a way to launch a successful morning meeting, how about a catered breakfast? Staff and clients alike will appreciate the platters of fresh breads and fruit served with condiments and beverages. These impressive eye openers are guaranteed to have everyone ready to get down to business.

The next time you want to make an event special, remember The Company Chef for catering. You'll find the perfect blend of quality and convenience.

PLEASE
*turn the page
for our menu
selections* ▶

RESTAURANT: The Company Chef
LOCATION: Chevy Chase, Maryland
DESIGNER: Scott Mahr
FIRM: Great Scott Graphics
SPECIFICATIONS:
SIZE: 11½" x 15"
PAPER: 60# white offset
PRINTER: Ad Design

The owner, who is also a real estate developer, wanted a corporate feeling in the menus for this gourmet office catering and take-out chain. Located only in office buildings, The Company Chef provides an upscale take-out menu and also caters business meetings and special events. Catered items are delivered in cherry red boxes with the logo on top. The copywriting describes the concept and merchandises the food. Particularly nice is a reference to the office staff as the "9 to 5 family."

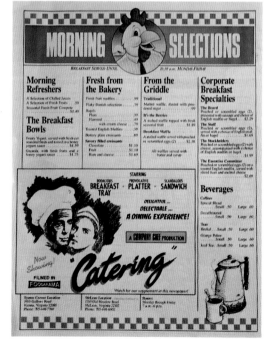

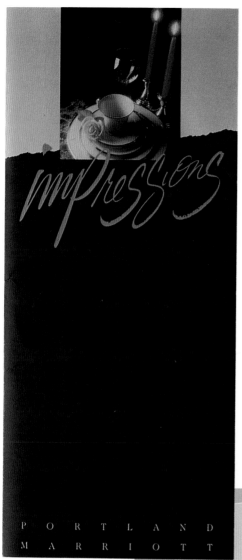

RESTAURANT: Portland Marriott Hotel
Catering Department
LOCATION: Portland, Oregon
DESIGNER: Karen Matheson
FIRM: Whitman Advertising
PHOTOGRAPHER: Steve Bonini
FIRM: Bonini Photography
SPECIFICATIONS: "Impressions" Menu
SIZE: 4" x 9" (folded)
PAPER: Kromekote

This menu won first place in the "Banquet/Catering" category of the National Restaurant Association's 1986 Great Menus Contest. The full-color cover holds a stepped series of inserts printed on an uncoated stock. The dot over the "i" on the cover was chosen as a unifying design element and appears both on the interior of the folder and on the insert forms. The insert items that will vary are printed in one color—the green that is the predominant color on the folder. The base colors of the inserts are chosen from a range within the colors of the folder.

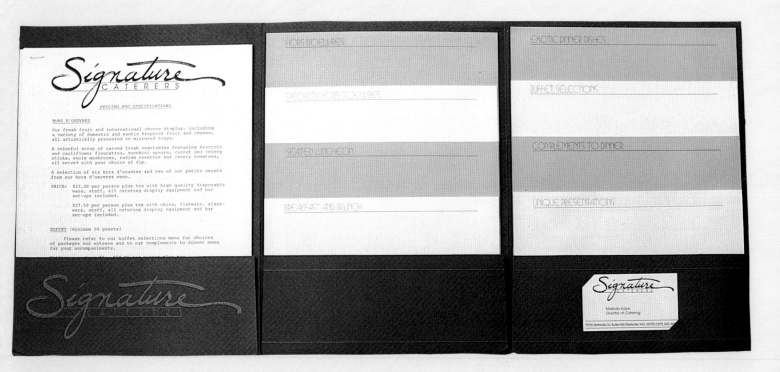

RESTAURANT: Signature Caterers
(Carrollton Enterprises)
LOCATION: Beltsville, Maryland
DESIGN FIRM: Eisner & Associates
SPECIFICATIONS:
SIZE: 9″ x 12″
PRINTER: Executive Printers

This menu won third place in the "Banquet/Catering" category of the National Restaurant Association's 1986 Great Menus Contest. The understated dark green folder is designed to permit easy updating of each menu section. Because each section is printed in one color on a separate sheet, one or more sheets may be changed without affecting the others. The folder is sturdy and designed to fit conveniently into a file folder. There is also a special die-cut to hold the contact's business card. The typeface specified for the menu items is elegant and presents a clean appearance.

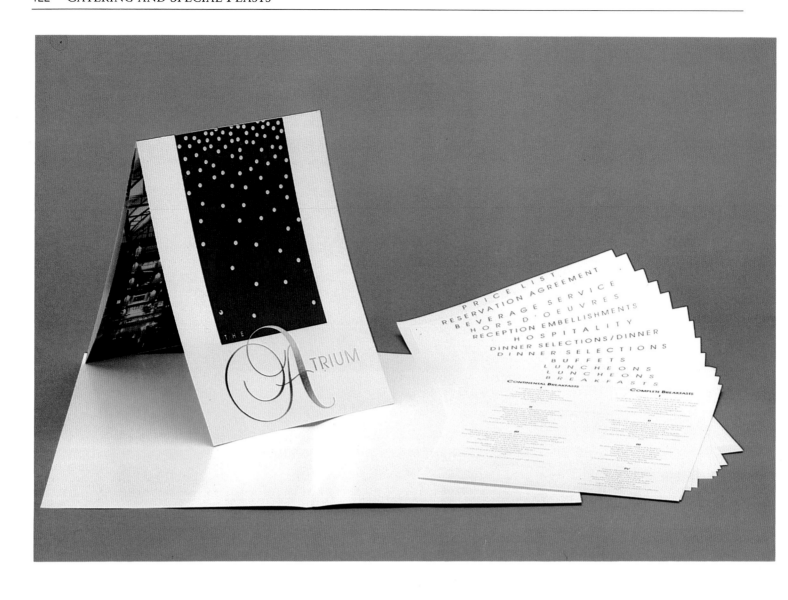

RESTAURANT: The Atrium

LOCATION: Minneapolis, Minnesota

DESIGNER: Jennifer Closner

FIRM: Jennifer Closner Designs

SPECIFICATIONS:

SIZE: 7½″ x 12″ (folded)

PAPER: 80# Lustro Enamel and Dull

PRINTER: Litho Specialists

This menu won second place in the "Banquet/Catering" category of the National Restaurant Association's 1986 Great Menus Contest. The Atrium is an L-shaped, five-story-high complex designed for special evening events. It is located at the International Market Square, a design center and home furnishings mart located in the renovated Munsingwear Factory in downtown Minneapolis.

The Atrium's peaked glass roof with the stars visible above was the inspiration for the menu's main design look. The price list is a separate insert that corresponds to a two-digit alphanumeric code listed on the main inserts next to each available menu item. The customer is thus encouraged to order on the basis of the menu item's appeal, not its price.

ON FEASTS

"It's a shame that in America, only the hunters enjoy the game. And the hunters are notoriously bad cooks. There's a woman in Barcelona who renders a masterpiece in wild boar. And the game birds, fresh as frost. Stuffing is her art, though. Red berries on brown bread. Ibiza cold water oysters. She had a fair cellar of wine, too. Fall is for feasting and fasting. Gets a body ready for winter."

"Tales in Earnest"
by
Duc Maynard d'Catalognia

Winter Game Festival

appetizers & soups
(choice of one)
Breast of Duck A l'Indienne / Game Pate, Sauce Cumberland
Cream of Pheasant Soup with Wild Rice

entrees
(choice of one)
Filet of Venison
Lingonberry Sauce served with Potato Croquettes
Roast Pheasant
served with Chestnut Puree and Potato Croquettes
Kebab of Rabbit
Australian Style served with a Wild Mushroom and
Pepper Sauce over a Bed of Rice
Wild Goose Hunter Style
served with a Piquante Mushroom Sauce
and Potato Croquettes
Grilled Quails on Croutons
au Natural served with Wild Rice

Entrees are served with Vegetables of the Day
and Hemingway's Special Salad.

desserts
(choice of one)
Papaya Custard / Strawberry Romanoff / Cranberry Pudding

beverages
Coffee / Tea / Decaffeinated Coffee / Espresso

$19.95 Per Person
November 1st to December 15th

RESTAURANT: Hemingway's
LOCATION: Holiday Inn Crowne Plaza,
Rockville, Maryland
DESIGN FIRM: Paisley & Romorini
SPECIFICATIONS: Winter Game Festival Menu
SIZE: 4¼" × 6" (folded)
PAPER: Kromekote

A beautiful pen-and-ink drawing on watercolor of the writer Ernest Hemingway adorns the cover of this menu. The inside was printed in one color and describes a fare that is available for only six weeks in mid-winter. The prix fixed menu features wild game with appropriate accompaniments. This is a nice use of a menu master for a special purpose. It would be equally appropriate for a menu of spring or summer specialties, drinks, or "munchies." The literary selection in the style of Hemingway on the left-hand inside cover is a nice touch and enhances the menu's effectiveness.

RESTAURANT: Associated Students Food Service
LOCATION: California State University, Chico, California
DESIGNERS: Joe Martin, John Milano, Fred Swift, Susie Geshekter (all in-house; Associated Students, Chico Graphics)
SPECIFICATIONS: "Mediterranean Ports of Call Christmas Feast" Menu
SIZE: 6½" square
PAPER: Chromolux
PRINTER: Walker Litho

This menu, which won third place for "Best Design" in the National Restaurant Association's 1986 Great Menus Contest, was designed for an annual feast sponsored by the food service department at the university.

The 1985 feast was designed around a "Mediterranean Ports of Call" theme. The cover and interior forms were inspired by Italian graphics. The feast was literally an orchestrated event staged as a cruise that included a bon voyage party and streamers, an elegant sit-down dinner with reserved seating, and finally, a farewell party with dancing to live music. Tickets for the feast's 290 seats are usually sold within a week or two of their going on sale. The feast is designed as a showcase for the food service staff's talents and to promote goodwill between the faculty, the staff, and the townspeople. Each menu cover is unique.

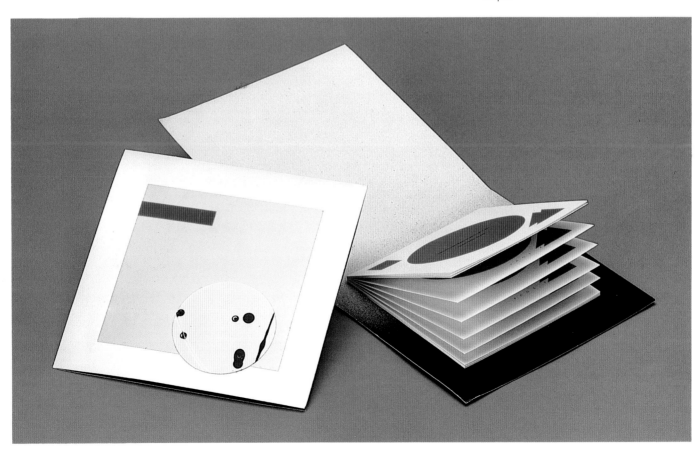

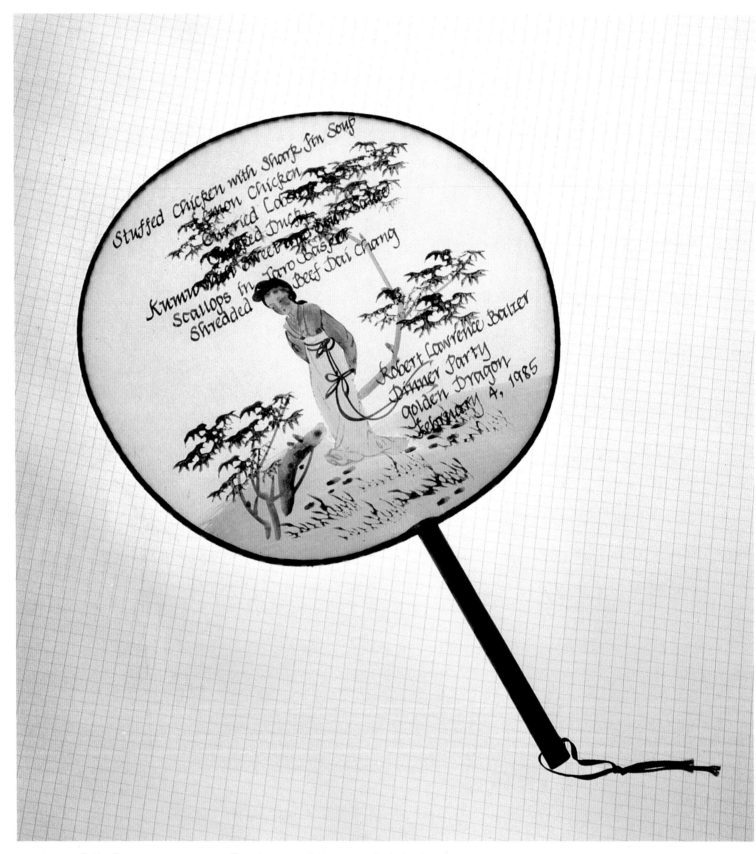

RESTAURANT: Golden Dragon

LOCATION: Hilton Hawaiian Village, Honolulu, Hawaii

DESIGNER: Noel G. Trainor

SPECIFICATIONS:

MEDIUM: Fabric fan with hand-painted watercolor

These fans are available as souvenirs in the shops along Waikiki Beach. The Hilton Hawaiian Village has used them as the "form" for special dinner party menus several times. This particular dinner party, hosted by Robert Lawrence Balzer, food editor of *Travel/Holiday Magazine*, was composed by the chef of the Golden Dragon for the occasion.

CHAMPAGNE BRUNCH BUFFET

The ideal way to start any day, especially a Saturday or Sunday, with fresh fruits, cheeses, cold cuts, hot meats, eggs, crepes and, of course, a chilled sparkling glass of champagne. 100 persons minimum. $10.95 per person.

Fruits and Juices

Fresh Fruit Basket
Hawaiian Papaya Wedges with Fresh Limes
Apricots and Prunes
Fresh Orange Juice
Guava Juice
Tomato Juice

Pastries

Fresh Baked Apple Turnovers, Muffins, Cinnamon Rolls, Croissants, and Marble Cake.

Cold Buffet

Tossed Greens, Choice of Dressing
Chef's Selection of Four Marinated Salads
Sliced Tomatoes and Cucumbers
Cottage Cheese
Assorted Sausages and Cheese
Haupia and Jello Mold

Hot Buffet

Sliced Roast Rack of Lamb
Chicken with Vegetables and Tofu
Veal and Chicken Crepes
Fruit Crepes
Scrambled Eggs
Eggs Florentine
Crisp Bacon, Pork Sausage Links, and Ham
Potatoes
Steamed Rice
Dinner Rolls

Desserts

Assorted Cakes, Pies, Tarts, French Pastries and Mousses

Beverages

Coffee, Tea

BREAKFASTS & LUNCHEONS

BANQUETS & PRIVATE PARTIES

HALE KOA HOTEL

RESTAURANT:	Hale Koa Hotel
LOCATION:	Honolulu, Hawaii
DESIGNER:	Anne Clare
FIRM:	Anne Clare Design
SPECIFICATIONS:	
SIZE:	8¾″ x 11¼″
PAPER:	65# Sundance Natural White Cover
PRINTER:	Service Printers

This catering menu uses stylized illustration to unify a broad range of catering services. In addition to providing meals and facilities for business meetings, the hotel also offers luaus, wedding receptions, and pupus (Polynesian hors d'oeuvres). Both the pink match color and the graphic elements in the line drawings have the flavor of the Islands, yet are subtle enough not to interfere with the information being communicated.

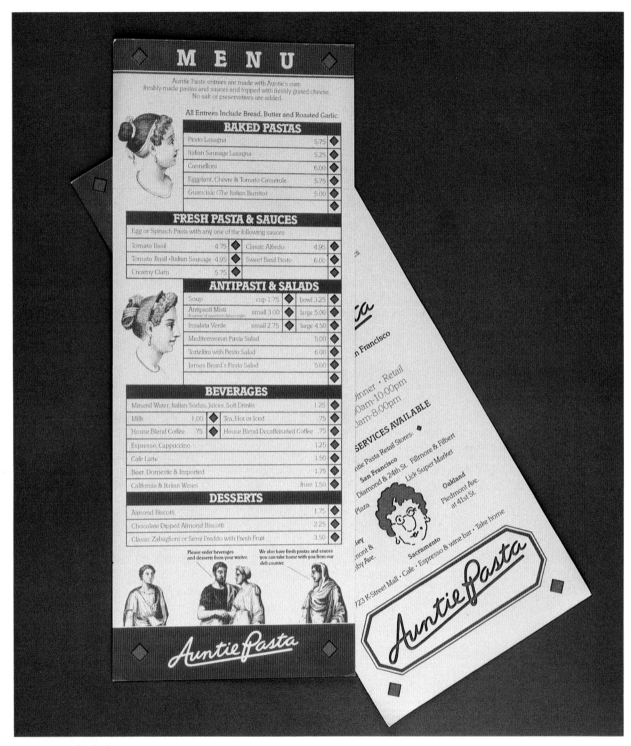

RESTAURANT: Auntie Pasta

LOCATION: San Francisco, California

SPECIFICATIONS:

    SIZE: 4¾″ x 12″

Auntie Pasta sells—what else?—homemade pastas and sauces to go and also provides catering. The sprightly menu card uses the colors of the Italian flag and a combination of clip art and illustration. The food listings, by contrast, are perfectly serious and assume sophistication about Italian food on the part of the consumer. The menu deliberately avoids price listing by running green diamonds where one would expect the prices to appear. This forces the purchasers to think more about the food and not be distracted by the prices—good merchandising!

RESTAURANT: "Cafe Society Awards Dinner"

LOCATION: Sheraton Corporate Headquarters, Boston, Massachusetts

DESIGNER: Paul Harnagy

FIRM: Art Group Inc.

ILLUSTRATOR: Al Himes

SPECIFICATIONS:

SIZE: 6" x 6⅝" (opens to 6" x 21⅞")

PAPER: Custom Kote

PRINTER: Ripple Printing/TH Enterprises

This special banquet menu is both fun to look at and an interesting example of several useful production techniques. The white card stock, coated on one side, is enlivened by the use of a silver foil sticker with a stylized white orchid. Opened, the inside of the folder reveals the name of the event, foil-stamped. The white orchid reappears hot-stamped on the insert. This menu was put together very quickly—in only three days. This was possible because the inserts were "stock on hand," permitting development of a very personalized menu under tight deadlines.

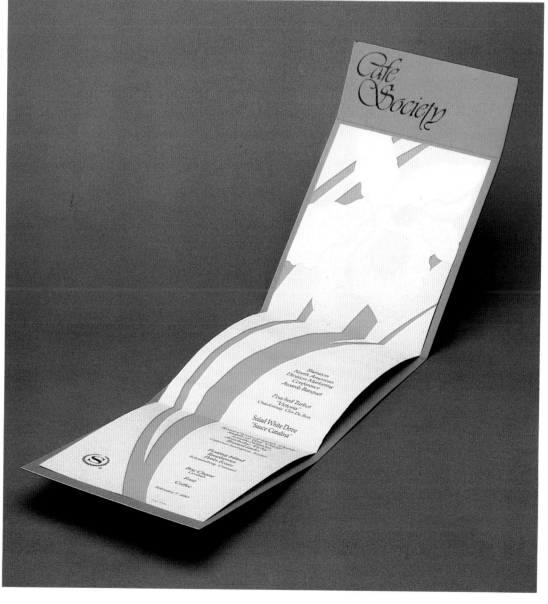

7

Hotel and Resort Menus

Hotels and resorts need a broad range of menus, all of them consistent with corporate identity, yet not sterile in appearance. A balance must be struck between the image associated with the hotel name and a sense of the location. The "sense of location" may be accomplished by graphics, colors, photography, or cultural motifs.

Hotel restaurants have become more sophisticated than in the past, when they were aimed mostly at the pragmatic needs of the traveller. Because the restaurant industry is booming, and thus making a wider variety of good food available, the hotel that hopes to capture the traveller's food dollar must provide him or her with a good reason beyond convenience to eat at the hotel restaurant.

The number of different menus needed by a hotel or a resort presents another design challenge. Consistency of image, if carried to an extreme, can create problems for the serving staff, who must have an easy way to distinguish among room service, breakfast, lunch, and dinner menus, as well as wine lists, bar menus, and other menus.

This chapter illustrates how some designers have successfully met these design challenges.

RESTAURANT: Jumby Bay Resort
LOCATION: Long Island, Antigua
DESIGNER: Mary McGinley
FIRM: Food & Wine Research, Inc.
ILLUSTRATOR: John Coles
SPECIFICATIONS: Dinner menu
SIZE: 7½" x 11"
PAPER: 130# Curtis Tweedweave
(cover); 80# Curtis
Tweedweave (inserts)
PRINTER: Thomas Todd Company, Printers

The Jumby Bay Resort is on a private island off Antigua. Its merchandising points are a tranquil atmosphere and an unspoiled tropical setting. All of its menus incorporate primitive watercolors to emphasize these ideas. Each has its own watercolor motif, but when the menus are seen together, it becomes obvious that all of the different watercolors are, in fact, small sections of the watercolor landscape on the front cover of the dinner menu.

THE · ESTATE · HOUSE

RESTAURANT: The Cathedral and Patio Royale
LOCATION: Boca Raton Hotel & Club,
Boca Raton, Florida
DESIGNER: Dayne Dupree
SPECIFICATIONS:
SIZE: 9½" x 14"
PRINTER: Blue Ocean Press

The clientele of this dining room is a bit older and more conservative than that of The Shell, also at the Boca Raton Hotel & Club. The room is reminiscent of grand ballrooms of the 1920s and 1930s. After dinner, old-fashioned ballroom dancing provides the evening's entertainment. Menu items are evenly balanced between meats and seafood. A daily specials insert slips under the cord that holds the main inserts in place; the double fold of the cover and a pre-printed flower lend the daily insert a more finished look. Pastel pink is used for category headings; menu items that will vary are printed in grass green. The leatherette menu cover features an embossed die-cut window revealing a pastel urn with orchids under glassine.

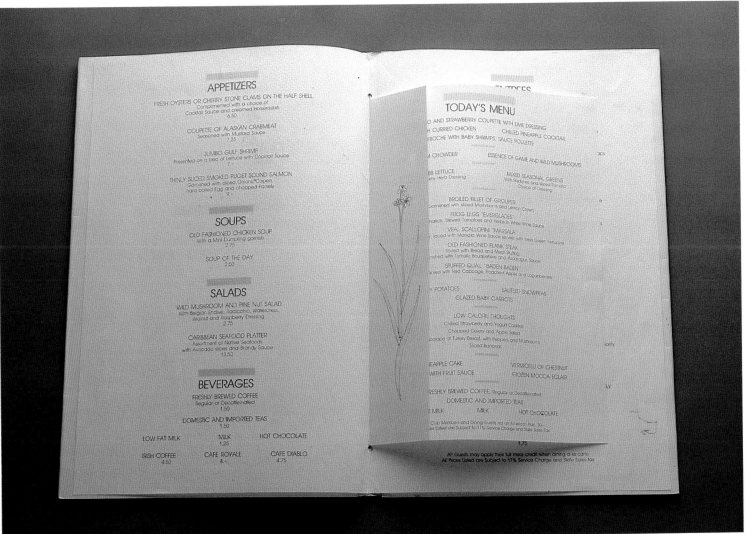

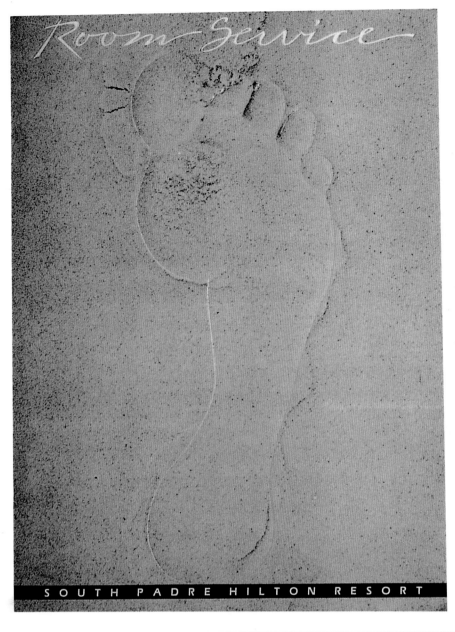

SOUTH PADRE HILTON RESORT

RESTAURANT: South Padre Hilton Resort
LOCATION: South Padre Island, Texas
DESIGNER: Ann Werner
FIRM: Associates Printing Service
SPECIFICATIONS: Room service menu
SIZE: 8″ x 10¾″
PAPER: Kromekote, embossed cover
PRINTER: Associates Printing Service

Embossing defines a footprint in the sand on the cover of this room service menu. The type style of category headings and the copywriting style enhance the breezy, beach atmosphere of the resort.

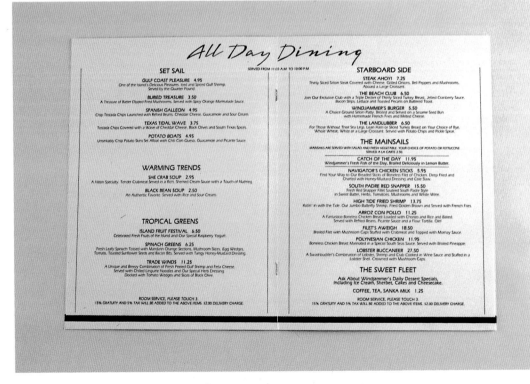

RESTAURANT: Westin Hotel
LOCATION: Washington, D.C.
DESIGNER: Don Clark
FIRM: Visual Communication Services
SPECIFICATIONS: Health menus
SIZE: 8" x 6" (closed)
PAPER: Silver Currency Cover

These slick silver menus with stylized sporting theme symbols reminiscent of Olympic signage are used for low-calorie menu selections throughout the hotel. The menu sheets are produced by computer and inserted. A calorie count for each item is also listed. Use of a word processor makes changing the menu an easy task and thus permits the hotel to take advantage of seasonal produce in providing a variety of light and healthful dishes.

menu

RESTAURANT: Prime Motor Inns, Inc.
LOCATION: Fairfield, New Jersey
DESIGNER: In-house Food and Beverage
Director
SPECIFICATIONS: Sandalwood menu
PRINTER: Grafik Haus

The Sandalwood menu, an artful creation of delicate illustration and subtle color, won second place in the "Best Design" Category of the National Restaurant Association's 1986 Great Menus Contest. Besides being striking, this menu is undisputably ingenious. It can be adapted by inserting any of a number of cards, among them breakfast and lunch cards, as well as seasonal cards showing monthly specials.

RESTAURANT: Jumby Bay Resort

LOCATION: Long Island, Antigua

DESIGNER: Mary McGinley

FIRM: Food & Wine Research, Inc.

ILLUSTRATOR: John Coles

SPECIFICATIONS: Lunch and dinner menus, wine list

SIZE: 7½" x 12" (lunch menu); 7½ x 11" (dinner menu); 6" x 11" (wine list)

PAPER: 130# Curtis Tweedweave (cover); 80# Curtis Tweedweave (inserts)

PRINTER: Thomas Todd Company, Printers

The Jumby Bay Resort is on a private island off Antigua. Its merchandising points are a tranquil atmosphere and an unspoiled tropical setting. The menu design incorporates primitive watercolors to emphasize these ideas. Although each menu is different, all are united by a common and beautiful paper stock. Each also has its own watercolor motif. When the menus are seen together, it becomes obvious that all of the different watercolors are, in fact, small sections of the watercolor landscape on the front cover of the dinner menu. Seen separately, the menus would all seem to have different illustrations. The walls of the "main house" are adorned by paintings in a similar style. Menu lists are in one color, and the dinner menu has a "specials" sheet, handwritten in calligraphy on coordinated stock, which is changed daily.

The Shell

RESTAURANT: The Shell
LOCATION: Boca Raton Hotel & Club,
Boca Raton, Florida
DESIGNER: Dayne Dupree
SPECIFICATIONS:
SIZE: 9½″ x 14″
PAPER: Strathmore Beau Brilliant
PRINTER: Blue Ocean Press

The Boca Raton Hotel and Club has seven different dining rooms that vary in degree of formality and specialize in different cuisines. The three represented here illustrate the broad range of atmosphere and cuisines offered. The Shell, which is the most elegant, features a nouvelle cuisine menu. A large shell sculpture at the entrance of the restaurant provides the theme for the menu. The restaurant, like the menu, uses soft pastels accented with silver. Menu inserts, printed in one color, use the same rich stock as the cover. Embossing and foil stamping lend the cover distinction. Attentive service and table-side preparation of many dishes make this the most formal of the three rooms represented here. This is a popular choice for business meetings.

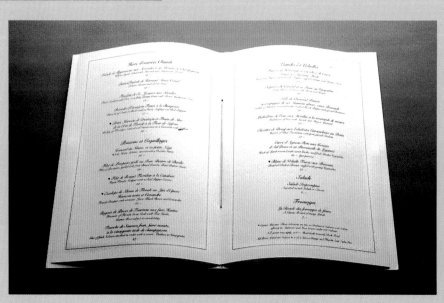

RESTAURANT: Ashley's

LOCATION: Albany Marriott Interstate Hotel Corporation, Albany, New York

SPECIFICATIONS:

SIZE: 7⁵⁄₁₆″ x 14⁵⁄₁₆″ with rounded top

PAPER: Creme Linen Index, with embossed border and gold-foil logo

PRINTER: Clevelend Menu Printing Company

This menu won second prize in the "Restaurant: Average Check Over $10.00 Per Person" category of the National Restaurant Association's 1986 Great Menus Contest. The emphasis of the restaurant is American cooking with fresh ingredients. An embossed border of artichokes and grapes adorns the die-cut menu. On the interior fold-out right-hand side, a "wheel" of herbs and spices illustrates this theme. Other menu illustrations include mushrooms and pepper plants.

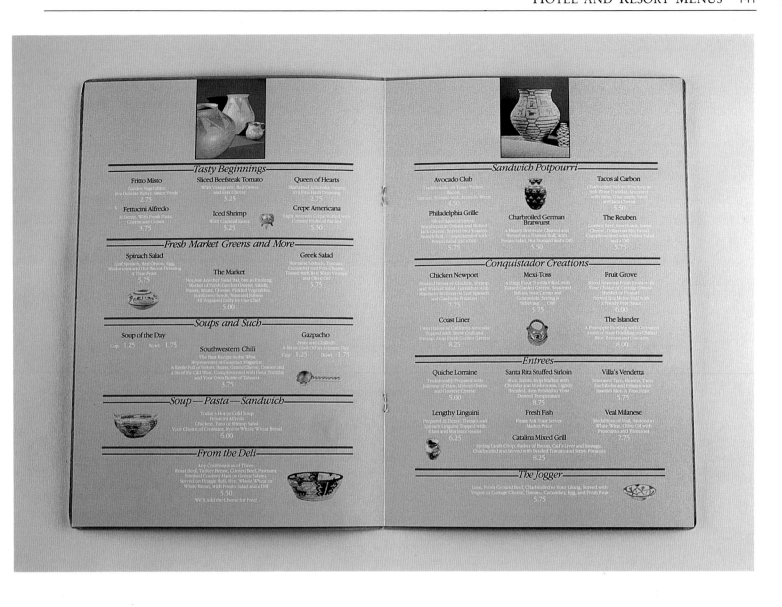

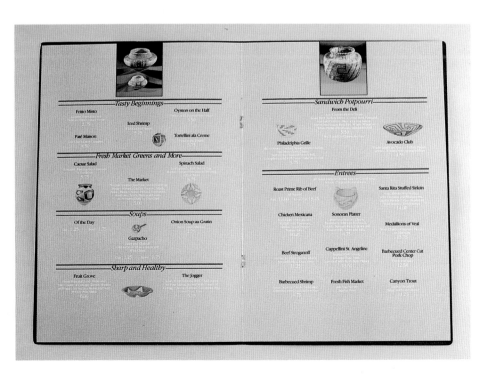

RESTAURANT: Sundance

LOCATION: Sheraton El Conquistador, Tucson, Arizona

PHOTOGRAPHY: Arizona State Museum, University of Arizona

SPECIFICATIONS:

SIZE: 10" x 14⅜"

PAPER: Beau Brilliant, with embossed and silver-foil-stamped logo (cover)

Foil-stamping and embossing in exact register embellish the covers of these exquisite menus. The glossy inside spreads use foil-stamping and a black holding line to separate categories. Color-process-printed photographs of American Indian basketry and pottery lend a "sense of location" to the menus. The regional theme is enhanced by the inclusion of Mexican specialties on the menu.

RESTAURANT: Garden Terrace

LOCATION: Red Lion's La Posada Resort Hotel, Vancouver, Washington

DESIGNERS: John Hill, Carol Stephens

FIRM: Visual Communications System

SPECIFICATIONS: Breakfast, lunch, and dinner menus

SIZE: 9″ x 14″

PAPER: Circa 83 Latigo Brown Cover (breakfast menu); Carnival Cover Coral (lunch menu); 80# Strathmore Cover, Esprit, Plum (dinner menu); 80# Karma Natural Text (inserts)

PRINTER: Visual Communications Systems

The breakfast, lunch, and dinner menus are all the same size and use the same die-cut of mountains, and embossing on the cover. The insert masters contain line drawings of palms against air-brushed mountains exposed by the die-cut covers. The menus are distinguished by the use of different colored and different textured covers. The breakfast menu uses a light brown laid stock; the lunch, a medium rose vellum finish; and the dinner, a deep mauve on felt finish. The insert masters feature category headings and a larger version of the palm and mountain scene.

◀

RESTAURANT: Le Cygne

LOCATION: Noga Hilton International Geneva, Geneva, Switzerland

DESIGN FIRM: Valblor

SPECIFICATIONS:

SIZE: 9½″ x 15″

PAPER: Chromolux

PRINTER: Impressa

The menu cover of Le Cygne, which in French means "the swan," features a swan in bas relief. The same graceful representation is foil-stamped on the insert. Extensive use of foil-stamping throughout the menu and the tasseled cord provide a note of luxury. The insert is held in place by both the cord and the corner slots on the inside of the cover. The glossy cover is a coated, two-ply stock, which is extremely sturdy.

RESTAURANT: Park Hyatt Hotel
LOCATION: Chicago, Illinois
SPECIFICATIONS: Room service menu
SIZE: 10" x 15"

A full-color watercolor of water lilies confined by a gold foil box is affixed to the front cover of the room-service folder in each room of the luxury hotel. The menu inserts are printed in green on a cream-colored stock. A line drawing of a single flower with a drop shadow effect is the cover motif for each of the stepped inserts. The rooms are decorated in this green with the terra cotta of the folder used as an accent color. If the flower can be taken as a visual metaphor for service, it is well-chosen—the menus offer a broad enough choice to suit any palate. This is a well-planned menu program. Any or all of the inserts can be replaced without disturbing the others.

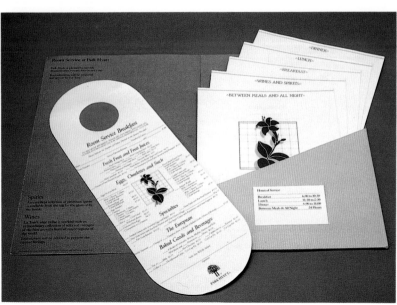

RESTAURANT: The Summerhouse
LOCATION: Hilton International Sydney,
Sydney, New South Wales,
Australia
PHOTOGRAPHER: Greg Desmond
SPECIFICATIONS:
SIZE: 9¾″ x 15⅛″

This menu won first place in the "Restaurant: Average Check Over $10.00 Per Person" category of the National Restaurant Association's 1986 Great Menus Contest. Both the menu cover and the inserts are printed on white stock tinted with flat color ink. A series of photographs entitled "When the Sun Shines" by award-winning Australian photographer Greg Desmond illustrates the menu. A large, legible typeface is used for menu items. The playful nature of the photography lends a touch of fun to the menu, enhanced by the menu-oriented captions provided for each photograph. The inside front cover has a boxed area for a tipped-in daily specials sheet.

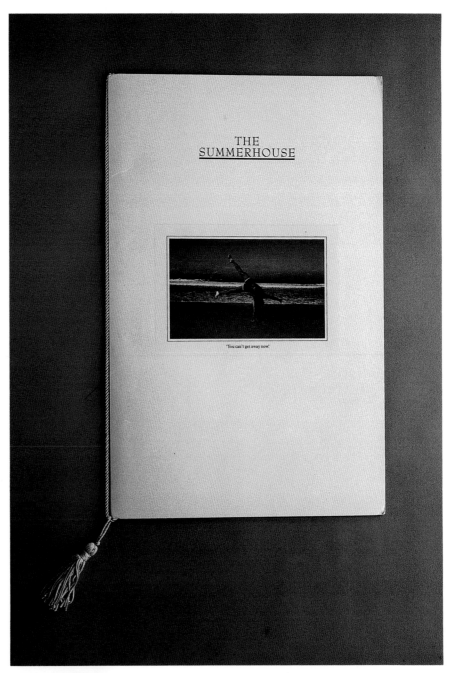

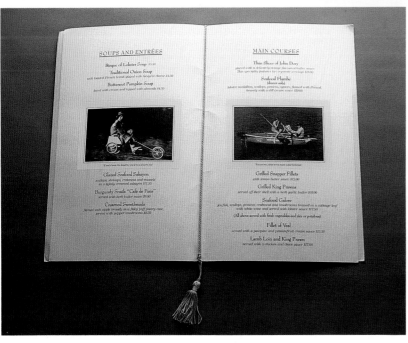

RESTAURANT: The Hale Koa Room
LOCATION: Hale Koa Hilton, Honolulu, Hawaii
DESIGNER: Richard Reese
FIRM: Graphic Works
ILLUSTRATOR: Durward Kirtley
SPECIFICATIONS:
SIZE: 6¾" x 12"
PAPER: 80# Gainsborough Cover, Spice Ivory
PRINTER: Sturgis Printing

Orchids, native to Hawaii, appear on the covers of all of the hotel's menus. The dinner and "afters" menus use the same color scheme, while on the wine list, the colors have been reversed for distinction. Copper foil-stamping and a cursive type style convey a note of elegance and style.

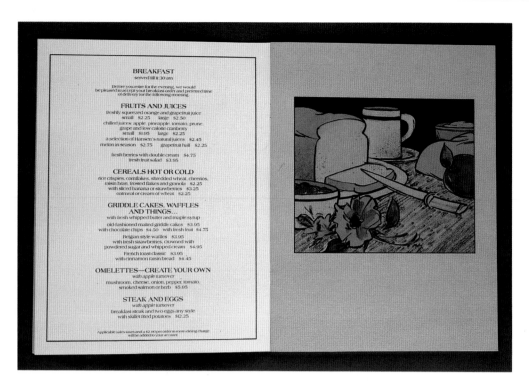

RESTAURANT:	Sheraton Premiere
LOCATION:	Universal City, California
DESIGNERS:	Paul Harnagy, Barry Berlin
FIRM:	Art Group, Inc.
ILLUSTRATOR:	Jim Conaway
SPECIFICATIONS:	"In Room Dining" Menu
SIZE:	8½" x 11"
PAPER:	Strathmore Beau Brilliant (cover); Mohawk Irish Linen (interior)
PRINTER:	Ripple Printing/TH Enterprises

The food and beverage director wanted a subtly artistic room service menu, yet needed the flexibility to change menu items and prices. The creative solution to this design challenge was to print the full-color cover back-to-back and print the variable items on other sheets. These are assembled book fashion and are interspersed with each other. The two-color menu pages are printed as needed and assembled with the master four-color illustrations to create the new menus.

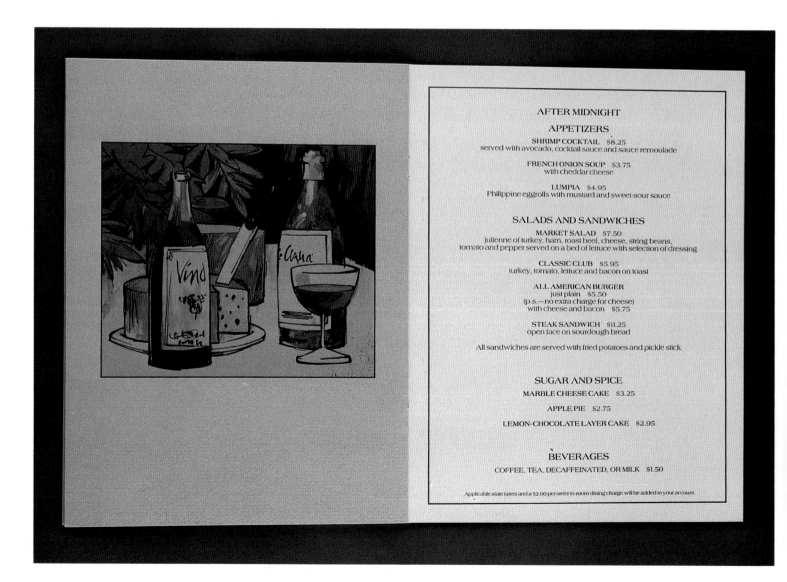

IN ROOM DINING

C A B A N A

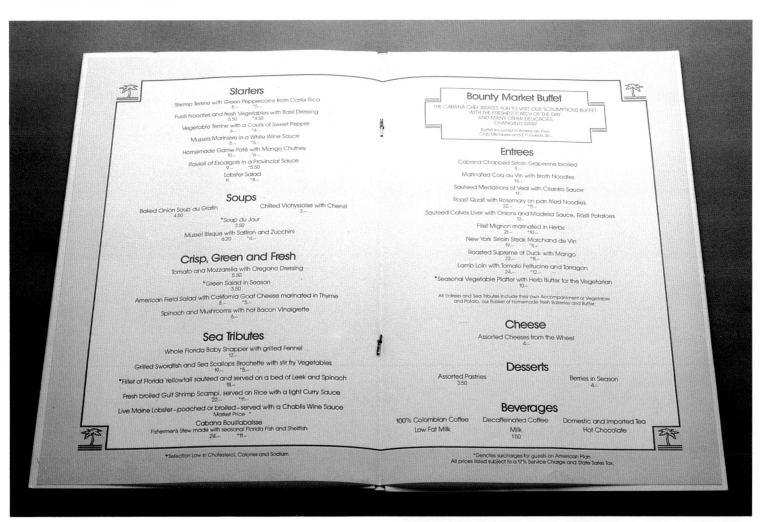

Starters

Shrimp Terrine with Green Peppercorns from Costa Rica
8.— *5.—

Fusilli Noodles and fresh Vegetables with Basil Dressing
6.50 *4.50

Vegetable Terrine with a Coulis of Sweet Pepper
6.— *4.—

Mussels Marinière in a White Wine Sauce
8.— *5.—

Homemade Game Paté with Mango Chutney
10.— *6.—

Ravioli of Escargots in a Provincial Sauce
9.— *5.50

Lobster Salad
11. *8.—

Soups

Baked Onion Soup au Gratin   Chilled Vichyssoise with Chervil
4.50   3.—

*Soup du Jour
2.50

Mussel Bisque with Saffron and Zucchini
6.20 *4.—

Crisp, Green and Fresh

Tomato and Mozzarella with Oregano Dressing
5.50

*Green Salad in Season
3.50

American Field Salad with California Goat Cheese marinated in Thyme
8.— *5.—

Spinach and Mushrooms with hot Bacon Vinaigrette
6.—

Sea Tributes

Whole Florida Baby Snapper with grilled Fennel
12.—

Grilled Swordfish and Sea Scallops Brochette with stir fry Vegetables
19.— *5.—

*Fillet of Florida Yellowtail sauteed and served on a bed of Leek and Spinach
18.—

Fresh broiled Gulf Shrimp Scampi, served on Rice with a light Curry Sauce
22.— *11.—

Live Maine Lobster—poached or broiled—served with a Chablis Wine Sauce
Market Price *

Cabana Bouillabaisse
Fishermen's Stew made with seasonal Florida Fish and Shellfish
24.— *11.—

*Selection Low in Cholesterol, Calories and Sodium.

Bounty Market Buffet

THE CABANA CHEF INVITES YOU TO VISIT OUR SCRUMPTIOUS BUFFET
WITH THE FRESHEST CATCH OF THE DAY
AND MANY OTHER DELICACIES
CHANGING DAILY.

Buffet Included in American Plan
Club Members and E.P. Guests 30.—

Entrees

Cabana Chopped Sirloin Grapevine broiled
8.—

Marinated Coq au Vin with Broth Noodles
14.—

Sauteed Medallions of Veal with Cilantro Sauce
17.—

Roast Quail with Rosemary on pan fried Noodles
22.— *11.—

Sauteed Calves Liver with Onions and Madeira Sauce, Rösti Potatoes
17.—

Filet Mignon marinated in Herbs
21.— *10.—

New York Sirloin Steak Marchand de Vin
19.— *8.—

Roasted Supreme of Duck with Mango
22.— *11.—

Lamb Loin with Tomato Fettucine and Tarragon
24.— *12.—

*Seasonal Vegetable Platter with Herb Butter for the Vegetarian
10.—

All Entrees and Sea Tributes include their own Accompaniment or Vegetable
and Potato, our Basket of homemade fresh Bakeries and Butter.

Cheese

Assorted Cheeses from the Wheel
4.—

Desserts

Assorted Pastries   Berries in Season
3.50   4.—

Beverages

100% Colombian Coffee   Decaffeinated Coffee   Domestic and Imported Tea
Low Fat Milk   Milk   Hot Chocolate
                                            1.50

*Denotes surcharges for guests on American Plan
All prices listed subject to a 17% Service Charge and State Sales Tax.

RESTAURANT: The Cabana

LOCATION: Boca Raton Hotel & Club, Boca Raton, Florida

DESIGNER: Dayne Dupree

SPECIFICATIONS: Main and lunch menus

SIZE: 9½″ x 14″ (main menu); 8½″ x 11″ (lunch menu)

PAPER: 100# Quintessence Dull Text (main menu cover); 25 pt. White Pajo (main menu insert)

PRINTER: Blue Ocean Press

The most informal of the three dining rooms of the Boca Raton Hotel & Club represented in this book, The Cabana is most like Florida in atmosphere. The room serves three meals, and patrons may be dressed in anything from bathing suits to business suits. The lunch menu features a screened down version of the sailboat and palm graphic from the dinner menu cover. The dinner menu is printed in marine blue on masters with pale pink borders. This dining room features a buffet as well as a selection of meat, poultry, and fish dishes.

RESTAURANT: The Pelican Club

LOCATION: Antigua, West Indies

DESIGNER: Dale Glasser

FIRM: Dale Glasser Graphics, Inc.

ILLUSTRATORS: Glen Head, Patricia Kovic

SPECIFICATIONS:

SIZE: 8½″ x 13½″ (closed)

PAPER: 100# Vintage Velvet, laminated (cover); 100# Mohawk Superfine (insert)

PRINTER: Wilson Elm Graphics

The design motifs for the menu were drawn directly from the decor in this seaside restaurant. The dining room is surrounded by latticework and the peach-colored background of the menu, with flowers and "squiggles," is the fabric design of the undercloth on the individual tables. The mint-green diamond is die-cut to form an interesting closure for the center-opening menu. The lattice border is repeated on the menu insert, which is designed for easy one-color revisions. Peach-colored diamond shapes repeating the flower motif head each menu category.

Institutional Menus

Institutions, unlike other food purveyors, must sell more than food with their menus. The menu must reflect what the institution as a whole provides, even though the menu itself is only a small part of the institution's corporate identity program and often must take a back seat to the overall program.

Successful institutional menus require imaginative use of the graphic resources available and a thorough understanding of the primary service offered. A cruise line offers food but is selling transportation and ambiance; a hospital provides food but is selling health care. Yet the food services of these two very dissimilar institutions must have appealing menus that are in keeping with the overall goals of the organization.

8

RESTAURANT: Gulfstream Park
LOCATION: Hallandale, Florida
DESIGN FIRM: Ad Art Litho
SPECIFICATIONS:
SIZE: 11″ x 16″
PRINTER: Ad Art Litho

This vividly colored menu typifies the excitement of horse racing. A jockey on horseback gallops out of a tropical flower on the cover of the menu for this Florida racetrack.

UNION CLUB RESTAURANT
UNIVERSITY OF ARIZONA

RESTAURANT: Union Club
LOCATION: University of Arizona,
Tucson, Arizona
DESIGNER: Debbie Young
SPECIFICATIONS:
SIZE: 8½" × 11"
PAPER: White Bristol Cover
PRINTER: Arizona Lithographers

The Union Club's menus are designed by students from the Graphic Arts Department. Ideas for theme and design evolve from brainstorming sessions with staff members. This movie-theme menu was complemented by movie poster displays on the walls of the restaurant.

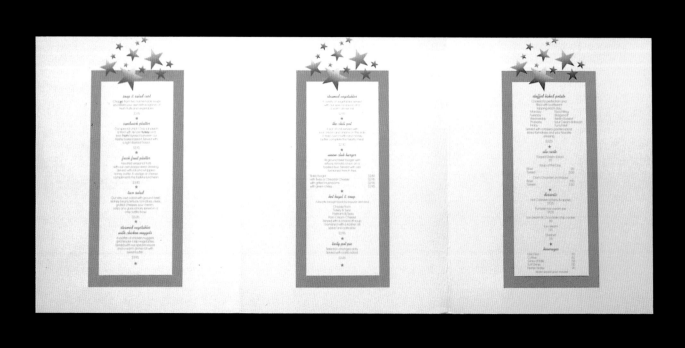

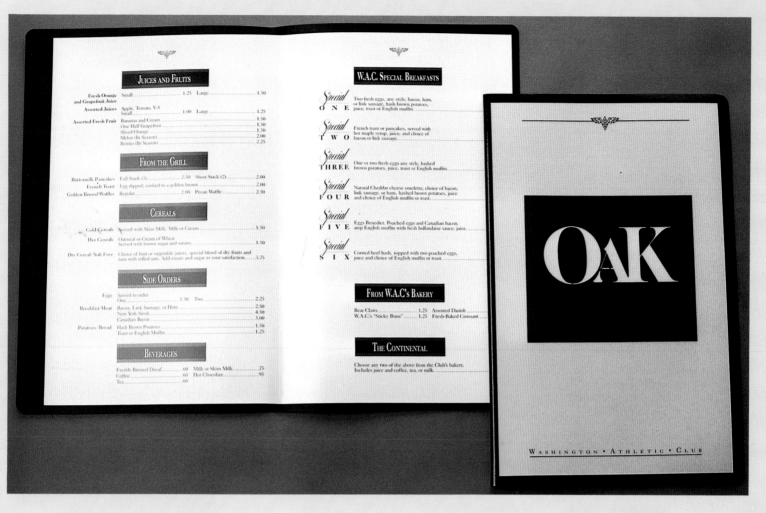

RESTAURANT: Oak Room

LOCATION: Washington Athletic Club, Seattle, Washington

DESIGN FIRM: Menu Workshop

SPECIFICATIONS:

SIZE: 8½″ x 13″

PAPER: Viviguard (cover)

The cheerful burnt orange and green of the menu cover reappear on the bright white insert. Reversed type on green with orange borders heads each category. Menu items are listed in orange, with description and prices in the more subdued green. This menu has a crisp look that is well-suited to an athletic club eating establishment.

COFFEE SHOP MENU

are printed in one color, category headings in the other color. The menu's overall effect is relaxed and pleasant.

APPETIZERS

HOMEMADE SOUP DU JOUR	Cup 1.75	Bowl 2.25	
JUMBO SHRIMP SUPRÊME			6.25
CHILLED MELON IN SEASON			2.95
FRESH FRUIT CUP			2.95
WATERMELON			2.95

Extra Plate Charge 1.50

SALADS

PRESIDENT'S SALAD BOWL	4.95
Crisp Greens, Julienne of Turkey, Cheese, Ham, Tomato, Garnish and Roll,	
with Your Choice of Dressing.	
STUFFED TOMATO	6.25
With Tuna or Diced Chicken, Garnish and Roll.	
CAESAR SALAD	2.75
MIXED GREEN SALAD	1.95
SLICED TOMATO	2.25
COLE SLAW	.65
COTTAGE CHEESE, With Pear or Peach Wedges	2.25
HEARTS OF LETTUCE	1.95
FRUIT PLATE	6.50
With Cottage Cheese or Sherbet, Roll and Butter.	
FRESH MELON SLICES AND ASSORTED CUT CHEESE	4.95
With Sliced Apple Garnish, Roll or Garlic Toast.	

Extra Plate Charge 1.50
Roquefort or Caesar Dressing .50 Additional

CHILLED FISH & SEAFOOD PLATES

NOVA SCOTIA LOX PLATE	7.25
Fresh Lox, Toasted Bagel, Cream Cheese, Sliced Onion, Tomato, Capers and Cucumbers.	
GULF SHRIMP PLATTER	9.50
Jumbo Shrimp on a Bed of Lettuce, Garnished with Tomato Wedges, Celery Hearts,	
Ripe Green Olives, Hard-Cooked Egg Wedge, Choice of Dressing, Roll and Butter.	
BILOXI SALAD PLATTER	6.95
Buefsteak Tomato Half, Topped with Cole Slaw, Surrounded by Sardines	
and Served with a Roll and Butter.	
WEIGHT WATCHERS PLAIN TUNA OR PLAIN SALMON	6.25
Tuna or Salmon Served with Egg Wedges, Celery, Radishes, Cucumbers, Green Pepper,	
and Tomato Wedges.	
CHILLED PLAIN TUNA OR SALMON	5.25
Simply Served on a Bed of Lettuce, with a Wedge of Lemon.	

Extra Plate Charge 1.50
Roquefort or Caesar Dressing .50 Additional

HOT SANDWICHES

CHEF SPECIAL	4.45
Sliced Ham, Turkey, Mushrooms, Supreme Sauce, Bacon and Cheese	
on Toast Points. (Lunch Only)	
MELTED CHEESE, BACON & TOMATO	4.30
With French Fried Potatoes and Garnish. (Lunch Only)	
REUBEN	4.50
Corned Beef, Turkey, Swiss Cheese and Sauerkraut on Black Bread,	
with French Fried Potatoes.	
GRILLED CHEESE	3.25
Your Choice of American or Swiss Cheese, Served with French Fried	
Potatoes and Garnish.	
BROILED JUMBO KOSHER FRANKFURTER	3.45
Served on a Toasted Bun, with French Fried Potatoes and Garnish.	
FRANCHEEZI	4.65
A Jumbo Frankfurter Filled with Cheese and Wrapped in Bacon, Served on a Toasted Bun	
with French Fried Potatoes and Garnish.	

Extra Plate Charge 1.50

SANDWICHES

BACON, LETTUCE & TOMATO, ON TOAST	3.25
TRIPLE DECKER CLUB, ON TOAST	4.95
JUNIOR CLUB, ON TOAST	4.65
SLICED TURKEY, ON TOAST	3.75
TUNA FISH SALAD, ON TOAST	4.95
SALMON SALAD, ON TOAST	4.95
CHICKEN SALAD, ON TOAST	4.95
EGG SALAD, ON TOAST	2.75
BAKED HAM, ON RYE	3.95
CORNED BEEF, ON RYE	4.95
HAM & CHEESE, ON RYE	3.95
ROAST SIRLOIN OF BEEF	4.25
Sliced Thin and Served on a Roll or Bread, Garnish.	

Extra Plate Charge 1.50

HAMBURGERS

HAMBURGER COMBINATION	4.50
A Hamburger Served on a Bun or Pita Bread, with French Fried Potatoes, Garnish,	
and Your Choice of Two of the Following: Swiss Cheese, 1000 Island Dressing,	
American Cheese, Shredded Lettuce, Bacon, Bleu Cheese, Slice of Tomato, Green Olives,	
Mozzarella Cheese, Spanish Sauce, Mushrooms, Green Pepper, Each Additional Item .75.	
HAMBURGER DELUXE	3.05
Served on a Bun or Pita Bread, with a Slice of Raw or Grilled Onion.	
PATTY MELT	4.50
A Hamburger Covered with Melted Cheese on Grilled Rye Bread, Slice of Raw or Grilled Onion,	
French Fried Potatoes and Garnish.	
LOW-CALORIE HAMBURGER PLATE	5.25
With Cottage Cheese and Fresh Fruit.	

Extra Plate Charge 1.50

ENTRÉES

TENDERLOIN STEAK SANDWICH	6.95
Served on Toast Points with French Fried Potatoes and Garnish.	
FRESH GROUND ROUND STEAK	6.25
Served with Onion Rings, French Fried Potatoes, Roll and Butter.	
On a Plankett	7.75
BROILED ONE HALF CHICKEN	5.95
Served with French Fried Potatoes, Roll and Butter.	
BREADED CHICKEN FINGERS	6.25
Served with Sweet and Sour Sauce, Apricot Sauce or Barbecue Sauce, French Fried Potatoes,	
Garnish, Roll and Butter.	
CHICKEN LIVERS	4.45
Sautéed in Butter, with Onions and Mushrooms, Potato, Garnish, Roll and Butter.	

Extra Plate Charge 1.50

DESSERTS

ASSORTED SUNDAES	2.95	FRESH FRUIT PIES	2.45
		A La Mode	4.40
ASSORTED ICE CREAM	1.95	STRAWBERRY SHORTCAKE	3.25
PARFAIT	2.95	CAKE	2.45
JELLO	.95		

BEVERAGES

COFFEE OR SANKA	.75	ICED COFFEE OR TEA	.75
TEA	.75	CHOCOLATE MILK	1.25
HOT CHOCOLATE	.90	MILK	.90
With Mint	1.25	MILK SHAKE	2.75

RESTAURANT: Midland Hospital Center
Food Service

LOCATION: Midland, Michigan

DESIGNER: Ron Acker

ILLUSTRATOR: Ron Acker

SPECIFICATIONS:

SIZE: 9" x 12"

PAPER: 80# Regimental Ivory,
Brigadoon Cover

PRINTER: McKay Press

This menu won third place in the "Institutional Foodservice" category of the National Restaurant Association's 1986 Great Menus Contest. A tranquil duotone cover illustration lends gentility to this menu. Interior sheets are printed in one color for easy updating and a pocket has been included on the inside back cover for a daily specials sheet.

RESTAURANT: Royal Viking Cruise Line
LOCATION: Headquartered in San Francisco, California
SPECIFICATIONS: Dinner and farewell party menus
SIZE: 8¼" × 10¾"
PAPER: Uncoated, foil stamping
PRINTER: F. Beyer

The hallmarks of this luxury cruise line are its personalized service and wonderful food. These themes are married nicely in its menus. The luncheon and dinner menus are printed every day so that the chef can take advantage of fresh foods obtained at each port of call. About 400 menus are printed for each meal. Menu masters are printed in advance and stored aboard ship. Each night the two menus are typeset and imprinted onto the masters, aboard ship. Menu selections are never duplicated on a cruise. The dinner menus feature gold-foil-stamped representations of Viking artifacts and symbols. The blue menu is for the captain's farewell party—the symbol is the captain's insignia. Passengers are encouraged to take the menus as souvenirs. Extras are also printed for use by the sales and public relations departments in the main office.

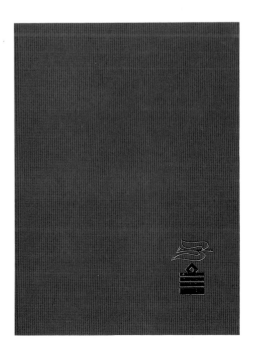

Details of a Norwegian tapestry, c. 1700.
The Oslo Museum of Applied Art.

RESTAURANT: Royal Viking Cruise Line
LOCATION: Headquartered in San Francisco,
California
ARTWORK: Details of a Norwegian tapestry,
circa 1700, courtesy of the Oslo
Museum of Applied Art
SPECIFICATIONS: Tapestry menu
SIZE: 16½" × 11"
PAPER: Coated on one side
PRINTER: F. Beyer

The Royal Viking tapestry menu maintains the
ancient Norse theme seen in the cruise line's
dinner menus, one of which appears above. The
line encourages passengers to take its menus as
souvenirs and also uses their menus for sales and
other promotional activities.

RESTAURANT: United Airlines "Ocean to Ocean Service"

LOCATION: Headquartered in Chicago, Illinois

United Airlines uses a variety of menus, some of which are geared to specified routes. The first class menu for its flight from Seoul to Taipei includes a Korean translation of the menu on the same card that holds the wine list. United's service between California and Hawaii is quite famous. As a result, a series of menus featuring vivid blue tapa cloth patterns and blossoms native to the Hawaiian Islands has been developed especially for these routes. Menu interiors are printed in one color except for the first class menu.

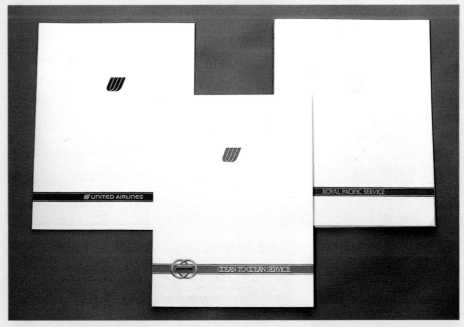

RESTAURANT: Seattle Tennis Club
LOCATION: Seattle, Washington
DESIGN FIRM: Menu Workshop
SPECIFICATIONS:
SIZE: 9″ x 11¾″
PAPER: Hardbound (cover); 25% cotton
(inserts)

This is a good example of a menu program
designed for updating. The padded leatherette
cover is enlivened by gold foil stamping. Inside,
corner pockets hold the inserted pages, which are
a standard-size 8½″ x 11″ and can be printed by
computer, word processing, or quick print offset.

RESTAURANT: La Paloma

LOCATION: La Paloma Country Club, Tucson, Arizona

DESIGNER: Cynthia Lehman

FIRM: Associates Printing Service

ILLUSTRATOR: Cynthia Lehman

SPECIFICATIONS:

SIZE: 8″ x 12″ (closed)

PAPER: Strathmore Rhododendron

PRINTER: Associates Printing Service

Peach and celery green are played against a cream stock on this pleasant and relaxing menu. Peach squares bracketed by green holding lines separate the categories inside. The palm tree and stylized window provide a tropical feeling suitable for a country club.

RESTAURANT: Creative Gourmets, Ltd.

LOCATION: Boston, Massachusetts

DESIGNER: Jobie DeVinney

FIRM: Clark/Linsky Design, Inc.

ILLUSTRATION: Joe Trepiccione Designs

SPECIFICATIONS: "Corporate Cafeteria" menus

SIZE: 8½" x 14"

PAPER: 70# Tomahawk

PRINTER: United Lithograph

Preprinted menu masters designed by this foodservice management company brighten the company's catered cafeteria service. Appetizing descriptions of each menu item are included. This type of menu is an inexpensive alternative suitable for frequently changing menus. The four menu masters shown are keyed to the four seasons of the year. The days of the week are printed in colors that complement the watercolor illustrations on each master form.

RESTAURANT: Union Club

LOCATION: University of Arizona, Tucson, Arizona

DESIGNER: Monica Pizarro

SPECIFICATIONS:

SIZE: 8½" × 11"

PAPER: White Bristol Cover

PRINTER: Arizona Lithographers

Students from the Graphic Arts Department at the University design the Union Club menus. Theme and design ideas evolve from brainstorming sessions between the students and staff members. This mountain theme menu plays off art produced in batik, oils, and acrylics by local artists. Tucson is set amid mountains, so, this menu reflects the geographic location, too.

9

Specialty Menus

When is a menu not a menu? When it's a first aid kit, or a strawberry, or a wine bottle, or a piano . . . in short, when it's a specialty menu. Specialty menus may also be table tents or dignified wine lists, but all have one characteristic in common: they are designed to sell items beyond the meal originally sought by the customer. In effect, the specialty menu permits the restaurateur to make additional sales to someone who has already agreed to buy.

Whether or not to have separate specialty menus is largely determined by what items the restaurant wishes to market most aggressively. If wine sales are a high profit source, it makes sense to have a separate wine list. This lends an air of importance to the selection of an appropriate wine and gives the customer an impetus towards impulse purchasing. The same is true of dessert menus, novelty drink lists, and the like.

A powerful tool for the restaurant, the specialty menu is also the menu designer's opportunity to flex his creative muscles. A specialty menu can be used to merchandise anything from seasonal fruits to beverages to specific cuisines, and it gives the designer a chance to use more dramatic techniques— die-cuts, pop-ups, embossing, expanded copywriting, and the like—to make the specialty menu truly special.

RESTAURANT:	Hyatt Hotel Corporation
LOCATION:	Headquartered in Chicago, Illinois
DESIGNER:	Georgia Pavelich
FIRM:	Associates Printing Service
STOCK PHOTOS:	Image Bank
SPECIFICATIONS:	"Autumn Mist" menu
SIZE:	5" × 8" (folded)
PAPER:	12 pt. Kromekote, coated two sides

Stock photography was used for the cover of this menu. Quality printing and the selection of appropriate supporting colors distinguish the work, which was designed for use in all Hyatt Regency food and beverage outlets at airports.

RESTAURANT: Rusty Pelican Restaurants, Inc.
LOCATION: Nationwide restaurant chain headquartered in Irvine, California
SPECIFICATIONS: Beer list
SIZE: 3½" x 10" (folded, measuring outer edges of die-cut)

The pelican featured on the restaurant's main menu makes a cameo appearance on the neck of this "beer bottle" menu where the brewer's label would ordinarily appear. The menu cover, which is laminated and trimmed flush, is designed to simulate the heraldic motifs used on European beer labels. As is often the case with these labels, a variety of design motifs vie for attention. Because the cacophony is expected, it works here.

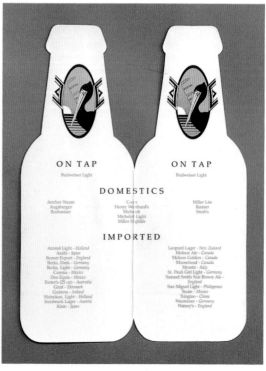

RESTAURANT: Hudson's Seafood House
LOCATION: Hilton Head, South Carolina
SPECIFICATIONS: "Wine Not" Wine List
SIZE: 13" high
MEDIUM: Glass bottle
PRINTER: Perry Printing

A clear glaze was applied to protect and seal the "labels" on this real wine bottle, which was corked and sealed by winemaker August Sebastiani of California, one of whose wines is included on the wine list. Though all the wines listed are available only in fifths, a 1.5 liter bottle was chosen for use with the wine list to aid readability and provide additional space for the listings.

Wine Not?

1. **Cavit Pinot Grigio.** . . . . white wine
   An exceptional, dry, crisp, ...
   an exquisite bouquet and light taste.
2. **Macon-Lugny "Les Charmes"**
   Pinot Chardonnay. . . . .
   An estate-bottled wine. Delicate and rich,
   yet dry, with a distinctive aroma.
3. **Beaulieu Vineyards - Chablis.** . . . . .
   A medium dry, estate-bottled California
   wine. Fruity with a crisp, lively finish.
4. **Bolla - Soave.** . . . .
   A delicious dry white wine from Italy,
   pale in color and well-balanced.
5. **B&G - Ste Louise Chardonnay.** Dry
   Made from 100% Chardonnay grape.
6. **La Femme Chenin Blanc.** . . . .
   A light, full bodied wine with a clean
   brilliance and delightful taste.
7. **Sebastiani Vineyards - Pinot Noir Blanc.** . .
   A full-bodied dry wine with an intensive
   The "Eye of the Swan".

RESTAURANT: Fedora Cafe & Bar
LOCATION: Kansas City, Missouri
SPECIFICATIONS: Table tent
SIZE: 4½″ x 12″ (die cut)
PAPER: Tetron Tiara
PRINTER: Reliance Printing

Illustrations of specialty drinks in varying heights, die cut in four steps, form the cover of this accordion-folded table tent. Opening each fold leads to a new category. The customer is welcomed to Fedora as he opens the first fold and is presented with a list of cognacs, armagnacs, and champagnes as he opens the second. Since many customers will get no further than this, it makes good merchandising sense to list high-profit items here. Non-alcoholic beverages, wines, and specialty drinks are listed behind the last fold. The table tent uses the same typeface as the main menu for a sense of continuity.

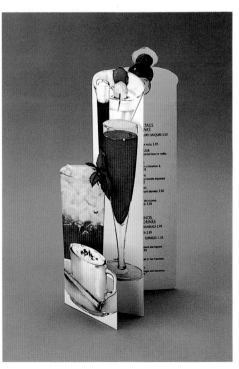

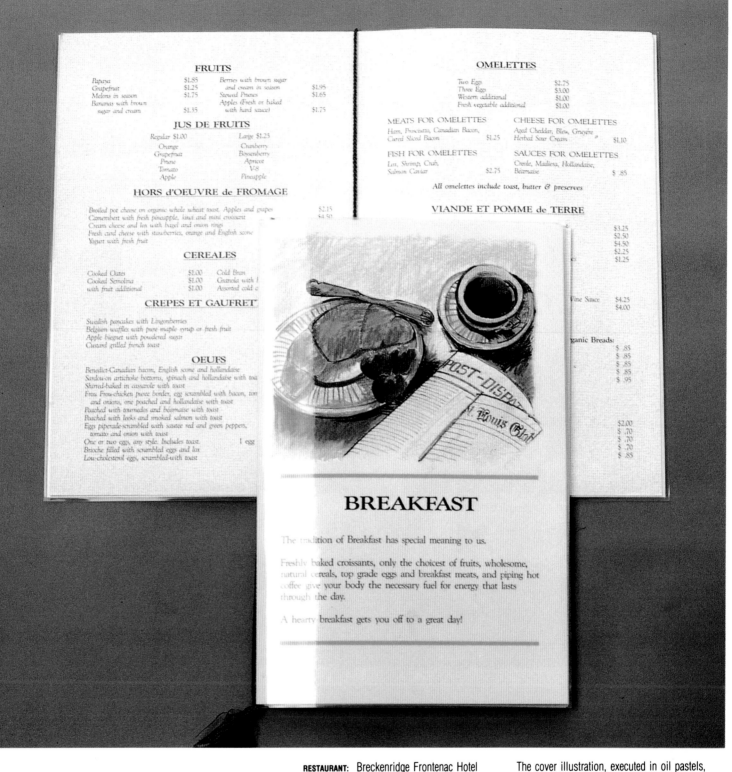

FRUITS

Papaya	$1.85	Berries with brown sugar	
Grapefruit	$1.25	and cream in season	$1.95
Melons in season	$1.75	Stewed Prunes	$1.65
Bananas with brown		Apples (Fresh or baked	
sugar and cream	$1.35	with hard sauce)	$1.75

JUS DE FRUITS

Regular $1.00   Large $1.25

Orange	Cranberry
Grapefruit	Bossenberry
Prune	Apricot
Tomato	V-8
Apple	Pineapple

HORS d'OEUVRE de FROMAGE

Broiled pot cheese on organic whole wheat toast. Apples and grapes $2.15
Camembert with fresh pineapple, kiwi and mini croissant $4.50
Cream cheese and lox with bagel and onion rings
Fresh curd cheese with strawberries, orange and English scone
Yogurt with fresh fruit

CEREALES

Cooked Oates	$1.00	Cold Bran	
Cooked Semolina	$1.00	Granola with	
with fruit additional	$1.00	Assorted cold c	

CREPES ET GAUFRET

Swedish pancakes with Lingonberries
Belgian waffles with pure maple syrup or fresh fruit
Apple biegnet with powdered sugar
Custard grilled french toast

OEUFS

Benedict-Canadian bacon, English scone and hollandaise
Sardou-on artichoke bottoms, spinach and hollandaise with toa
Shirred-baked in casserole with toast
Frou Frou-chicken puree border, egg scrambled with bacon, tom
and onions, one poached and hollandaise with toast
Poached with turnedos and béarnaise with toast
Poached with leeks and smoked salmon with toast
Eggs piperade-scrambled with sautee red and green peppers,
tomato and onion with toast
One or two eggs, any style. Includes toast.   1 egg
Brioche filled with scrambled eggs and lox
Low-cholesterol eggs, scrambled with toast

OMELETTES

Two Eggs	$2.75
Three Eggs	$3.00
Western additional	$1.00
Fresh vegetable additional	$1.00

MEATS FOR OMELETTES		CHEESE FOR OMELETTES	
Ham, Prosciutto, Canadian Bacon,		Aged Cheddar, Bleu, Gruyère	
Cured Sliced Bacon	$1.25	Herbed Sour Cream	$1.10

FISH FOR OMELETTES		SAUCES FOR OMELETTES	
Lox, Shrimp, Crab,		Creole, Madiera, Hollandaise,	
Salmon Caviar	$2.75	Béarnaise	$.85

All omelettes include toast, butter & preserves

VIANDE ET POMME de TERRE

	$3.25
	$2.50
	$4.50
	$2.25
	$1.25

Vine Sauce $4.25
   $4.00

ganic Breads:

	$.85
	$.85
	$.85
	$.85
	$.95

	$2.00
	$.70
	$.70
	$.70
	$.85

BREAKFAST

The tradition of Breakfast has special meaning to us.

Freshly baked croissants, only the choicest of fruits, wholesome, natural cereals, top grade eggs and breakfast meats, and piping hot coffee give your body the necessary fuel for energy that lasts through the day.

A hearty breakfast gets you off to a great day!

RESTAURANT:	Breckenridge Frontenac Hotel
LOCATION:	St. Louis, Missouri
DESIGNERS:	Shelley Dietrichs, Harold Garber
FIRM:	Garber Graphic Services
SPECIFICATIONS:	Breakfast menu
SIZE:	7½″ x 10¾″
PAPER:	Quintessence Cover (cover); Gainsborough Canvas (insert)
PRINTER:	Garber Graphic Services

The cover illustration, executed in oil pastels, harmonizes nicely with both the menu's contents and the hotel's location. The menu, in a nod to St. Louis' French heritage, uses French category headings and features such French breakfast foods as croissants, beignets, and brioches. The two newspapers on the cover are clearly the St. Louis local papers. Menu covers are laminated for durability, and inserts are printed in one color and held in place with brightly colored, tasseled cords.

RESTAURANT: Hilton International Sydney
LOCATION: Sydney, New South Wales, Australia
DESIGNER: Sky Kwan
SPECIFICATIONS:
SIZE: 7⅝" x 14"
PAPER: Black Velvet Malt
PRINTER: Stax Condor Press

The lighting was tightly controlled and manipulated to create this dramatic harlequin-effect photograph of glasses of champagne. Inside, the left-hand page features champagne cocktails and a marvelous quote on drinking champagne from Mme. Lilly Bollinger. The right-hand side features the great French champagnes, both vintage and non-vintage. At bottom right is a laid-in card listing the champagne of the week, available by the glass.

RESTAURANT:	Westin Hotel Galleria
LOCATION:	Dallas, Texas
DESIGNER:	Tim Girvin
SPECIFICATIONS:	Beer list
SIZE:	4½″ x 11½″ (folded)
PAPER:	80# Vintage Gloss Cover (cover); Kilmory Text (interior)
PRINTER:	Visual Communication System Inc.

The gold used on the cover is almost the same color as beer. Inside, beers are listed by country of origin, with accompanying notes worthy of a wine tasting. The menu, aimed at serious beer drinkers, lists lagers, pilsners, stouts, and ales from twenty different countries. The space above and below the menu listings is used to advertise various hotel restaurants and specialty shops. The center signature provides historical notes and humorous comments on the subject. Clip art is used effectively throughout the menu. Famous beer labels and a glossary of beer terms are also included.

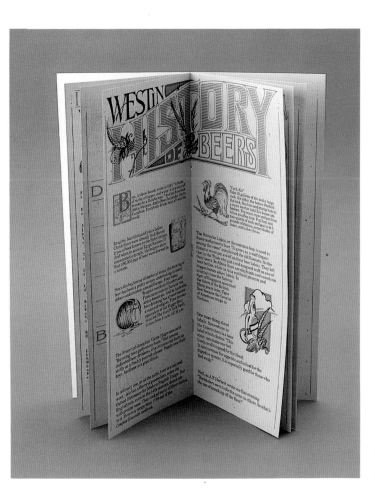

RESTAURANT: St. George's Bar
LOCATION: London Hilton on Park Lane,
London, England
DESIGNER: M. Neydon
FIRM: Arch Press (London) Ltd.
LETTERER: M. Neydon
SPECIFICATIONS:
SIZE: 4 x 8¼" (folded)
PAPER: Wiggins Teape, High Seed Blade
PRINTER: Arch Press (London) Ltd.

The exquisitely embossed gold foil and rich
cinnamon on the cover inform the patron that St.
George's Bar is a far cry from the informal theme
bars of the United States. Park Lane is in London's
West End. The major embassies, Hyde Park, and
many of London's finest hotels are nearby. The
tradition of the area is reflected in the traditional,
rather formal menu.

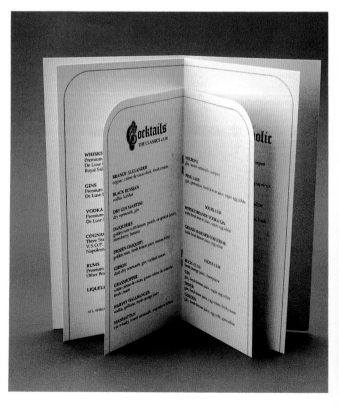

RESTAURANT: Girard's Casual Creative
American Food
LOCATION: Clearwater, Florida
DESIGNER: Caron Gordon
FIRM: Caron Gordon Graphics
SPECIFICATIONS:
SIZE: 5¼" x 5"
MEDIUM: Cocktail napkin
PRINTER: Hoffmaster Napkins

It's difficult to think of a more effective way to market appetizers and specialty drinks than to print the menu on the cocktail napkin. In case the patron misses the point, the server opens the "menu" as he or she places it on the table. Later, the menu does double duty when it is used for its original purpose. Deep burgundy ink on a pale gray napkin makes the menu easy to read, even in dimly lit places.

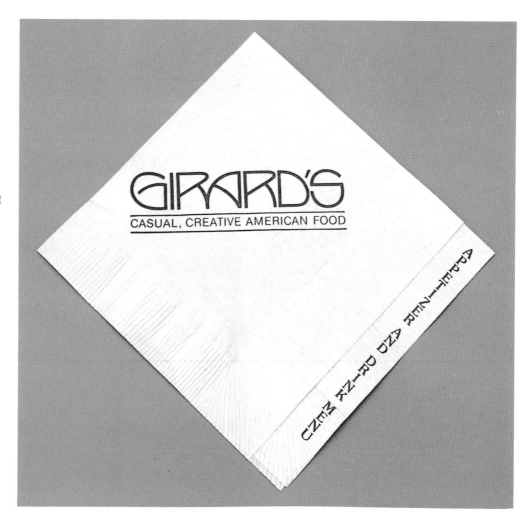

SPECIALTY DRINKS

Chandon Judy The ultimate aperitif! A special recipe from California's famous sparkling wine producer, Domaine Chandon. A combination of Panache and Sparkling Wine.

Georgia Peach An elegant blend of Champagne and Peaches.

Long Island Iced Tea A traditional favorite.

Plant City Daiquiri Rum and Strawberries blended our special way.

Florida Sunrise Vodka, freshly squeezed Orange Juice, and Grenadine.

Margarita Gold A South-of-the-Border specialty made with Cuervo Gold Tequila!

Blue Hawaiian Vodka, Rum, Blue Curacao, and Tropical Fruit Juices.

ALL SPECIALTY DRINKS **$3.25**

Non-Alcoholic Cocktails Available upon request.
"Artesia" Sparkling Texas Mineral Water . . . **$1.25**

BEER SELECTION

Domestic

Anchor Steam	$2.50
Budweiser	$1.75
Michelob (Draft)	$1.60
Michelob Light (Draft)	$1.60
Miller Lite	$1.75

Imported

Bass Ale (England)	$2.50
Beck's Dark (Germany)	$2.25
Heineken (Holland)	$2.25
Molson's Golden (Canada)	$2.25
Spaten Weiss (Germany)	$2.75

WINES

House Wines We feature California Chablis, Rosé, and Burgundy. Available — By the glass $1.75
By the carafe $6.50

Featured Wines By The Glass We offer a daily selection of special wines of exceptional quality and value. Ask for today's selections.

Ask to see our "Taste of America" Wine List!

APPETIZERS

Peel and Eat Gulf Shrimp	$4.25
Chilled, Marinated Mussels	$3.95
Alabama Oysters on the Half Shell	$3.50
Onion Ring Basket w/fried cheese cubes	$3.75
San Antonio Nachos	$5.25
St. Louis Style Toasted Ravioli	$4.50
Spicy Buffalo Wings	$3.95
Cup of Girard's Cheesy Clam Chowder	$1.75
Cup of the Chef's Featured Daily Soup	$1.50

APPETIZER AND DRINK MENU

RESTAURANT: Restaurant Las Chivas

LOCATION: Hilton International Cartagena, Cartagena, Columbia

DESIGNER: Ingrid Angel

FIRM: Ingrid Angel S. & Associates

PHOTOGRAPHER: Carlos Delgado

SPECIFICATIONS:

SIZE: 18½″ x 12½″ open

PAPER: Cardboard Duplex WPC, plastified both sides

PRINTER: Litotechnoin Ltda.

This menu won third place in the "Merchandising Power" category of the National Restaurant Association's 1986 Great Menus Contest. The vanilla ice cream with fresh strawberries on the cover demurely identifies this as a dessert menu. When the cover is opened and the spectacular display of ice cream varieties is displayed, the mouth waters. The art direction and photography are both superb.

Café

Helado de Vainilla co
Vanilla Ice Cream

Helado de Ron con pasas y Coco,
Rum and Coconut Ice Cream, to

Helado de Chocolate, Vainilla, Fresa y Pistacho s
Chocolate, Vanilla, Strawberry and Pistachio I

Helado de Piña, Coco y Banano con sa
Pineapple, Coconut and Banana Ice Cream v

Helado de Vainilla con sals
Vanilla Ice Cream

Helado de Vainilla y Bana
Vanilla

Helados

…ema 320.oo
…cream.

…erto con coco dorado. 320.oo
…nix and tosted coconut.

…s cubierto con salsa de moras. 350.oo
…d topped with Blackberry sauce.

…ngo y tajadas de coco. 280.oo
… fruit sauce served with sliced coconut.

…lla

…nte y crema de Chantilly. 280.oo
…uce and whipped cream.

…ero

…amelo y nueces picadas. 280.oo
… with Caramel sauce and crushed nuts.

…e de dos sabores a su elección: 200.oo

Vainilla, Chocolate, Fresa, Pistacho,
Vanilla, Chocolate, Strawberry, Pistachio,

…erbets

Mango, Tamarindo, Guayaba,
Mango, Tamarind, Guava,

Fantasía Negra

Helado de Chocolate con salsa de Vainilla, Caramelo y Chocolate con almendras y nueces. 280.oo
Chocolate Ice Cream with Vanilla, Caramel and Chocolate sauce, topped with crushed nuts and almonds.

Acuarela

Una combinación de Helados de: Chocolate, Guanabana, 380.oo
Mango, Pistacho, Mora servido con sus salsas.
A delightful combination of Chocolate, Sour Sop, Mango, Pistachio and Blackberry
Sherbets and Ice Creams topped with a variety of sauces.

Tropicana

Sorbetes de Mango, Tamarindo, Maracuya y Guanabana servido con Brevas y salsa de Frutas. 320.oo
Mango, Tamarind, Passion Fruit and Sour Sop Sherbets served with Figs and Fruit sauce.

Bella Vista

Helado de Fresa y Vainilla cubierto con salsa de Moras y crema 280.oo
Strawberry and Vanilla Ice cream with Blackberry sauce and whipped cream.

Guayabal

Sorbete y Cascos de Guayaba servido con salsa de Vainilla 280.oo
Guava fruit and Sherbet served with Vanilla sauce.

Two flavours of Ice Cream Sherbet of your choice: 200.oo

Ron con Pasas, Coco, Banano ó Piña.
Rum and Raisins, Coconut, Banana of Pineapple.

Maracuya, Mora ó Guanabana.
Sour Sop, Blackberry of Passion Fruit.

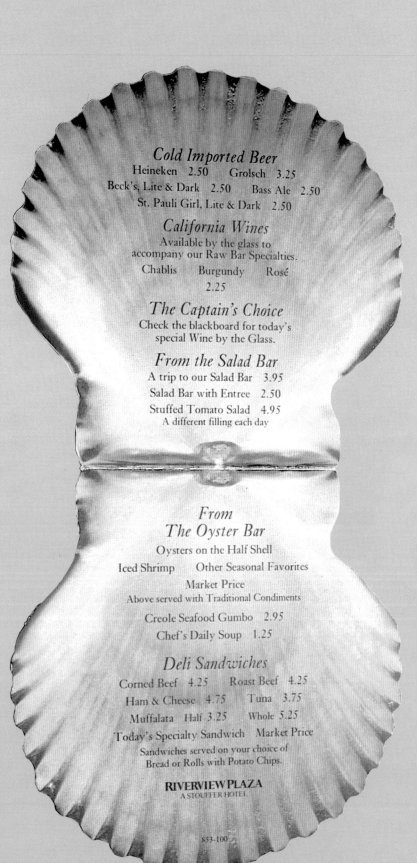

Cold Imported Beer
Heineken 2.50   Grolsch 3.25
Beck's, Lite & Dark 2.50   Bass Ale 2.50
St. Pauli Girl, Lite & Dark 2.50

California Wines
Available by the glass to
accompany our Raw Bar Specialties.
Chablis   Burgundy   Rosé
2.25

The Captain's Choice
Check the blackboard for today's
special Wine by the Glass.

From the Salad Bar
A trip to our Salad Bar 3.95
Salad Bar with Entree 2.50
Stuffed Tomato Salad 4.95
A different filling each day

*From
The Oyster Bar*
Oysters on the Half Shell
Iced Shrimp   Other Seasonal Favorites
Market Price
Above served with Traditional Condiments
Creole Seafood Gumbo 2.95
Chef's Daily Soup 1.25

Deli Sandwiches
Corned Beef 4.25   Roast Beef 4.25
Ham & Cheese 4.75   Tuna 3.75
Muffalata Half 3.25   Whole 5.25
Today's Specialty Sandwich Market Price
Sandwiches served on your choice of
Bread or Rolls with Potato Chips.

RIVERVIEW PLAZA
A STOUFFER HOTEL

853-100

RESTAURANT: Riverview Plaza
LOCATION: Mobile, Alabama
SPECIFICATIONS:
SIZE: 6″ x 6″ (die cut)

A die-cut oyster shell opens to display a selection
of appetizers, snacks, beers, and wines. The menu
items are displayed in clear type against the shell's
interior. The menu works because it is an actual
photograph, enlarged, of the inside and outside of
an oyster shell. The die-cut is carefully matched to
the perimeter of the shell to preserve the illusion.

RESTAURANT: The Plantation Veranda
LOCATION: Kapalua Bay Hotel & Villas,
Kapalua Maui, Hawaii
DESIGNER: Robert Glick
FIRM: Kapalua Advertising Company
ILLUSTRATOR: Pegge Hopper
SPECIFICATIONS: Wine list
SIZE: 9½″ x 10½″ (cover folded)
PAPER: 10½ pt. Buff Chromolux (cover);
Natural Parchtone Cover (inserts)
PRINTER: Edward Enterprises

The deceptively simple cover with its copper-foil-stamped logo gives little hint of what lies inside. The painting of a young Polynesian woman lying at ease amid palms and blossoms on the inside front cover establishes a lavish and relaxed mood. This wine list is devoted entirely to California wines and the very best, at that. The beautiful paper and the italic typeface provide the simple dignity appropriate for showcasing this magnificent wine cellar. This menu demonstrates a fine use of several interesting techniques: foil-stamping, full-color printing, combining paper stocks, and combining type styles.

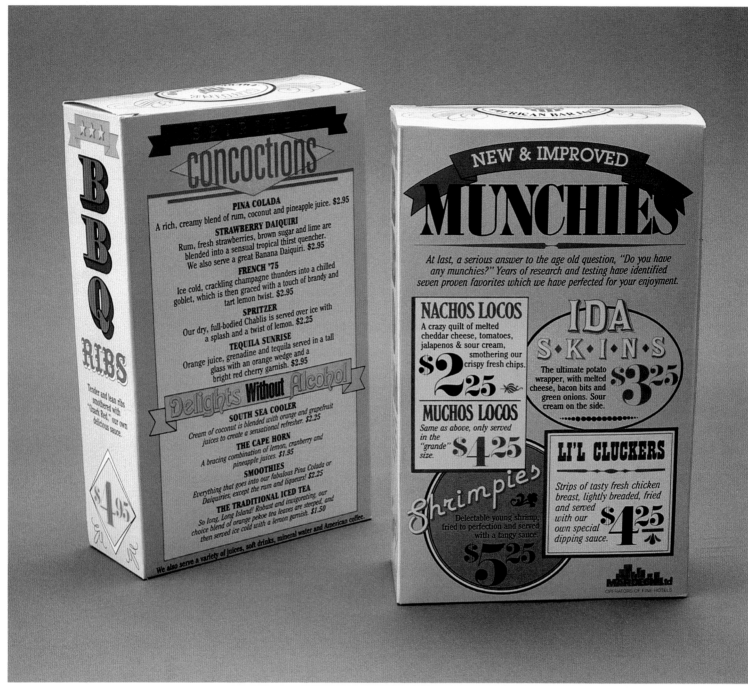

RESTAURANT: Mardeck, Ltd.

LOCATION: Rockville, Maryland

DESIGNER: Paisley-Ramorini

SPECIFICATIONS: "New and Improved Munchies" Menu

SIZE: 4¾" x 2" x 7½" (assembled box)

This menu won first place in the "Merchandising Power" category of the National Restaurant Association's 1986 Great Menus Contest. It's easy to see why this colorful, playful, yet clear table tent is effective. Seven appetizers and five specialty drinks, plus four non-alcoholic drinks, are featured. The copywriting is heavy on adjectives without being long-winded. Every surface except the bottom is used to sell. Because the patron must pick up the box or turn it around to read the entire menu, it is a good point-of-purchase piece. The first step to selling the patron additional items is to involve him in the choice. This box does that quite effectively.

RESTAURANT: Hale Koa Territorial Coffee House

LOCATION: Hale Koa Hotel, Honolulu, Hawaii

DESIGNER: Richard Reese

FIRM: Graphic Works

ILLUSTRATOR: Durward Kirtley

SPECIFICATIONS:

SIZE: 15" x 8½"

PAPER: Gainsborough Cover, Spice Ivory

PRINTER: Sturgis Printing

In a radical departure from the beautiful menus used in its formal dining room, the Hale Koa uses illustration and entertaining copywriting on its breakfast menu. Breakfast items are given thematic names, and Hawaii's tropical fruits are among the featured items. The reverse side of the breakfast card advertises the hotel's other restaurants and bars as well as special events such as luaus on the beach and champagne brunches.

Lobster Mania!

Lobster Salad 10.95

New England Lobster Roll 7.95

Lobster with Drawn Butter 11.95

Lobster with Swordfish Steak 14.25

Lobster with Top Sirloin Steak 15.75

Something's Sizzling

New York Sirloin Steak, 20 Ounces 16.75

Roast Prime Ribs of Beef with Yorkshire Pudding 11.95

The Rest Of The Best

Oyster Stew 5.50

Shrimp Scampi 8.95

Seafood Salad 9.75

Marseille Bouillabaisse 10.50

Whitney's Tossed Salad 4.25

Chicken Caprice 6.75
Tender Breast of Chicken Prepared with Ham,
Bananas and Herb Butter.

Fresh Fish Selections at the Market Price

Wine Not?

Try Whitney's Variety of Great Wines—
By The Taste, By The Glass, or By The Bottle!
The Selection Changes Every Day, but the Prices Are
Always Reasonable . . . so You Can Satisfy Your
Curiosity without Blowing Your Budget!

RESTAURANT: Whitney's
LOCATION: Executive Suites Hotel,
Schiller Park, Illinois
DESIGNER: Georgia Pavelich
FIRM: Associates Printing Service
SPECIFICATIONS: "Late Night" Menu
SIZE: 5" x 7" (die cut)
PAPER: 80# Smooth Starwhite Cover
PRINTER: Associates Printing Service

The image of a drink on a piano means late nights in a visual sense. The menu, as befits its location at O'Hare International Airport, offers a variety of full-scale meals to cater to travelers whose biological clocks have not yet adjusted to local time. The hot pink, played against black on the cover, and used as a background for black type inside, adds a touch of glamour. The die-cut baby grand piano is a fun touch. With a print run of 20,000, the menu is used as an in-room promotional piece, a menu, and a direct-mail flyer.

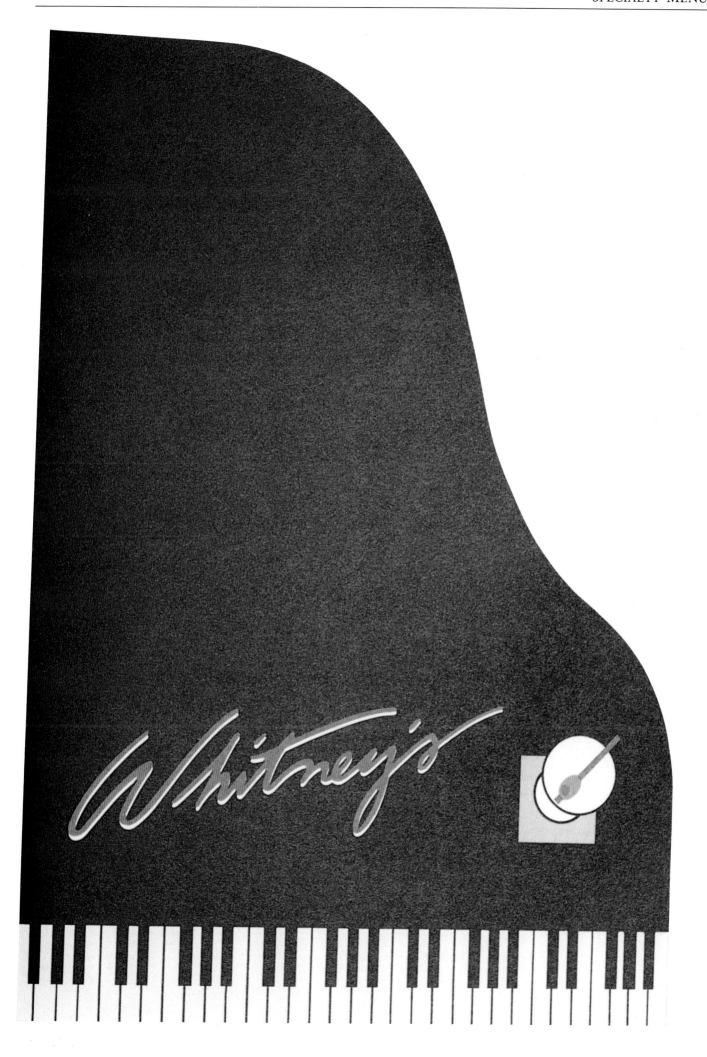

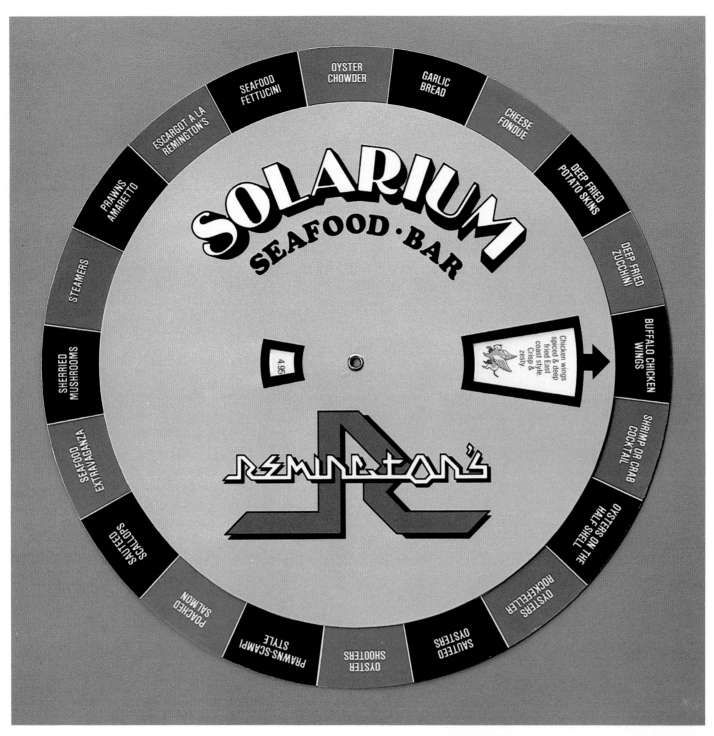

RESTAURANT: Remington's Solarium Seafood Bar

LOCATION: Ramada Inn, Spokane, Washington

DESIGNER: Gary Peterson

FIRM: Apex Printing

SPECIFICATIONS:

SIZE: 12″ diameter circle

PAPER: Laminated

PRINTER: Apex Printing

This menu won third place in the "Most Imaginative" category of the National Restaurant Association's 1986 Great Menus Contest. A variation on a child's toy, this menu features two concentric disks, the smaller of which has two die-cut windows and a heavy black "pointer." To obtain a description and a price for a specific offering, the diner points the arrow at his choice. Some clip art is used to illustrate the descriptions. For the convenience of those who prefer to see everything at once, the menu is printed in one color, with all the prices and the descriptions fully visible, on the menu's reverse side. This is an entertaining menu and encourages customer involvement.

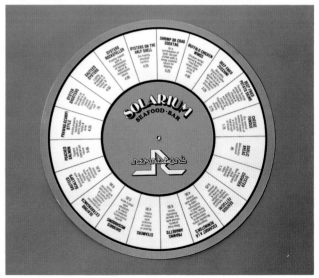

P O P   A R T

Celebrate

. . . With Festive Champagnes,
Fine Wines And
Spirited Cocktails.

RESTAURANT:	Hyatt Hotel Corporation
LOCATION:	Headquartered in Chicago, Illinois
DESIGNER:	"Pop Art": Ann Werner; "Autumn Mist": Georgia Pavelich
FIRM:	Associates Printing Service
STOCK PHOTOS:	"Pop Art": Comstock; "Autumn Mist": Image Bank
SPECIFICATIONS:	"Pop Art" and "Autumn Mist" menus
SIZE:	5" x 8" "Autumn Mist," (folded); 4¾ x 7½" "Pop Art," (folded)
PAPER:	12 pt. Kromekote, coated two sides
PRINTER:	Associates Printing Service

Stock photography was used for the covers of both these seasonal drink menus. Quality printing and selection of appropriate supporting colors distinguishes the work. These menus were designed to be used in all Hyatt Regency food and beverage outlets at airports.

RESTAURANT: Whitney's

LOCATION: Executive Suites Hotel/O'Hare, Schiller Park, Illinois

DESIGNER: Georgia Pavelich

FIRM: Associates Printing Service

ILLUSTRATOR: Georgia Pavelich

SPECIFICATIONS:

SIZE: 9¾" x 12¾"

PAPER: Strathmore Rhododendron Cover, double thick

PRINTER: Associates Printing Service

The restaurant's theme piano is silhouetted here against a light lavander background, surrounded by musical notes against a violet-blue background. Category headings on the reverse of the card are in the same lavander. And the violet-blue is used for the menu items that will vary.

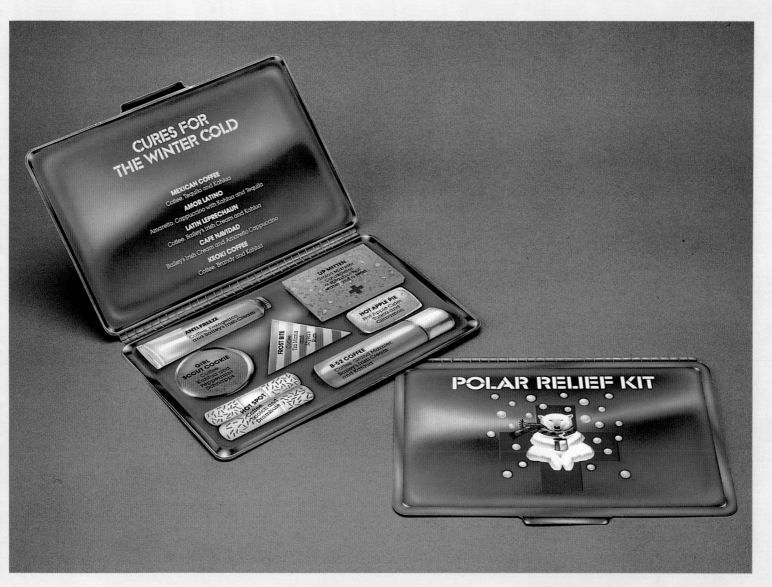

RESTAURANT: El Torito

LOCATION: Nationwide restaurant chain headquartered in Irvine, California

DESIGNER: Claude Prettyman

ART DIRECTION: Diane Richards (El Torito in-house creative dept.)

ILLUSTRATOR: Eddie Yip

SPECIFICATIONS: "Polar Relief Kit"

SIZE: 7½" x 5¼" (closed)

PAPER: 12 pt. Brilliant Art Gloss Cover

PRINTER: Frye & Smith

This menu won the second Grand Prize in the National Restaurant Association's 1986 Great Menus Contest. Designed to counteract flagging liquor sales in the chain's restaurants across the country, this drink list as first aid kit offers alternatives to chicken soup to relieve the winter cold. Bandages, a sponge, a tube of salve, and soap, each labeled with a cleverly named drink, form the contents of the relief kit. This is classic merchandising at its best. Because the restaurant realized that word about this menu would get around, they *removed* it from the tables at an early stage of the campaign. Customers had to ask for the relief kit to see it. Note also that no prices are listed.

Max &
SUMMER 1985 MENU
Erma's

RESTAURANT: Max & Erma's
LOCATION: Columbus, Ohio
DESIGNERS: Teri Schuller (in-house)
Karen Brennan (in-house)
PHOTOGRAPH: Supplied by California
Strawberry Advisory Board
SPECIFICATIONS: Summer 1985 Menu
SIZE: 8¾" x 13" (die-cut)
PAPER: 24 pt. King James Cover,
finished
PRINTER: Prestige Envelope & Printing
Company

This menu won second place in the "Merchandising Power" category of the National Restaurant Association's 1986 Great Menus Contest. What better way to sell strawberries than to turn your menu into a strawberry? Reversed type makes the menu easy to read. The photograph was provided by the California Strawberry Advisory Board. In return, the strawberries offered on the menu are genuine "California grown." This is an interesting example of co-op advertising. To take full advantage of the strawberry, the seeds and leaves on the back are embossed for a more realistic effective.

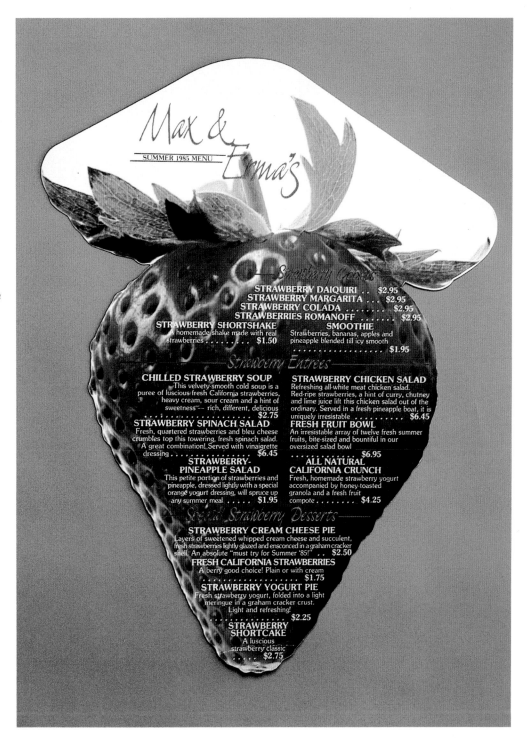

EXPRESS BREAKFASTS

THE EXPRESS
Choice of Juice;
Scrambled Eggs; Bacon or Sausage;
Home Fries; Fruit Garnish;
Croissant or Muffin;
Coffee
8.75

THE BUFFET
Fresh Juice;
Choice of Cereals;
Fresh Fruit Medley; Yogurt;
Granola; Carrot & Zucchini Breads;
Coffee
6.95

THE CONTINENTAL
Choice of Juice;
Croissant and Danish;
Fruit Garnish;
Coffee
5.50

FRESH FRUITS OR JUICES

GRAPEFRUIT, HONEYDEW,
CANTALOUPE, BANANAS 2.25

STRAWBERRIES, BLUEBERRIES 3.25
In Season.

ORANGE OR
GRAPEFRUIT JUICE 2.25

CEREALS

CHOICE OF CEREAL 1.75
Corn Flakes, Bran Flakes, Frosted Flakes,
All Bran, Raisin Bran, Special K, Cheerios
and Wheaties.

With Fresh Fruit 3.00

HOT OATMEAL 1.75

OMELETTES

SMOKED SALMON 6.95

MUSHROOM 5.50

THREE CHEESES 5.50

THE COPLEY BREAKFAST 8.75
Two Eggs, Any Style; Ham, Bacon or
Sausage; Home Fries; Fruit Garnish;
Toast; Fresh Juice; Coffee.

EGGS

TWO EGGS, Any Style	3.50
With Bacon, Sausage or Ham	5.50
EGGS BENEDICT	7.75
SCRAMBLED EGGS In Vol au Vent with Brie.	5.75
POACHED EGGS With Corned Beef Hash.	6.50

BAKERY PRODUCTS

CROISSANT AU BEURRE	2.75
DANISH PASTRIES	2.50
BLUEBERRY MUFFINS	2.50
ENGLISH MUFFIN	2.00

PANCAKES & WAFFLES

APPLE-BUCKWHEAT PANCAKES	4.75
BLUEBERRY-BUTTERMILK PANCAKES	4.75
BUTTERMILK PANCAKES	4.25
PECAN WAFFLES	4.95
FRENCH TOAST	4.75

A LA CARTE

YOGURT WITH GRANOLA	3.50
BREAKFAST STEAK	6.00
CANADIAN BACON	3.00
HAM, BACON, SAUSAGE	2.75
LOX & BAGEL 6.75 With Cream Cheese.	
APPLE CRÊPES 3.25	

Brasserie

RESTAURANT: Brasserie
LOCATION: Westin Copley Place, Boston, Massachusetts
DESIGNER: Roberta Warehan
FIRM: Associates Printing Service
ILLUSTRATOR: Roberta Warehan
SPECIFICATIONS:
SIZE: 10″ x 13½″
PAPER: Strathmore Rhodedendron Cover, double thick
PRINTER: Associates Printing Service

Stylized illustrations and a combination of screen tints enliven this two-color breakfast card. The illustrations are used to separate and identify the various menu categories. The inclusion of yogurt, fresh juices, and whole grain breads is evidence of the tendency toward nutritious and wholesome foods at the Brasserie.

RESTAURANT: Metro Hotel Corporation
LOCATION: Nationwide chain headquartered in Dallas, Texas
DESIGNER: Ann Werner
FIRM: Associates Printing Service
ILLUSTRATORS: Ann Werner, Cynthia Lehman
SPECIFICATIONS: Cassidy's "Fresh Approach" Menu
SIZE: 9" x 13½"
PAPER: Gainsborough
PRINTER: Associates Printing Service

Beautifully screened illustrations are used to emphasize fresh, wholesale ingredients on this menu. The soft pink and deep blue provide a tranquil feeling. Again, in response to the public interest in health, yogurt, fresh fruit, and breakfast shakes are featured along with more traditional fare. The back of the menu provides detailed information on eggs—how to tell if they are fresh, how they are sized, even how many calories and how much cholesterol an egg contains.

BREAKFAST

CASSIDY'S FRESH APPROACH

— CASSIDY'S FRESH APPROACH TO BREAKFAST —

CASSIDY'S FRESH APPROACH TO
FRUIT JUICES

FRESHLY SQUEEZED ORANGE JUICE
FRESHLY SQUEEZED GRAPEFRUIT JUICE
FRESH GAZPACHO COOLER
NATURAL TOMATO JUICE AND APPLE JUICE
OUR OWN VERSION OF V-8
1.25

CASSIDY'S FRESH APPROACH TO
FRESH FRUIT

CHILLED FRESH MELON BASKET 1.75
With Grand Marnier and Homemade Whipped Cream 1.95

BAKED HALF GRAPEFRUIT 1.95
Glazed with Honey and Cinnamon.

FRESH FRUIT MELANGE 1.95
With Homemade Whipped Cream.

— CASSIDY'S FRESH APPROACH TO BREAKFAST —

CASSIDY'S FRESH APPROACH
PANCAKES & WAFFLES

A STACK OF PANCAKES
A Stack of Buttermilk or Blueberry-Almond Pancakes with Whipped Honey-Orange B

APPLE-CINNAMON PANCAKES
Pancakes Layered with Sautéed Apples and Served with Honey-Orange Butter, Maple, Fresh Whipped Cream.

THE SUNRISE
Two Pancakes with Two Eggs and Two S of Bacon.

THE BELGIAN WAFFLE
Our Special Malted Waffle with Whipped Honey-Orange Butter.

WAFFLE BERRY
Our Belgian Waffle with Sour Cream, Fr and Maple Syrup.

SANTA FE WAFFLE 4.25
Toasted Piñon Waffle Topped with Grated Chocolate, Berries and Homemade Whipped Cream.

FRENCH TOAST 3.75
Served with Grand Marnier and Honey Syrup, Fresh Fruit and Homemade Whipped Cream.

CASSIDY'S STEAK AND EGGS 6.75
Two Fresh Eggs, Cooked as You Like Them, with a Six-Ounce Prime New York Strip Steak. Served with Sautéed Green Chili.

CASSIDY'S OMELETTE 3.95
A Three-Egg Omelette with Fine Herbs and Cheddar Cheese.

SANDIA OMELETTE 4.25
Ricotta Cheese, Fresh Basil and Hot Tomato Coulis.

TAOS OMELETTE 4.75
Wisconsin White Cheddar, Bacon and Sautéed Fresh Spinach.

SANTA FE OMELETTE 4.50
Green Chili and Onions, Topped with Homemade Chili Con Queso.

HILL COUNTRY OMELETTE 3.95
Fresh Seasonal Vegetables with Toasted Piñon Nuts.

Our Eggs and Omelettes Are Served with a Basket of Fresh Breakfast Bakeries and New Mexican-Style Fried Potatoes or Fried Vermicelli.

CASSIDY'S FRESH APPROACH TO
BREAKFAST BAKERIES

CASSIDY'S CONTINENTAL 2.95
The Chilled Fresh Juice of Your Choice, Orange, Grapefruit, Gazpacho or Vegetable; a Basket of Fresh Breakfast Bakeries with Whipped Honey-Orange Butter, and Coffee or Tea.

CROISSANTS   FRUIT BREADS
FRESH BAKED PASTRIES
ENGLISH MUFFINS   FRUIT OR BRAN MUFFINS

CASSIDY'S FRESH APPROACH TO
COFFEE

We Grind Our Coffees Fresh Daily.

BREAKFAST BLEND
.95 Per Cup   3.95 Per Chambord (Four Cups)

— CASSIDY'S FRESH APPROACH TO BREAKFAST —

C A B A N A

CONTINENTAL

Freshly Squeezed Chilled Juice, Tropical Fruits
A Selection from our Bakery Basket, Sweet Butter, Preserves or Honey
Coffee, Tea, Hot Chocolate or Milk
5.95

The following selections are included in the Modified American Plan (MAP).
Guests on the European Plan (EP) may enjoy a full breakfast for 10.- per person.

BUFFET CHOICES

Chilled Fruits and Juices
Assorted Fruit Nectars and Juices
Freshly squeezed Orange or Grapefruit Juice,
Assorted Fruit, Berries and Melon in Season
Low Fat Yogurt, Plain or Fruit

Hot and Cold Cereals
Served with Milk or Cream and fresh Fruit
in Season

From the Bakery
Freshly baked Breads, Danish and Muffins

Choice of Omelettes
Three Egg Omelettes Prepared to Order
with Ham, Mushroom, Cheese
Chicken Liver, Fine Herbs or Jelly
Served with your choice of Breakfast Meats.

*UNIQUELY DIFFERENT

Soft cooked Eggs with Beluga Caviar, Mouillette Toast 9.-
Eggs Scrambled with Ribbons of Fresh Salmon 5.-
Apples Sauteed with Cinnamon and Vanilla in a Pancake topped with Caramel 3.50
Foie Gras crowned with one perfect sunnyside Egg 7.-
Exotic Fruit Fritters with Maple Syrup 4.-
Puget Sound Salmon with Bagel and Cream Cheese 6.-
Expresso 2.-   Cappuccino 2.50
Bloody Mary 3.50   Screwdriver 3.50   Mimosa 4.50
A Glass of Taittinger Champagne 12.-

* The above items are surcharged in addition to the full breakfast price listed above

Fruits and Juices
Freshly squeezed Orange.or Grapefruit Juice, Passion Fruit Juice
Melon on Ice, Seasonal Berries, Fruit Compote

AMERICAN

Two Eggs as you like with Ham, Bacon or Sausage
Assorted Omelettes: Cheese, Ham, Mushroom, Fine Herbs, Chicken Liver, Jelly
Waffle or Pancakes with Maple Syrup

From the Bakery
Fresh Croissants and Small Chocolate Roll   Creamcake
Toasted French Country Bread   Toasted English Muffin

Beverages
100% Columbian Coffee   Decaffeinated Coffee   Domestic and Imported Teas
Milk   Low Fat Milk   Hot Chocolate with Cinnamon

All Prices Listed are Subject to a 17% Service Charge and Florida State Sales Tax

RESTAURANT: The Cabana
LOCATION: Boca Raton Hotel & Club,
Boca Raton, Florida
DESIGNER: Dayne Dupree
SPECIFICATIONS:
SIZE: 10″ x 13″
PAPER: Quintessence Dull
PRINTER: Blue Ocean Press

This menu uses the same colors, screened down, as the restaurant's luncheon and dinner menus. The audience is well-to-do and accustomed to the best; many are on vacation. Menu items were selected specifically for these patrons. Fresh juices, French champagne by the glass, and eggs with Beluga caviar or fresh salmon contrast with the more mundane breakfast selections. The menu is a flush-cut laminated card.

RESTAURANT: Windows

LOCATION: North Shore Hilton, Skokie, Illinois

DESIGNER: Cynthia Lehman

FIRM: Associates Printing Service

ILLUSTRATOR: Cynthia Lehman

SPECIFICATIONS: Dessert menu

SIZE: 5¾" x 10" (closed)

PAPER: Curtis Linen Cover, double thick (cover); Curtis Linen text (interior)

PRINTER: Associates Printing Service

The night sky forms a backdrop for the Chicago skyline, visible across the Lake, on the cover of this dessert menu. Foil stamping and the use of silver and white heightens the drama. Inside, desserts on one side and coffee specialties on the other are printed in one color for easy changes.

RESTAURANT: Metro Hotel Corporation

LOCATION: Nationwide chain headquartered in Dallas, Texas

DESIGNER: Ann Werner

FIRM: Associates Printing Service

SPECIFICATIONS: "Spirited Delights" Menu

SIZE: 6 x 6¾" (folded)

PAPER: Mead Gloss Enamel, cover and book weights

PRINTER: Associates Printing Service

This oversized "book of matches" invites the patron to pull each "row of matches" forward to see additional items. Strong copywriting makes the offerings very appealing. Four-color process printing was used for the matches. Neon-style typography, used on the cover and as category heads, adds sparkle. Prices are not listed to encourage impulse purchases. This menu is used in all of the chain's night clubs and bars.

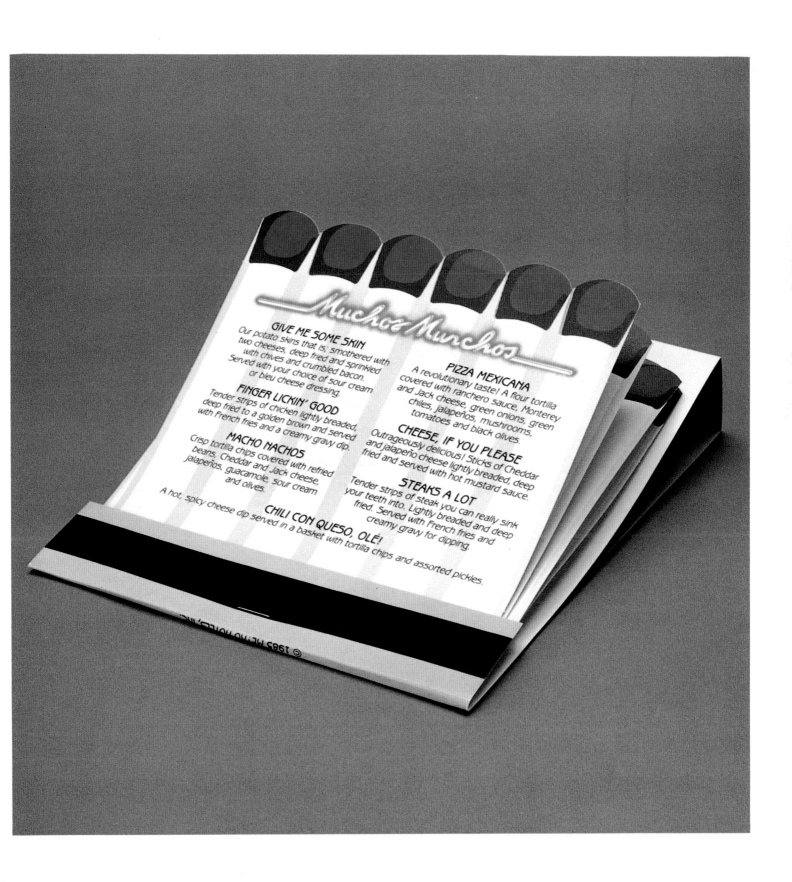

A Wine-Maker's Calendar

JANUARY

Trimming, or pruning, is traditionally done in January but nowadays starts in December while the ground is frozen or covered with snow. The vines withstand temperatures down to -18°C.

FEBRUARY

The trimming of the vines is finished and new cuttings are taken for grafting. Meanwhile the racking of the new wine into clean barrels takes place.

MARCH

Towards the middle of the month, the vine starts to emerge from the soil. Then the ploughing starts to aerate the soil and uncover the bases of the vine.

APRIL

The vineyard is cleared of remaining trimmings and rotten stakes and new cuttings are planted. The casks are topped up, not to leave any empty space above the wine. About five percent of the wine evaporates through the wooden sides of the barrel each year.

MAY

Overnight frost may damage the delicate vegetation and stoves are needed to protect the vineyard. Towards the end of May, the second racking of the wine into clean barrels takes place.

JUNE

The vines start to flower when the temperature reaches 18–20°C. After flowering the shoots are trimmed and tied against the wiring. The second racking is finished. Casks are constantly inspected for weeping.

JULY

The vines are sprayed regularly with a mixture of copper sulphate, slaked lime and water. In hot weather, the bottling of the wines can not take place and all efforts are geared to keep the cellars cool.

AUGUST

The vineyard is weeded and the vine trimmed. Casks and equipment are inspected and cleaned in preparation for the harvesting and pressing.

SEPTEMBER

Towards the end of September the harvesting can begin if weather permits.

OCTOBER

The harvest continues for another two weeks. Then the land is prepared for new plantation by spreading manure or pressed grape skin over it. The new wine is fermenting, meanwhile the cellars are cleaned to accommodate the barrels with the young wine.

NOVEMBER

Now the vineyard is ploughed to cover the trimmed vines and protect them from frost. The wine is racked one more time before bottling.

DECEMBER

Before Christmas, the pruning can start, while the bottling of older wine goes on. The new wines can now be tasted and casks are topped up frequently.

RESTAURANT: Hong Kong Hilton
LOCATION: Hong Kong
SPECIFICATIONS: "The Atlas of Wine"
SIZE: 9" x 15" (folded)

Beautiful full-color illustrations of various varieties of grapes and a calendar of the winemaker's year are reinforced by informative copywriting in the introduction to this wine list. The wines, drawn from five continents, are simply listed on two-color printed pages. Both front and back covers are sturdy and double-folded.

10

Children's Menus

After more than a decade in decline, the birthrate in the United States is once again rising. It's likely, as a result, that family-oriented restaurants will increase over the next few years to meet the needs of this market. Children's menus will be an important outgrowth of this trend.

A well-known but seldom openly-acknowledged fact about children's menus is that their chief function is to occupy the child long enough for the parents (and the other patrons) to eat in peace. Listing smaller and simpler meals is a secondary function. Amusing the child is vital.

Interactive menus seem to work best in occupying children. Bright colors, masks or toys to fit together, and word games for older children are all successful. If a menu is not designed for one-time-only-use, it must be constructed of extremely sturdy materials. Above all, the menu must be designed without tassels or staples that can be easily removed and swallowed, or other potentially dangerous materials.

The menus that follow illustrate how creative design can capture a child's attention and imagination.

RESTAURANT: Skippers, Inc.
LOCATION: Seattle, Washington
DESIGNER: Paula Rees
FIRM: Rees Thompson Designers
ILLUSTRATOR: Nancy Woodman
SPECIFICATIONS:
SIZE: 9¼" diameter
PAPER: 24 pt. White Feedcote with Marcoating
PRINTER: Impression Northwest

This brightly colored menu may by itself seem captivating, but it is only part of the merchandising story. A coordinating table tent (shown later in this chapter) invites the under-12 set to become "Skipper's Shipmates" and ends with the irresistible line, "If you're an adult, stop reading this!" A Fun Pack® available with each meal is the third part of the merchandising program.

SHIPMATES' PLATES

A special menu just for Skipper's Shipmates
(All Kids 12 or under)

Skipper's Clipper™
One Fish Fillet with Fries,
Jell-O® and Fun Surprise
$1.79

Chicken Ahoy™
Three Chicken Breast Strips
with Fries, Jell-O®
and Fun Surprise
$2.19

Chicken and Shrimp Trawler™
Two Chicken Breast Strips
and Shrimp with Fries, Jell-O®
and Fun Surprise
$2.79

Skipper's Bounty™
(All-You-Can-Eat)
Fish Fillets, Fries, Chowder,
Jell-O® and Fun Surprise
$3.29
(per Child)

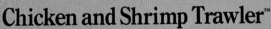

RESTAURANT: Benihana of Tokyo

LOCATION: Nationwide restaurant chain

DESIGNER: Ted Tanaka (in-house designer)

SPECIFICATIONS:

SIZE: 8½″ x 9½″

PAPER: 65# Hammermill Ivory Cover

PRINTER: Continental Graphic

One side of this one-color menu features amusing cartoons of teppan chefs and a kimonoed waitress as well as the menu selections. The other side features one of the five different "color your own" designs used on the various versions of this menu. This menu is not elaborate, but it meets its primary purpose beautifully—coloring is something to interest the child.

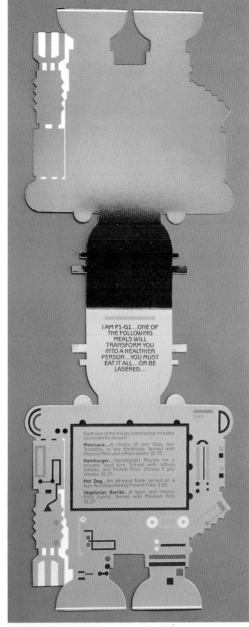

RESTAURANT:	Plata Grande
LOCATION:	Beltsville, Maryland
DESIGNER:	Kathleen Wilmes Herring
FIRM:	MDB Communications
ILLUSTRATOR:	Kathleen Wilmes Herring
SPECIFICATIONS:	"P1-G1" Menu
SIZE:	7¼" x 10" (measuring outside edges of die cut)
PAPER:	Kromekote
PRINTER:	Peake Printers, Inc.

This colorful robot earned the restaurant third place in the "Specialty" category of the National Restaurant Association's 1986 Great Menus Contest. The copywriting is simple and humorous. The selections have been designed to provide a full nutritious meal. Desserts are not listed but are included after the main course. The vivid colors and intricate patterns are attention-getters.

KID'S STUFF

BREAKFAST

The Cabbage Patch
Choice of hot or cold cereal with a slice of buttered
toast and preserves

Humpty Dumpty
One egg, any style, with crisp bacon and a slice of buttered
toast and preserves

Fat Mat Cakes
Two buttermilk pancakes with cinnamon honey/butter and
warm maple syrup

Frenchies
Our special French Toast with powdered sugar and warm
maple syrup

CHILDREN'S FARE

Charley the Tuna $2.50
A tuna fish sandwich on white bread served with potato chips

Chicken Little $3.50
Tender fingers of white breast meat breaded and deep fried

Dennis the Menace $1.75
Peanut Butter and Jelly sandwich on white bread

Miss Piggy $2.50
Cold ham and cheese sandwich on white bread served with potato chips

The E.T. $1.95
A grilled cheese sandwich with ham and potato chips

The Porky Pig $2.25
A hot dog and bun served with french fries

Wimpy's Burger $2.95
A burger served plain or with American cheese and french fries
Choice of Chilled Juice, Milk or Soda $.75

DESSERT

Candy's Clown $1.50
A clown made of vanilla ice cream, sugar
cone, M&M's and whipped cream.

Bullwinkle Pudding $.95
Creamy Chocolate Moose

The Rainbow Connection $.95
A bowl of orange, raspberry and lime
sherbet.

RESTAURANT: Ambassador Grille
LOCATION: Embassy Suites Hotel,
Wayne, Pennsylvania
DESIGNER: Maura Harnagy
FIRM: Art Group, Inc.
ILLUSTRATOR: Al Himes
SPECIFICATIONS:
SIZE: 15″ x 15¾″ die-cut hat
PAPER: Carolina Cover
PRINTER: Ripple Printing/TH Enterprises

The restaurant is contemporary, but the hotel is
located in the Valley Forge area. The children's
menu is therefore theoretically correct for the area
and its associations with George Washington. The
menu has perforations that permit the child to wear
the menu as a Revolutionary War era general's hat,
complete with powdered wig at the back. The
copywriting is quite contemporary, drawing on
movies, cartoons, and current children's toy and
games for the item names and associations.

McHenry's
CHILDREN'S MENU
For Children under 12

Sandwiches

Grilled Cheese Sandwich $1.95
Hamburger/Cheeseburger $2.25
Hot Dog $1.50
Peanut Butter n' Jelly $1.95

All of the above sandwiches are accompanied by French fries and beverage

Hot Entrees

Fried Chicken $3.75
Fried Shrimp $4.25
Spaghetti with Tomato Sauce $3.25
Mini Pepperoni Pizza $4.00

All of the above entrees are accompanied by hardroll and beverage

Ice Cream $1.50

Sheraton Inner Harbor Hotel
Baltimore

RESTAURANT:	McHenry's
LOCATION:	Sheraton Harbor Hotel, Baltimore, Maryland
DESIGNERS:	Paul Harnagy, Jeff Metzler
FIRM:	Art Group, Inc.
ILLUSTRATOR:	Al Hines
FIRM:	Art Group, Inc.
SPECIFICATIONS:	
SIZE:	14½″ x 18¾″ (die-cut hat)
PAPER:	Carolina Cover
PRINTER:	Ripple Printing/TH Enterprises

The restaurant is named for Fort McHenry but is not colonial in theme. The coonskin cap is just a fun device for the child. In designing children's menus, thematic consistency is less important than it is for adults. If the child is entertained by an idea, that is sufficient.

RESTAURANT: Herbig's Gum Tree

LOCATION: Hilton International Adelaide, Adelaide, South Australia, Australia

DESIGNER: Ian Kidd (Hilton in-house designer)

SPECIFICATIONS:

SIZE: 10½″ x 13½″

PAPER: Mirrorkut Folding Board

PRINTER: Mitchell Press

This menu won first place in the "Specialty" category of the National Restaurant Association's 1986 Great Menus Contest. The menu appeals to children of all ages. It includes a story to read (or read to the really small child), a crossword puzzle based on the story, a maze, a picture to color, and a word game on the back cover. Food and beverages are listed amid the games. All menu items are well-chosen. This restaurant is located in the Hilton Hotel in Adelaide, so most of its clientele are tourists. The story mentioned above is about the Barossa Valley, south Australia's primary wine-producing region and a favorite area among tourists. This makes the story more effective as the children are likely to see or have seen the gum tree (eucalyptus) mentioned in the story.

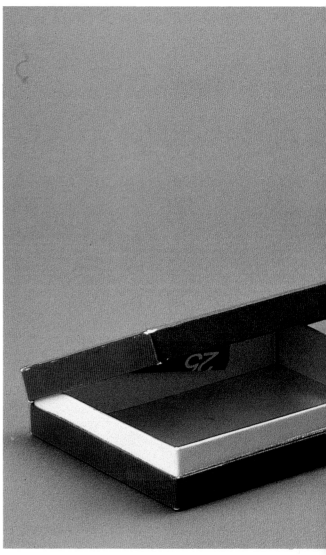

RESTAURANT:	Eat 'n Park Restaurants, Inc.
LOCATION:	Pittsburgh, Pennsylvania
DESIGNER:	Kensington Falls
FIRM:	Family Communications, Inc.
SPECIFICATIONS:	
SIZE:	2″ x 3¼″
PAPER:	Williamsburg High Bulk, Frankote Cover
PRINTER:	Geyer Printing

These little books use simple illustrations of the selections available to children, with a brief description and price (for the parents' benefit) next to the spine. Each item in the meal is depicted, and a partially consumed glass of milk is suggestively placed alongside. At the front and back are "flip sections" that simulate animation. If the book is turned over, a complete "flip story" is available for the child's amusement. The picture menu is an effective way to involve the child in planning his own meals. Nobody needs to read the words to him—he can choose, all by himself.

RESTAURANT:	Ramada Inns, Inc.
LOCATION:	Phoenix, Arizona
DESIGNER:	Robert Lansdell
FIRM:	E. F. M. Graphics
SPECIFICATIONS:	
SIZE:	9½″ round
PRINTER:	E. F. M. Graphics

This menu won second place in the "Specialty" category of the National Restaurant Association's 1986 Great Menus Contest. Fancifully colored animals can be reassembled at will by turning the three disks to align one animal's head with another's body and a third's feet. Since each cut in the menu is made at a point where the outlines match exactly, the game is even more fun. Some variations of the "mix and match" game have been played by children for many years, yet the game never loses its excitement. Menu items are described simply on the outermost disk. This menu provides the perfect excuse to read the menu upside down—and get away with it. The animals' faces are drawn with appealing artistry.

RESTAURANT: La Paloma Country Club

LOCATION: Tucson, Arizona

DESIGN FIRM: Associates Printing Service

LETTERING: Sean, age 7

SPECIFICATIONS:

SIZE: 10" x 13"

MEDIUM: Paper bag

PRINTER: Associates Printing Service

This menu is written on the back of a paper bag and was carefully lettered by Sean, age 7. He got a little tired toward the end and used ditto marks for "ice cream" and "chocolate". But the menu is perfectly clear. Where abbreviations are used, they are understandable to a child. (Childless adults may have some trouble with a "PB+J" sandwich at first.) Note that the young artist understood that he must somehow make the category headings stand out. With perfect logic, he simply circled them. The bag could double as a temporary parking place for "treasures."

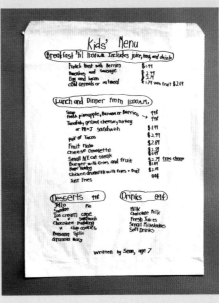

RESTAURANT: Midland Hospital Center

LOCATION: Midland, Michigan

DESIGNER: Ron Acker

FIRM: Bentley & Associates

ILLUSTRATOR: Ron Acker

SPECIFICATIONS: "Just Kid Stuff" Menu

SIZE: 8½" x 11" (cover)

PAPER: 8 pt. White King James Cover (cover); 80# White Carnival Offset

PRINTER: McKay Press

This menu won first place in the "Institutional Foodservice" category of the National Restaurant Association's 1986 Great Menus Contest. An army of fruit and vegetables marches across the cover of this menu of "Just Kid Stuff." Inside pages for the child to color flank the carefully planned menus. In marked contrast to the "whole meal package" approach used by restaurants, the Hospital Center offers a broad variety of accompaniments to choose from at each meal. Because sick children are easily bored and often don't want to eat, this approach works well because it encourages the child to take action in choosing. It also counteracts the helplessness most people—especially children—feel when they are confined to a hospital.

RESTAURANT: Sakura

LOCATION: Hilton International Tokyo, Tokyo, Japan

SPECIFICATIONS:

SIZE: 5″ x 11¼″

PAPER: Hard-cover bound

Die cuts and pop-ups create a fanciful landscape with food, spaceships, and baseball players all relatively the same size. Trying to decide what all of the figures are and how they relate to one another should prove entertaining to most children. The menu uses two languages—Japanese and English—and a combination of Japanese and American cultural images to provide both reassurance and a sense of adventure. The menu items have names relating to popular movies, children's stories, and baseball. The menu portion is set off by a knife and a fork.

Children's Gourmet Paradise
さくら
めりーごーらんど

RESTAURANT: Skippers, Inc.

LOCATION: Seattle, Washington

DESIGNER: Paula Rees

FIRM: Rees Thompson Designers

ILLUSTRATOR: Nancy Woodman

SPECIFICATIONS: Point-of-purchase menu, table tent

SIZE: 9¼" diameter (point-of-purchase menu); 5" x 8" (table tent)

PAPER: 24 pt. White Feedcote with Marcoating (point-of-purchase menu); 12 pt. Feedcote Cover with varnish (table tent)

PRINTER: Impression Northwest

The brightly colored full-circle menu is only part of the story. A coordinating table tent invites the under-12 set to become "Skipper's Shipmates." The copywriting is targeted to its audience, promises a Fun Pack® with each meal, and ends with the irresistible line "If you're an adult, stop reading this!" The Fun Pack® changes so that a child revisiting the restaurant will find something new. This three-part approach is a well-crafted merchandising program with a well-defined and well-addressed audience.

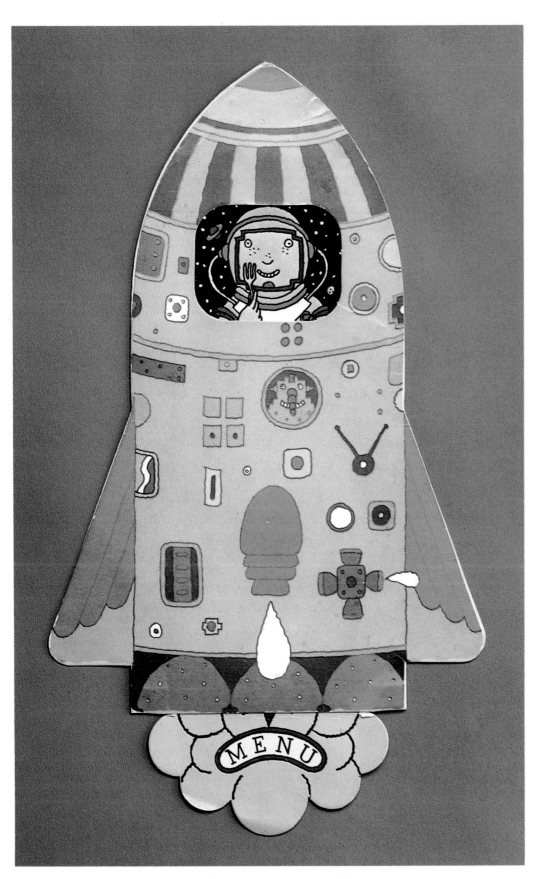

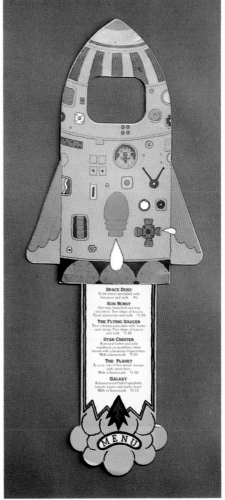

RESTAURANT: Holiday Inns, Inc.
LOCATION: Memphis, Tennessee
SPECIFICATIONS:
    SIZE: 7″ x 11″ (measuring outer edges of die cut)

The grinning astronaut and his fork disappear as the rocket's vapor trail is pulled down to reveal the menu. Tabs concealed just below the astronaut prevent the child from pulling the menu all the way out. This probably saves quite a few menus from early destruction. The spaceship theme is carried out in the copywriting. The body of the spaceship features happy aliens concealed amid the circuitry.

11

Casual Dining

The phrase "casual dining" covers a broad range of restaurants from coffee shops to upscale but informal dinner houses. One of the trends in this category is towards diners. Having run the full gamut of nouvelle cuisine, with its often small portions and foreign ingredients, Americans are reacting by turning back to the cooking they grew up with. And, for many, the American cooking of their youth is typified by diners.

The diner of the 1980s is only superficially like that of the 1950s. The pastel booths and jukeboxes are still there and no self-respecting diner would exclude burgers from its menu. But the music on the jukebox is usually contemporary, the burgers are generally charcoal-broiled, and there is a greater emphasis on fresh produce. Broiled chicken sandwiches are often offered as an alternative to beef burgers.

The emphasis on fresh ingredients and "home-style cooking" extends beyond the diner, of course. "Locally grown produce" seems to be a catch phrase of the 1980s. Fresh foods, simply prepared, have become part of an overall approach to food.

The menus in this chapter amply demonstrate these phenomena. Copywriting is used liberally on most to establish the tone of the restaurant. Clear descriptions of the food are intermingled with humorous advice on etiquette and stories about the restaurant's vision and history. Graphic support is humorous, beautiful, even exotic, and copy and art are especially well-integrated.

POOL BAR & GRILL

SABINO'S CHAR-BROILED BURGERS
Plain; Chili & Cheese; Bleu Cheese;
Jack Cheese; Guacamole & Sprouts.
5.25

BALL PARK HOT DOG
2.75

DELI SANDWICHES
Ham, Turkey, Roast Beef, Swiss and Cheddar
on French, Whole-Wheat or Corn Rye.
4.95

FRESH PINEAPPLE BOAT
Fruit Salad with Cottage Cheese
or Soft Serve Yogurt.
5.25

SABINO SALAD
Deli Meats, Shrimp and Cheeses.
Choice of Dressing.
5.25

SOFT SERVE YOGURT
Regular 1.00   Large 1.50

ICE CREAM SANDWICHES
1.25

COFFEE, TEA, MILK, SOFT DRINKS
1.00

FRUIT JUICES
1.50

CANDY, NUTS, CHIPS
.75

M E N U

RESTAURANT: Sabino's Pool Bar & Grill

LOCATION: Westin La Paloma,
Tucson, Arizona

DESIGNER: Ann Werner

FIRM: Associates Printing Service

SPECIFICATIONS:

SIZE: 6¼" x 9¼"

PAPER: Kromekote

PRINTER: Associates Printing Service

Sabino's is literally a pool bar and grill. You can
walk in or you can swim up. The pool motif is
highlighted with the use of a beachball instead of
the letter "o" in the restaurant's name, the aqua
waves as a holding line, and the water droplet in
place of an apostrophe. The red and white stripes
are reminiscent of a cabana.

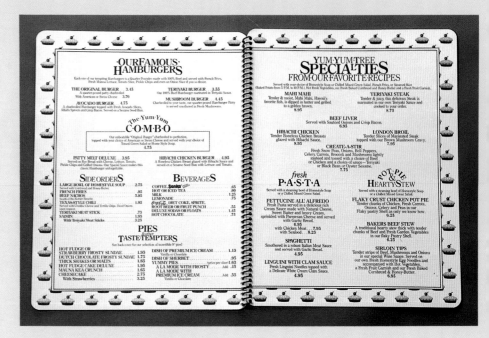

RESTAURANT: Yum Yum Tree

LOCATION: Honolulu, Hawaii, (and other Oahu locations)

DESIGNER: Robert Bates

FIRM: Bates/Lee Advertising

ILLUSTRATOR: Susi Johnson

SPECIFICATIONS:

SIZE: 8½" x 11"

PAPER: 130# Curtis Linen Snow White Antique

PRINTER: Printers Ink

This upscale coffee shop has a "Grandma's Kitchen" theme that is enhanced by the use of old kitchen utensils, milk cans, and the like as decorative accessories in each restaurant. The spiral-bound menu is designed to look like a homemade cookbook. The pies that form the recurring motif on the menu are the restaurant's specialty. Within the restaurant, they are served by the slice; they are also available, whole, as a take-out item.

RESTAURANT: The Costa Mesa Omelette Parlor
LOCATION: Costa Mesa, California
DESIGNER: Vickie Lee Goodale
FIRM: Grand American Fare
SPECIFICATIONS:
SIZE: 8½″ x 11″ (folded)
PAPER: 80# Howard Offset Felt Text
PRINTER: Cornhusker Printing Co., Inc.

This menu won first place in the "Restaurant: Average Check Under $5.00 Per Person" category of the National Restaurant Association's 1986 Great Menus Contest. The cover is printed in two colors, one a very subtle yellow, and features an antique photograph on the back. Clip-art has been cleverly used both on the cover and inside. The copywriting is exceptionally good. In addition to an exaggeratedly formal treatise on etiquette that frames the main part of the menu, copywriting has been used to tie the names of the various dishes to the appropriate geographical areas. The menu is also used to sell promotional items—it advises "Ask about our Original Omelette Parlor T-Shirts." This menu is a well-planned merchandising piece.

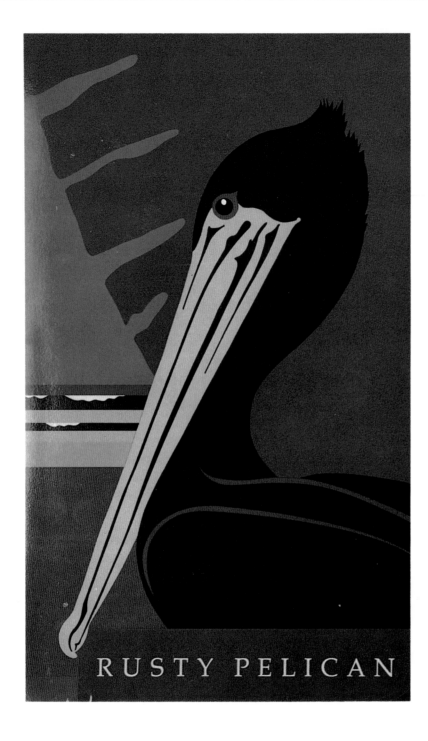

RUSTY PELICAN

RUSTY'S
SEAFOOD BAR

RESTAURANT: Rusty Pelican Restaurants Inc.
LOCATION: Nationwide restaurant chain headquartered in Irvine, California
DESIGNER: Dean Gerrie
FIRM: Guzman & Gerrie
ILLUSTRATOR: Dean Gerrie
SPECIFICATIONS:
SIZE: 7½" x 12"
PRINTER: Dot Printer

The illustrations that form a graphic link among all the menus for this restaurant chain use a stylized technique; the colors—cool blues, greens, and turquoises, all contrasted with flamingo pink—create a fantasy-like impression. The typeface is large and legible. The contrast between illustrations rendered proportionately and those rendered unproportionately—such as the huge bird of paradise, which runs the full height of the menu, or the anthurium, which slightly overflows its confining box—provides visual interest.

The design program uses serigraphic technology to produce a menu of fine arts quality. In an interesting "life imitates art" twist, the menu cover has been produced as a signed, numbered lithograph. A one-color paper menu is available as a souvenir for those who request it.

RESTAURANT: The Bakery Cafe

LOCATION: Westin Hotel,
O'Hare International Airport,
Rosemont, Illinois

DESIGNER: Roberta Warehan

FIRM: Associates Printing Service

ILLUSTRATOR: Roberta Warehan

SPECIFICATIONS:

    SIZE: 9″ x 11½″ (folded)

    PAPER: Rhododendron

    PRINTER: Associates Printing Service

The border on both the cover and the interior resembles an old-fashioned tablecloth pattern updated with tranquil colors. This, together with the cover line art, lends a homey feeling to the menu. This two-color menu is printed on a satisfyingly heavy stock. Food items are eclectic, as befits a restaurant near the world's busiest airport.

RESTAURANT: Captain Bilbo's River Restaurant

LOCATION: Memphis, Tennessee

DESIGNER: Craig Thompson

FIRM: Kelley & Associates Advertising, Inc.

ILLUSTRATOR: Craig Thompson

SPECIFICATIONS:

SIZE: 9½ x 14½" (folded)

PAPER: Sorg Leather Embossed, varnished (cover); Beckett Text Laid Bamboo (interior pages)

PRINTER: Dawson's Printing

This menu won third place in the "Restaurant: Average Check Over $10.00 Per Person" category of the National Restaurant Association's 1986 Great Menu Contest. The richly textured cover has the look and feel of leather, and the stylized illustrations on the inserts also have a textural quality. The category headings are set so they simulate a rubber stamp; this lends the menu an air of immediacy. The restaurant is located on "The Bluff" in downtown Memphis, overlooking the Mississippi River. Its specialties are fish and seafood. As an interesting touch, a specific wine is recommended to accompany each dish.

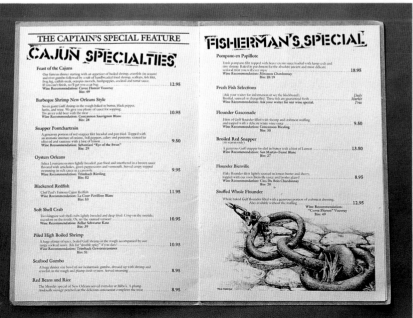

RESTAURANT: Lime Rickey's

LOCATION: Concord, Ontario, Canada

DESIGNER: Ray Marjury

ILLUSTRATOR: Kenneth Stompnick

SPECIFICATIONS:

SIZE: 8" x 19" (folded);
24" x 19" (open)

PAPER: Cornwall Coated White

PRINTER: Spirit Graphics, Inc.

This menu won first place in the "Restaurant: Average Check Between $5.00–$10.00 Per Person" category of the National Restaurant Association's 1986 Great Menus Contest. The menu, with its bold hand-lettered category heads executed in quick strokes of pastels, is very effective for this upscale diner. The free-form designs underlying the various menu categories lend interest to the menu. The waitress with a ponytail adds a nostalgic 1950s flavor to the menu, as the jukebox does for the restaurant. But the menu items are clearly rooted in the 1980s and the jukebox plays contemporary music. This menu strikes a nice balance between two eras.

RESTAURANT: Quicksilver Dining & Diversions
LOCATION: Herndon, Virginia
DESIGNER: Chris Meyer
FIRM: Meer Design
SPECIFICATIONS:
SIZE: 5¾" x 14" (folded);
17¼" x 14" (open)
PRINTER: Westland Enterprises

The spattered ink reminiscent of Jackson Pollack gives this menu both excitement and a new wave look. The spattered background is repeated in the interior but does not intrude on menu copy, which is contained in boxes. The three-panel menu positions specials in the best location, the center panel, and places desserts on the back of the third fold.

RESTAURANT: Valley Deli
LOCATION: Albuquerque, New Mexico
DESIGNER: Steve Wedeen
FIRM: Vaughn/Wedeen Creative, Inc.
SPECIFICATIONS:
SIZE: 7¼" x 29"
PAPER: Carliner Stock
PRINTER: Academy Printers

The range of foods offered and the need for varying type arrangement from section to section presented a real design challenge on this menu project. The graphic elements were used to provide uniformity. The paper is the same as that used to line freight cars; it's very sturdy. The menus hang from a hook in this quaint deli. The design of the menu fits the deli's decor perfectly.

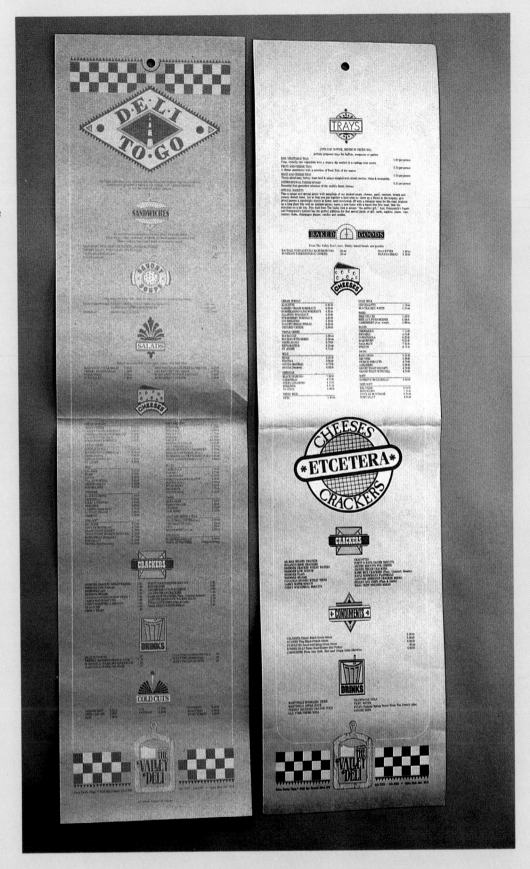

RESTAURANT: City

LOCATION: Los Angeles, California

DESIGNERS: Jill Sprayregen Henkel (cover);
Steve Saneos (logo)

SPECIFICATIONS:

SIZE: 8½″ x 11″

PAPER: White offset (cover); bright
yellow offset (insert pages)

Susan Seniger, co-owner of City, has an ongoing
commitment to art. At one time, the walls of the
restaurant showcased changing exhibitions of
original art. She eventually decided she wanted a
menu cover that would change with the menu and
would also feature art. Her creative solution was to
use color photo copies of paintings, changing
them each month. The menu itself is produced
with the aid of a computer. Both menu pages and
cover sheet are three-hole-punched and inserted in
a plastic report cover. The whole program is an
exciting use of the most up-to-date techniques to
permit inexpensive menu updates. The program is
ideally suited to this restaurant.

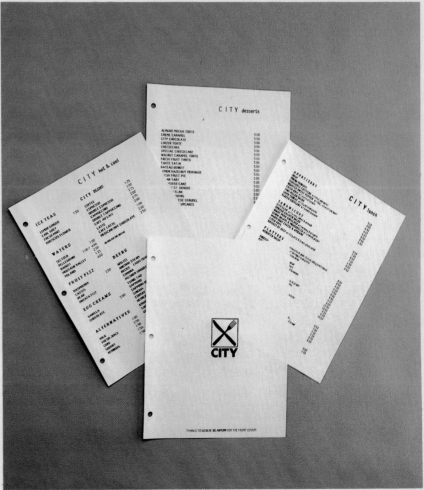

RESTAURANT: 1411 Collection Cafe
LOCATION: New York, New York
DESIGNER: Dale Glasser
FIRM: Dale Glasser Graphics, Inc.
ILLUSTRATOR: Larry Kazal
SPECIFICATIONS:
SIZE: 5½″ x 8½″
PAPER: Chromolux White, coated
one-side (cover); 70#
Hammermill Offset Vellum White
(insert)
PRINTER: C. M. Industries, Inc.

This tiny jewel of a spot is located in the Sportswear Building in the heart of the Garment District in New York City. It caters to the needs of garment buyers and clothing manufacturers. These business people wanted a lunch spot with the feeling of a private club. Plush blue banquettes, brass and wood cabinetry, and telephones and fresh flowers on each table all contribute to this effect. The spring bouquet on the menu cover fits perfectly with this mood. The blue of the inside back cover is repeated in the one-color menu insert, which is held in place by a soft pink cord. Because the type of cord used is more commonly found in clothing than in menus, it adds a personal touch to the menu.

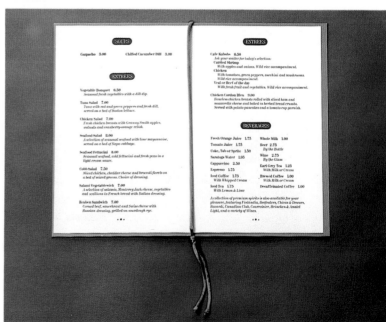

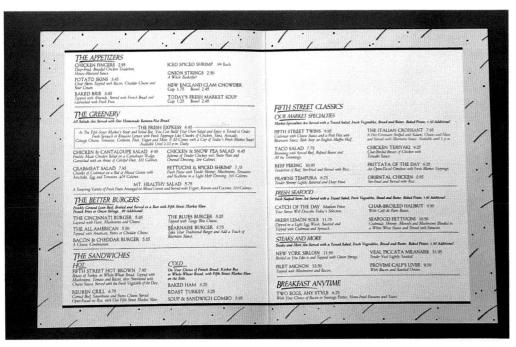

RESTAURANT: Fifth Street Market

LOCATION: Westin Cincinnati at Fountain Square, Cincinnati, Ohio

DESIGNER: Cynthia Lehman

FIRM: Associates Printing Service

ILLUSTRATOR: Cynthia Lehman

SPECIFICATIONS:

SIZE: 8½″ x 11″ (closed)

PAPER: Strathmore Rhododendron

PRINTER: Associates Printing Service

Abstract flowers and brush strokes lend this menu an informal flavor. The strokes form a border around the menu listings inside and underscore the menu categories for emphasis and separation. Menu items that will vary are printed in one color with prices noted after item identification and set in a block with the descriptive copy.

RESTAURANT:	Monterey Bay Canners
LOCATION:	Irvine, California
	(and several other locations in
	California and Hawaii
DESIGN FIRM:	Bates/Lee Advertising
SPECIFICATIONS:	
SIZE:	9″ x 13″
PAPER:	Kromekote
PRINTER:	Printers Ink

The cheerful red cover and bright yellow type are reminiscent of the canned salmon labels one remembers from childhood. The simple graphic and type are enclosed in a box, furthering this idea. The cover invites exploration of the menu. A brief story on the back cover states the restaurant's vision and inspiration.

RESTAURANT: New Yorker Coffee House
LOCATION: Harrah's at Trump Plaza,
Atlantic City, New Jersey
DESIGNER: Paul Harnagy
FIRM: Art Group, Inc
ILLUSTRATOR: Al Himes
FIRM: Art Group, Inc
SPECIFICATIONS:
SIZE: 7" x 16"
PAPER: White, coated two sides,
laminated
PRINTER: Lee J. Blumberg

The signage, restaurant interior, and menu were
designed simultaneously for this 24-hour restaurant
in a hotel casino. The menu cover depicts the
Chrysler Building in New York, while a
12-foot-high black marble sculpture at the
restaurant's entrance recreates the building, and the
menu display case also features it. All signage and
the menu were designed by the same firm. The net
result is a strong, consistent theme that says "New
York," without being trite.

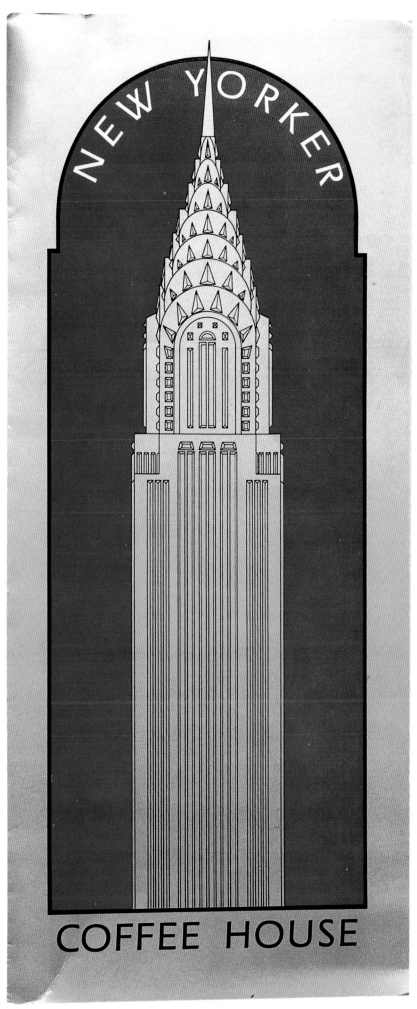

RESTAURANT: Papa's Cafe
LOCATION: Holiday Inn, Crowne Plaza
Rockville, Maryland
SPECIFICATIONS:
SIZE: 9½" x 13½"
PAPER: 80# Americana Cover

Papa's is named for Ernest "Papa" Hemingway.
The restaurant, located in a six-story atrium, has a
"nautical" theme that is carried out by the real
lifeboat suspended from the ceiling. The menu
cover has a stipple airbrush background that
resembles beach sand. The various animals and
plants native to Hemingway's beloved Key West are
depicted on the cover; they reappear to separate
the various food categories in the menu insert. The
paper selected for the insert has a wavy pattern
that reminds one of ocean waves. The inserts are
printed in two colors to create a simple, appealing
effect.

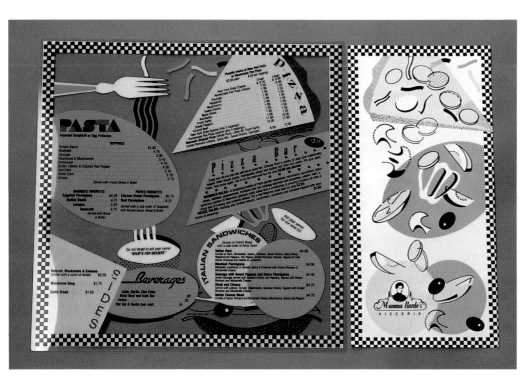

RESTAURANT: Mamma Ilardo's Ristorante
LOCATION: Baltimore, Maryland
DESIGNERS: W. Scott Mahr, Tim Thompson
FIRM: Great Scott Graphics
SPECIFICATIONS:
SIZE: 13″ x 13″
MEDIUM: Silk-screened on acetate

This menu was the Grand Prize winner in the National Restaurant Association's 1986 Great Menus Contest. The restaurateur wanted an exciting menu, something completely different, and the designer had always wanted to create an acetate menu. This treatment works well for this particular restaurant. The menu colors are drawn directly from the colors used in this post-modern/new-wave restaurant. Its graphics are coordinated with the 4′ x 8′ murals on the walls. Three of the menus are displayed, back-lit, in a triangular black lacquered unit near the restaurant's entrance. The acetate menus are relatively costly to produce so, when souvenirs are requested, the two-color carry-out version, on paper, is provided.

RESTAURANT: Muckleberry's

LOCATION: Holiday Inn,
Memphis, Tennessee

SPECIFICATIONS:

SIZE: 11″ x 10¼″ (folded)

Home-style cooking is the theme of this restaurant. The short-folded cover was photographed from an actual piece of fabric, and the lower border is reminiscent of regional folk art. The pleasingly textured paper is lightly coated for durability.

RESTAURANT: Old Broadway
LOCATION: Fargo, North Dakota
DESIGNER: Paul Dezotel
FIRM: Spider Graphics
SPECIFICATIONS:
SIZE: 6¾" x 7½"
PRINTER: Kaye's Printing

The Old Broadway not only serves breakfast, lunch, and dinner, but also features dancing and games every night. Located in a former clothing store dating from 1903, it has and still uses the first espresso machine installed in the state. The menu is supplemented by wine, beer, drink, and "Mocktail" (non-alcoholic cocktail) menus. Organized party nights and flyers are also part of the program. Humorous copywriting lends just the right touch to this menu, which lists mostly sandwiches and light entrees. Sandwiches are numbered for ease in ordering. The menu cover features an illustration of a happy chef with clip art, and is laminated for durability. The inserts, printed on nicely textured paper with a dark green border to match the cover, are held in place by an elastic cord.

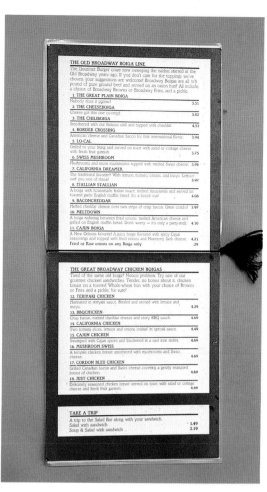

RESTAURANT: All American Cafe

LOCATION: Holiday Inn,
Petoskey, Michigan

FIRM: Hinkle Frye Scannell
Advertising, Inc.

SPECIFICATIONS:

SIZE: 9″ x 12″ (folded)

PAPER: 24# white offset

"Please feel free to steal this menu" reads the inside of the menu for this Petoskey, Michigan, gathering spot. The restaurant's sign, framed in the brass rods used throughout the restaurant, is the basis for the front cover and inside spread. The American Cafe's menu is directed at a young professional crowd. Added enticement is provided by the Reunion Bar, separated from the restaurant by a glass partition.

The All American Cafe uses "Menu Engineering," a program developed by Don Smith of Michigan State University. The restaurant's receipts are put into a computer system every four weeks and the profitability of the various items is analyzed. When the menus are updated annually, the results of this analysis are incorporated in decisions on pricing, placement, and deletion and addition of specific menu items.

PAPER SUPPLIERS

Appleton Papers, Inc.
P.O. Box 359
Appleton, WI 54912
(414) 734-9841

Decorated Paper Corporation
8th & Erie Streets
Camden, NJ 08102
(609) 365-4200

Howard Paper Mills, Inc.
P.O. Box 982
Dayton, OH 45401
(513) 224-7315

Beckett Paper Company
400 Dayton Street
Hamilton, OH 45012
(513) 863-5641

Diamond International Corporation
333 Bolivar Street
Canton, MA 02021
(617) 828-4200

International Paper Company
77 West 45th Street
New York, NY 10016
(212) 599-3194

Champion International Corporation
Paper Division, One Champion Plaza
Stamford, CT 06921
(203) 358-7000

Eastern Fine Paper, Inc.
Division of Eddy Paper Co. Ltd.
P.O. Box 129
Brewer, ME 04412
(207) 989-7070

Linweave Inc.
10 Linweave Drive
Holyoke, MA 01040
(413) 536-6410

Cross Siclare/New York, Inc.
150 Granite Avenue
Staten Island, NY 10303
(212) 442-8900

Georgia-Pacific Corporation
Printing & Specialty Paper Division
320 Post Road
Darien, CT 06820
(203) 655-1100

Mead Paper
Fine Paper Division
Courthouse Plaza N.E.
Dayton, OH 45463
(513) 222-6323

Crown Zellerbach
Printing Paper Division
1 Bush Street
San Francisco, CA 94104
(415) 823-5000

Gilbert Paper Company
P.O. Box 260
430 Ahnaip Street
Menasha, WI 54952
(414) 722-7721

Midtec Paper Corporation
North Main Street
Kimberly, WI 54136
(414) 788-3511

Curtis Papers
Division of James River Corporation
Paper Mill Road
Newark, DE 19711
1-800-441-9292

Hammermill Paper Company
1540 East Lake Road
Erie, PA 16533

Mohawk Paper Mills, Inc.
P.O. Box 497
465 S. Saratoga Street
Cohoes, NY 12047
(518) 237-1740

Monadnock Paper Mills, Inc.
Bennington, NH 03442
(603) 588-3311

Riegel Division
James River Corporation
Milford, NJ 08848
(201) 995-2411

Strathmore Paper Company
Westfield, MA 01085
(413) 568-9111

Neenah Paper
Division of Kimberly-Clark Corporation
1400 Holcomb Bridge Road
Roswell, GA 30076
(404) 587-8000

Rising Paper Company
Park Street
Housatonic, MA 01236
(413) 274-3345

Westvaco Corporation
Fine Papers Division
299 Park Avenue
New York, NY 10017
(212) 688-5000

Nekoosa Papers, Inc.
Port Edwards, WI 54469
(715) 887-5111

St. Regis Paper Company
Laminated and Coated Products Division
421 S. Union Street
Troy, OH 45373

Weyerhaeuser Co.
Paper Division
One Plymouth Meeting
Plymouth Meeting, PA 19462
(215) 825-1100

Northwest Paper Div.
Potlatch Corp.
Cloquet, MN 55720
(218) 879-2300

St. Regis Paper Company
Printing Paper Division
West Nyack Road
West Nyack, NY 10994
(914) 578-7000

Zanders Feinpapier AG
Paper Sources Int'l., Inc.
P.O. Box 368
Rutherford, NJ 07070
(201) 933-6664

Plainwell Paper Co., Inc.
200 Allegan Street
Plainwell, MI 49080
(616) 685-5851

Scott Paper Company
S.D. Warren Company Division
225 Franklin Street
Boston, MA 02101
(617) 423-7300

Potsdam Paper Corporation
Route #4
Potsdam, NY 13676
(315) 265-4000

Simpson Paper Company
One Post Street
San Francisco, CA 94104
(415) 391-8140

NRA MENU DESIGN COMPETITION

Each year since 1963, the NRA (National Restaurant Association) has sponsored a menu contest to help raise standards in menu design by displaying the most creative and successful menus of the year.

There are three criteria for judging the menus.

1. Imagination: The menus must show originality of design, choice, balance, naming of items, and an effectiveness in coordinating these elements.
2. Design: Criteria is based on effective layout, use of color, illustration, typeface, and paper, which combine to present a clean, readable document.
3. Merchandising Power: Criteria in this area is based on the selling power of the menu for certain dishes. Judging is based on visual strategies, such as graphic layout and description, which will entice a customer to order a featured item.

There are nine categories in which menus can be entered.

1. Menus in which the average check is under five dollars per person.
2. Menus in which the average check is five to ten dollars.
3. Menus in which the average check is over ten dollars per person.
4. Institutional food services (including hospitals, schools, college food services, museums, travel related menus, such as airlines, and industrial menus, such as corporate food services).
5. Banquet and Catering menus.
6. Specialty menus (including dessert menus, wine lists, appetizer menus, children's menus, and room service menus).
7. The most imaginative menu.
8. Menus exhibiting the best design.
9. Menus exhibiting the greatest merchandising power.

The contest is held annually. Menu submissions are generally made in February; contact the NRA for the exact date. All entries become the property of the NRA. Menus must be submitted through the restaurant they were designed for. The entry fee is $10.00 per menu for members, $15.00 per menu for nonmembers.

STATE RESTAURANT ASSOCIATIONS

Alaska Cabaret, Hotel and Restaurant
Association
P.O. Box 4-1260
Anchorage, AK 99509
(907) 272-8133

Alabama Restaurant and Food Service
Association
2100 Data Drive, Suite 207
Birmingham, AL 35224
(206) 988-9880

Arizona Restaurant Association
112 North Central, Suite 417
Phoenix, AZ 85004
(602) 258-3256

Southern Arizona Restaurant Association
Tucson Chamber of Commerce Building
465 West St. Mary's Road., Suite 300
Tucson, AZ 85705
(602) 791-9106

Arkansas Hospitality Association
603 Pulaski Street
P.O. Box 1556
Little Rock, AR 72203
(501) 376-2323

California Restaurant Association
3780 Wilshire Boulevard,
Suite 600
Los Angeles, CA 90010
(213) 384-1200

California State Restaurant Association
1225 8th Street, Suite 325
Sacramento, CA 95814
(916) 447-5793

California Restaurant Association
355 Grand Avenue
Oakland, CA 94610
(415) 836-2588

Golden Gate Restaurant Association
291 Geary Street, Suite 515
San Francisco, CA 94102
(415) 781-5348

Colorado-Wyoming Restaurant
Association
1365 Logan Street
Denver, CO 80203
(303) 830-2972

Connecticut Restaurant Association
236 Hamilton
Hartford, CT 06106
(203) 247-7797

Delaware Restaurant Association
P.O. Box 7838
Newark, DE 19711
(302) 366-8565

Restaurant Association of Metropolitan
Washington, Inc.
South Tysons Office Park
2112-D Gallows Road
Vienna, VA 22180
(703) 356-1315

Florida Restaurant Association
1065 NE 125th Street, Suite 409
North Miami, FL 33161
(305) 891-1852

Georgia Hospitality and Travel
Association
148 International Boulevard
Suite 625
Atlanta, GA 30303
(404) 577-5888

Hawaii Restaurant Association
130 Merchant Street, #2020
Honolulu, HI 96813
(808) 536-9105

Idaho Restaurant and Beverage
Association
P.O. Box 8205
Boise, ID 83707
(208) 336-7930

Illinois Restaurant Association
20 North Wacker Drive, Suite 1130
Chicago, IL 60606
(313) 372-6200

Indiana Restaurant Association
2120 North Meridian Street
Indianapolis, IN 46202
(317) 924-5106

Iowa Restaurant Association
415 Shops Building
Des Moines, IA 50309
(515) 282-8304

Kansas Restaurant Association
359 South Hydraulic
Wichita, KS 67211
(316) 267-8383

Kentucky Restaurant Association
455 River City Mall
Suite 417-421 Starks Building
Louisville, KY 40202
(502) 587-8629

Louisiana Restaurant Association
3350 Ridgelake Drive, Suite 101
Metairie, LA 70002
(504) 831-7788

Maine Restaurant Association
124 Sewall Street
Augusta, ME 04330
(207) 623-2178

Massachusetts Restaurant Association
825 Washington Street
Newtonville, MA 02160
(617) 969-3140

Michigan Restaurant Association
Executive Building, Suite 205
690 East Maple
Birmingham, MI 48011
(313) 645-9770

Minnesota Restaurant and Foodservice
Association
2001 University Avenue
St. Paul, MN 55104
(612) 647-0107

Mississippi Restaurant Association
P.O. Box 16395
Jackson, MS 39206
(601) 982-4281

Missouri Restaurant Association
P.O. Box 10210
Kansas City, MO 64111
(816) 753-5222

Missouri Restaurant Association
St. Louis Area
2385 Hampton Avenue, Suite 111
St. Louis, MO 63139

Montana Restaurant Association
P.O. Box 908
Helena, MT 59624
(406) 442-1432

Nebraska Restaurant Association
1220 Lincoln Benefit Building
Lincoln, NB 68508
(402) 475-4647

Nevada Restaurant Association
3661 Maryland Parkway, Suite 108
Las Vegas, NV 89109
(702) 733-1962

New Hampshire Hospitality Association
172 North Maine
Concord, NH 03301
(603) 228-9585

New Mexico Restaurant Association
2130 San Mateo Boulevard NE
Suite C
Albuquerque, NM 87110
(505) 268-2474

New York State Restaurant Association
250 West 57th Street
New York, NY 10019
(212) 246-3434

New York State Restaurant Association
3686 Gardenia Drive
Baldwinsville, NY 13027
(315) 652-6555

North Carolina Restaurant Association
P.O. Box 6528
Raleigh, NC 27628
(919) 782-5022

North Dakota Hospitality Association
P.O. Box 428
Bismark, ND 58501
(701) 223-3313

Northeastern Ohio Restaurant
Association
129 Main Street #1
Chardon, OH 44024
(216) 621-7914

Northwestern Ohio Restaurant
Association
1955 South Reynolds Road, Suite 16
Toledo, OH 42614
(419) 389-0501

Ohio State Restaurant Association
1061 Country Club Road
Columbus, OH 43227
(614) 864-2800

Oklahoma Restaurant Association
3800 North Portland
Oklahoma City, OK 73103
(405) 334-3180

Restaurant Association of Maryland, Inc.
5602 Baltimore National Pike
Suburbia Building, Suite 305
Baltimore, MD 21228
(301) 788-6400

Restaurants of Oregon Association
3724 North east Broadway
Portland, OR 97232
(503) 249-0974

Pennsylvania Association of Travel and
Hospitality
5403 Carlisle Pike
Mechanicsburg, PA 17055
(717) 697-3646

Pennsylvania Restaurant Association
900 Eisenhower Boulevard, Suite C
Harrisburg, PA 17111
(717) 939-7881

Philadelphia-Delaware Valley Restaurant
Association
1131 L.V.B. Building
1700 Market Street
Philadelphia, PA 19103
(215) 567-6528

Western Pennsylvania Restaurant and
Hospitality Association
1422 Bigelow Apartments
Pittsburgh, PA 15219
(412) 288-0157

Rhode Island Hospitality Association
P.O. Box 415
Ashton, RI 02869
(401) 334-3180

South Carolina Restaurant Association
510 Barringer Building
1338 Main Street
Columbia, SC 29201
(803) 254-3906

South Dakota Restaurant Assoc
805 ½ South Main Avenue
Sioux Falls, SD 57104
(605) 338-4906

Tennessee Restaurant Association
229 Court Square
Franklin, TN 37064
(615) 790-2703

Texas Restaurant Association
P.O. Box 1429
Austin, TX 78767
(512) 444-6543

Utah Restaurant Association
2520 South State, Suite 221
Salt Lake City, UT 84-15
(801) 487-4821

Vermont Hotel-Motel and Restaurant
Association
P.O. Box 9
Montpelier, VT 05602
(802) 229-0062

Virginia Restaurant Association
2101 Libbie Avenue
Richmond, VA 23230
(804) 288-3065

Restaurant Association of the State of
Washington, Inc.
722 Securities Guilding
Seattle, WA 98101
(206) 682-6174

West Virginia Restaurant & Licensed
Beverage Association
P.O. Box 2391
Charlestown, WV 25328
(304) 342-6511

Wisconsin Restaurant Association
122 West-Washington Avenue
Madison, WS 53703
(608) 251-3663

Typographic Terms

Typeface—styles of type. Typesetters' catalogs display the amazing array of styles available.

Sans Serifs—alphabets without cross lines at the end of main strokes of the letters. Generally, the face is simply designed, even in overall weight, with very little contrast between thick and thin strokes.

Serifs—the short cross lines at the ends of the main strokes of many letters in some typefaces.

Scripts—letterforms that simulate handwriting and have no serifs, little contrast between the thick and thin strokes, and letters that seem to touch each other.

Swash—an ornamental stroke on a letterform to simulate handwriting.

Printing Terms

Embossing—a process by which an image is stamped in relief (either positive or negative) on a piece of paper. Blind embossing refers specifially to an image stamped in relief with no ink added to define the image. Embossing is usually handled by specialty printers.

Die cutting—a process by which any shape can be cut out of a sheet of paper. A "die" with sharp cutting must first be made in the desired shape. Die cutting is usually handled by specialty printers.

Foil stamp—application of a thin foil film on paper. A die must be made first. Foil stamping is usually handled by a specialty printer.

4-color/full color—color reproduced as your eye sees it with the use of four color (black, magenta, cyan, and yellow) printing. These colors combine to give the entire color spectrum.

Full bleed—when ink coverage extends to the edges of the page on all four sides (no white border).

Lamination—a plastic film bonded by heat and pressure to a printed sheet for protection or appearance.

Short fold—when a piece does not fold so that extreme edges meet. Example: a fold that causes some of the bottom panel to be visible when looking at a cover panel.

Paper Terms

Coated one side— paper having a smooth finish and reflective surface on one side only, the other side remaining with a toothy finish.

Coated paper—paper having a surface coating which produces a smooth finish. Surfaces can vary from eggshell to glossy.

Card stock—inexpensive but opaque and somewhat rigid paper. Can be used for improved durability (over text stock) or for mailing without use of envelopes.

Cover stock—heavier in weight and therefore more expensive than text paper. Available in a variety of surface finishes.

Deckled edge—a rough, torn finish to a side of a sheet of paper. Simulates fine handmande paper techniques.

Dull-coated—paper with a chalky-like matte finish that enriches blacks and halftone reproduction (available in text and cover weights).

Duplex cover—two pieces of cover stock that have been laminated together. Used for extra durability and/or when a color different than that of the outside cover is desired on the inside front and back covers.

Pebble finish—texture applied to paper during manufacturing. Resembles tiny pebble surface. Not recommended for halftone reproduction.

Text—paper stock for the inside of a publication or for stationery. Lighter weight (and therefore less expensive) than cover stock.

Textured—paper with other than a smooth, flat surface. Can be embossed to simulate linen, felt, or other material.

Translucent parchment—a paper that allows light to pass through. Often used for fly sheets in the front of publications or as divider pages to separate sections of reports.

Notes to Assist You in Choosing Paper for Your Menu

Felt finish
Applied by marking felt or roll at the wet end of the paper machine.
Available in a variety of colors.
Resists soil marks.
Excellent opacity.
Perfect for matching envelopes.
Texture gives three-dimensional effect.
Fiber formation give strength for special effects.

Felt finish papers are suited for:
- Jobs with large non-printed areas to show texture.
- Embossing and stamping dies.
- Giving impression of quality.
- Special sections or fly leaf in brochures or annual reports.

Laid finish
A ribbed apppearance by a dandy roll.
Many similar characteristics to felt finish papers.

Can have a unique water mark visible in the finish.
Should be used with copy printing parallel to the laid lines to facilitate reading.

Laid finish papers are:
- Ideal for jobs which imitate printing of the 19th century or earlier.
- Perfect for reproduction of line art.
- Not suited for detailed halftones or where printed piece has to be folded against grain causing type to run perpendicular to laid line.

Vellum finish
Commonly referred to as toothy paper. Not as rough as an antique finish.
Absorbent and fast drying.
Uniform and level non-glare surface for ease of printing and readability.
Excellent bulk and rigidity.

Vellum finish papers are ideal for:
- Jobs requiring no pattern background and little surface texture.
- Brochures free from glare where felt finish would distract from subject.
- Clear halftone reproduction where soft effect is desired.

Embossed finish
Special designs imparted to finished paper usually one side at a time by engraved rolls.
Less bulk and rigidity than other text sheets but because compressed provides excellent ink holdout.
Distinct feel or quality through delicate pattern background.

Embossed finish papers are best used for:
- Jobs where a pattern background is desired.
- Excellent ink holdout to accent solids without glare.
- Jobs requiring die cutting, stamping, or embossing.

Source: Garrett-Buchanan Paper Company
Reprinted courtesy of the National Restaurant Association

INDEX I

RESTAURANTS

DESIGN FIRMS